Bridal BARGAINS

Secrets to throwing a fantastic wedding on a realistic budget.

DENISE AND ALAN FIELDS

WINDSOR PEAK PRESS

The copyright page and other rambling observations

Bassoon, oboe, and lead guitar by Denise Fields
Drums, stand-up bass, and spelling mistakes by Alan Fields
Additional percussion and backing vocals by Ben Fields
Accordion and other gas-filled instruments by Zuzu Fields
Backing vocals on "Bridal Magazines"
by John Hiatt and Ric Ocasek

Three berry-pie by The Fresh Pie Company
Cup of Joe (aka, decaf hazelnut mocha latte) by Beans of Boulder

Neato cover design by Hugh Anderson of Archetype
Interior design and guitar solo on "Flowers"
by Bob Schram of Bookends
Index and cowbell by Doug Easton
Marketing karma and expert funk by Mark Ouimet
Current standard of living by Charlie Winton

This book was written to the music of the Barenaked Ladies,
which probably explains a lot.

Special thanks to Jill Adams and Katy Davis.
More special thanks to Deborah Copaken, John Stehr and,
of course, Barb Koster. Yet more thanks to
Monica Bernstein, Jill Mulligan and Katy Burke.

To order this book, check your local bookstore or call (800) 888-0385. Or send $11.95 plus $3 shipping to Windsor Peak Press, 1223 Peakview Circle, Suite 7000, Boulder, CO, 80302. Quantity discounts are available. Questions or comments? Feel free to contact the authors at (303) 442-8792. Or fax them a note at (303) 442-3744. Or write to them at the above address.

Library in Congress Cataloging in Publication Data

Fields, Denise, 1964-
Fields, Alan, 1965-
    Bridal Bargains: Secrets to Throwing a Fantastic Wedding on a Realistic Budget/Denise and Alan Fields. 3rd Edition.

    Includes index.
    1. Wedding—United States—Planning. 2. Consumer education—United States. 3. Shopping—United States.
                                                          93-093752 LIC

ISBN 0-9626556-7-8

Distributed to bookstores by
Publisher's Group West, 1-800-788-3123

A Record of the Wedding

BRIDE

_____

GROOM

_____

WEDDING DATE

_____

HOW WE FIRST MET

_____

OUR FIRST ARGUMENT WAS OVER

_____

_____

PARENTS' REACTION TO ENGAGEMENT ANNOUNCEMENT

_____

_____

PARENTS' FIRST DISPARAGING REMARK MADE ABOUT FIANCE

_____

_____

FIRST ARGUMENT OVER WEDDING

_____

_____

MOST STUPID REMARK MADE BY A WEDDING ATTENDANT

_____

DATE AT WHICH YOU KNEW THINGS HAD GOTTEN OUT-OF-HAND

_____

DATE AT WHICH EITHER OF YOU UTTERED:

*"But I thought planning a wedding was
supposed to be a happy experience?"*

_____

Special thanks to our
editors panel of wedding professionals
who provided invaluable advice!

Extra special thanks to all the
brides and grooms who have provided
their personal insights on how to throw
a fantastic wedding on a realistic budget.
Without you, there would be no
Bridal Bargains.

This book is dedicated to Dee Dee McKittrick.
We love you.

Overview

Your Wedding teaches you how to find the best deals on bridal apparel for the bride and the wedding party. Then, you learn how to shop for your ceremony site, wedding flowers, and invitations. Each chapter gives you in depth money-saving tips and shopping strategies.

Your Reception shows you how to save money on everything from catering to entertainment. Our chapter on wedding photography gives you seven creative ways to save money plus eleven important questions to ask any photographer. You'll also learn how to find the best deals on wedding cakes and wedding videos.

Weddings Across America is a fascinating look at how couples are tying the knot in over 20 U.S. cites. You'll learn how bridal traditions and customs vary from region to region in the United States. We'll show you what's hot and what's not for nuptials in towns from coast to coast.

Table of Contents

Introduction

Part I: Your Wedding

Part II: Your Reception

CHAPTER 8
Catering 155

CHAPTER 9
Photography 174

CHAPTER 10
Cakes 197

Part III: Weddings Across America

Icons

What the Icons Mean

 What Are You Buying

 Sources

 Top Money-saving Secrets

 Getting Started: How Far in Advance

 Biggest Myths

 Step-by-step Shopping Strategies

 Questions to Ask

 Pitfalls to Avoid

 Real Wedding Tips

Chapter 1

STOP! READ THIS FIRST!

AAAAAIGH!!! So, you're engaged? Well, fasten your seat belts! Soon you will travel through a bizarre and crazy world, where the boundaries of good taste and sane thought are only fuzzy lines. Yes, you've done it now.

You've entered the WEDDING ZONE.

See, that's why we are here. We're sort of your tour guides through this wondrous journey of things bridal and ideas nuptial. Of course, right off the bat, you will probably notice a basic difference between this and all those other wedding books—this book contains actual COMMON SENSE.

Sure, we know we're going out on a limb here but what the heck? Why not write a book you can actually use to plan your wedding? Hey, it's the least we can do. At this point you may have a question: so, who are you guys? Let's put that into bold.

So Who Are You Guys?

When we got engaged, the first thing we did was trot down to our local bookstore. There has got to be a book that will help us survive this process, we thought. What we wanted was a consumer guide that would show us how to plan a wonderful wedding without spending an amount equivalent to the Federal Deficit. From recently-married friends, we heard all the horror stories—that wasn't going to happen to us. We would find out how to shop, what questions to ask and how to avoid scams and frauds. A small request, we thought.

Ha! All we found were etiquette books last revised when Eisenhower was president. Plenty of books wanted to tell us what was "proper," what was "socially acceptable" and what was "never to be done except under threat of death." Gee, that's nice, we said, but what we need is help, not useless etiquette.

So we left the bookstore with our heads down. Now what? Then the idea hit us: hey, why can't we write this book? There must be a few other engaged couples going through this experience needing practical advice too.

To make a long story somewhat shorter, we were right. In the past six years, we have "mystery shopped" over 1000 wedding businesses, from bridal shops to caterers; photographers to bakeries. From these anonymous visits, we learned a lot about planning a wedding. We now know how to spot a truly talented wedding photographer and which bakery will produce the best wedding cakes. At the same time, we learned how to identify dishonest merchants who will try to rip off brides with inferior products or dubious service.

We first took those experiences and wrote six regional guides to planning a wedding for cities in the Southwest. But we didn't stop there. For this book, we spent six years interviewing bridal professionals and wedding "experts" across the country. We then spoke to hundreds of engaged couples, carefully documenting problems and challenges they had encountered planning their weddings. When you read this book, you not only get our opinions but the wise advice of many recently married couples who have gone before you.

Of course, we are not wedding consultants or planners. We don't own a farmhouse in Connecticut and decorate it with gold-dipped walnuts and cut-up credit cards. Nope, we're just normal folks (well, as normal as two people can be and still live in Boulder, CO). We see our role as consumer activists, working to educate brides on how to be smart shoppers. Believe it or not, this is a full-time job—we write and research about the wedding biz for a living.

If you find this book helpful, please recommend it to your friends. If they can't find it at a local bookstore or library, call us toll-free (800) 888-0385. Also feel free to write to us at 1223 Peakview Circle, Suite 7000, Boulder, CO 80302. We value your opinions, comments and experiences—we plan to revise this book with future editions so please feel free to contact us.

The four truths about weddings you won't read in etiquette books.

1 SO YOU THINK YOUR WEDDING IS FOR YOU AND YOUR FIANCE? Ha! Forget it. Unfortunately, weddings often become less a celebration of marriage and more like a huge social event for the participants. Parents, and even some brides and grooms, are frequently guilty of turning weddings into spectacles to impress their friends or business associates. Money can become the sticking point since whoever pays for the wedding may feel a divine right to influence the proceedings with their own tastes.

Sometimes, parents and relatives try to make your wedding into the wedding they never had (and always dreamed of).

Your friends may be guilty of pressuring you to make your wedding fit some predetermined mold. Put another way, while you may be the stars of the show, you and your fiance may not be the wedding's directors, producers or choreographers.

Recognize this fact early and learn to negotiate without giving ultimatums. Yes, it is YOUR day, but remembering that others (parents, friends, relatives) are on the stage with you may prevent excessive bloodshed.

2 WEDDINGS ALWAYS END UP TWICE AS LARGE AS ORIGINALLY PLANNED. If only we had a dime for every couple we met who said "all we wanted was a small, intimate wedding and what we got was a huge affair for 500 guests." A wedding often takes on a life of its own, expanding into a hideous creature several times larger than you ever imagined. Other weddings start as informal gatherings and turn into formal spectacles that rival Princess Diana's shindig.

This process usually begins with what we call Guest List Inflation. Here the guest list grows because each family simply must invite personal friends, close business associates and people whom they haven't seen in fifteen years. The main problem: adding to the guest list has a direct, negative impact on your budget.

Several weddings have nearly unraveled when families have insisted on inflating the guest list without offering to help pay for the additional cost. We suggest you and your families be allowed to invite a certain number of guests each. Any invites beyond those targets must be financed by the offending party. Careful negotiations are often necessary to avoid open warfare on this point. Good luck.

3 PERFECT WEDDINGS DON'T EXIST IN THE FREE WORLD. No matter what anyone tells you, understand that the "perfect wedding" is an impossibility on planet Earth. That's because weddings always involve human beings who, on the whole, tend to be less than perfect creatures.

Now we know everyone tells you that you must have the perfect gown, perfect flowers, perfect cake unless you want to catch the Bridal Plague and die an agonizingly painful death. Don't listen to these demons. Instead, we suggest you aim for a "fantastic" or "wonderful" wedding. Or even just a fun wedding!

Since it's impossible to perfectly script something as complex as a wedding, we say why try? Attendants will miss cues, things will go wrong—if you need any proof of this just watch "America's Funniest Home Videos." Ever wonder why so many of those clips are of weddings? Hmmmmm.

Aiming for a wonderful wedding will also give you another benefit—you probably will be able to maintain your sanity.

4 THE "WEDDING INDUSTRY" ISN'T AS INNOCENT AS IT LOOKS. You might think the wedding industry is a collection of sweet old ladies whose only desire is to help young couples in love, but the reality is quite the opposite. Instead, think of the bridal business as a group of cut-throat small business persons who, in some cases, will do anything for a sale.

Newspaper columnist Dave Barry once wrote that the motto of the wedding industry is, "Money can't buy you happiness, so you might as well as give your money to us." Quite true. Weddings are big bucks. According to the latest research, over $30 billion dollars will be spent this year by couples tying the knot. That's billion with a "b." Making matters worse is the fact that many wedding businesses own a mini-monopoly in their city over gowns, cakes, photography, etc. These firms viciously block any new competition. Why should that matter to you? By blocking the competition, businesses can effectively stop discounters and keep the prices high.

Now we aren't against people in the wedding business making money. The problem we have is that too many wedding businesses have the morals of an average slug. Many simply don't realize that federal laws prevent price fixing. Others are surprised to learn that consumer protection laws outlaw deceptive marketing and advertising practices like "bait and switch." "No kidding," they say, "it's illegal to rip people off?"

So we say, be careful out there. We hope this book will teach you how to spot the scams and rip-off artists—and lead you to ethical and honest professionals who sincerely want you to have a wonderful wedding.

The Goal of This Book:
To help you save money and still have a fantastic wedding!

Consumer justice doesn't have to be a somber topic. Getting a great bargain should be fun. Outfoxing dishonest merchants should be a joyful experience. That's why we try to keep our perspective about this wedding stuff, and we urge you to do the same. Not maintaining your sense of humor during wedding planning may be hazardous to your health. That's why we've liberally sprinkled what could be loosely described as "humor" throughout this book.

In each chapter we give you Pitfalls to Avoid. As you learn about these bridal scams and wedding frauds, realize that just because you are a bride does not mean you have to be a victim. By using our consumer tips, you can protect yourself from losing hundreds, if not thousands, of dollars and have a good time doing it!

This book is for brides and grooms who want to hire professionals for their wedding. This book doesn't teach you how to sew a bridal gown or give you a recipe for a wedding cake. Instead, we'll show you how to get a nationally-advertised designer gown at a 20% to 40% discount. We'll also show you the secrets to finding an affordable baker who will bake you the best wedding cake you've ever tasted.

There's no advertising in this book?

There are no paid advertisements in this book. Furthermore, no company paid any consideration or was charged any fee to be mentioned in it. The publisher, Windsor Peak Press derives its sole income from the sale of this book and other consumer guides. As consumer advocates, the authors believe this policy ensures objectivity. The opinions expressed in this book are those of the authors.

So, how much does a wedding cost anyway?

Unless you are a Certified Public Account, you may not be inclined to use the words "fun" and "exhilarating" to describe setting the budget for your wedding. As you might expect us to say, however, this is a critical (albeit painful) part of the planning process.

Whether you're spending $100 or $100,000 on your wedding, every bride and groom has a limited amount of money to spend. This means you'll have to make tough choices regarding how you want to allocate your limited resources. In Appendix A, we provide an in depth look at setting a budget. Hopefully, this will help make this process easier.

So how much does a wedding cost? Here are the average costs for a formal wedding for 200 guests:

THE AVERAGE COST OF A U.S. WEDDING
(Based on industry estimates for 200 guests)

APPAREL	$1,175
FLOWERS	800
CAKE	500
RECEPTION/CATERING	8,400
PHOTOGRAPHY	1,500
VIDEOGRAPHY	850
INVITATIONS	200
MUSIC	1,000
MISCELLANEOUS	1,000
TOTAL	**$15,425**

When you add in the engagement and wedding rings ($3000 and $1000 respectively), the total bill could top **$19,000!** Wow!

Now, if you are a bride-to-be in New York City or Los Angeles, you may be looking at the above numbers and laughing (or crying). That's because many items there cost at least two to three times the average. Keep this in mind throughout the book when we quote "average prices."

As a side note, we have seen some dramatic inflation in the costs of some wedding services. For example, the cost of a professional wedding video has gone up dramatically—in the mid 80's, the average cost was about $400. Now, it's more than double. Likewise, many photographers have been jacking up their prices at the alarming rate of 20% or more per year.

On the upside, we've noticed deflation in the costs of some bridal apparel. Intensive competition and the recession of the early '90s prompted the introduction of several lower-cost lines of bridal apparel. Price hikes for other goods (such as invitations and flowers) have been held to a minimum too.

Now if you're going to spend the kind of money mentioned above, perhaps you'd like to track who's getting what. Our recommendation: get yourself organized.

Now, this doesn't mean you have to buy the $50 "bridal organizers" that the wedding industry hawks. We received several great suggestions about how to get organized from some of our past readers. For example, one bride suggested going down to a local office supply store and buying a plain accordion file for all the contracts, proposals and receipts every bride collects. The unglamorous brown file was a mere $5—significantly less than the $35 price for a "bride's" accordion file advertised in a bridal magazine with taffeta fabric and a satin bow.

Another bride organized her wedding using a three-ring binder. She hole punched all the contracts and bought pocket inserts for her receipts, photos and fabric swatches. Total cost: $4 to $5. If you bought a similar product specially designed for brides with lacy inserts and full color photos, you'd spend as much as $50.

Regardless of the method you use to organize your wedding, keeping all your receipts and contracts in one place is vitally important. Also, make copies of any written correspondence you have with the businesses you hire. Even keep a telephone log of your phone conversations.

Although chances are your wedding planning will be a smooth process, if any problems do crop up, you'll be glad you spent the time and money to be so well organized.

The Bridal Clock

"I'm late! I'm late for a very important date!" said the rabbit in Alice in Wonderland. At times, as you plan your wedding, you might feel a bit harried your self.

Of course, the first real crisis of any engagement is the realization that you must accomplish 1.6 million things in about 13 seconds in order to get to the church on time. The second crisis is wondering which of those 1.6 million things you should do first.

To solve this problem, we have invented our BRIDAL CLOCK, which is displayed below. Think of the numbers of the clock as months in the wedding planning process. At high noon is your wedding.

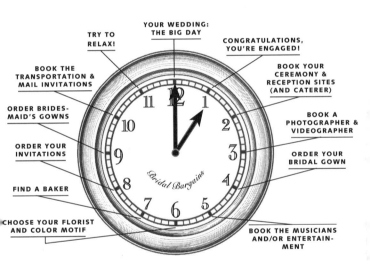

Start with reserving your ceremony site (two o'clock). Next, find and book a reception site and a caterer. From there, shop for your wedding gown . . . and so on.

In each chapter in this book, you'll find specific advice on how much time you need to order everything from invitations to a wedding cake. Of course, the BRIDAL CLOCK gives you a general sense of how far you've gone—and how much further you need to go until the bewitching hour!

To be fair, we should note that many of the bargain tips and advice in this book may require advance planning—it can take up to six months to order a gown through a discount mail-order service, for example. What if you've just got a few months (or weeks) before your wedding, can you still save money? Of course. Each chapter of this book contains cost-cutting alternatives anyone can use, no matter how much time you have to plan your wedding.

What's new in this edition?

We're proud to announce several improvements in this new, third edition of *Bridal Bargains*. First, you'll find "real wedding tips" sprinkled in each chapter—these are actual tips from readers of past editions and sage advice from previous brides. In addition to adding several more apparel designer reviews, you'll find an entirely new section on mail-order catalogs for discount invitations. Photos now illustrate our advice on flower bargains, as well as other tips in the book. We'll discuss how to use the Internet to plan your reception, a bargain source for wedding rings and how to use a laser printer to print invitations. Of course, we've updated all the prices and information on everything from bridal gowns to photography. Finally, check out the tear-out sheets in the back of the book—you'll find all of the "key questions to ask" various vendors in a convenient, take-along package.

PART I

Your Wedding

This traditional satin bridal gown costs $699 at David's Bridal, a 25-store warehouse-style chain. Is it a good deal? Check the "Spotlight: Best Buy #3" later in this chapter.

Chapter 2

Apparel for the Bride

Wonder how you can save 20% to 70% off those fancy designer bridal gowns? In this chapter, we'll show you how, plus teach you seventeen steps to buying the right bridal gown. Then you'll learn thirteen valuable money-saving tips. Finally, we'll expose how dishonest bridal shops rip-off brides, while we teach you how to outfox them. Last but not least, we'll take a candid look at the country's biggest bridal designers, rating them on price and quality.

The Bridal Gown. Nothing symbolizes a wedding more than the bridal gown. Prospective brides are taught from birth to fantasize about this ultimate dress, sparkling with beads, sequins and pearls delicately sewn onto French lace. Of course, the designers who make those gowns are well aware of this—their ads are laced with references to the "fairy-tale" wedding and "storybook" brides.

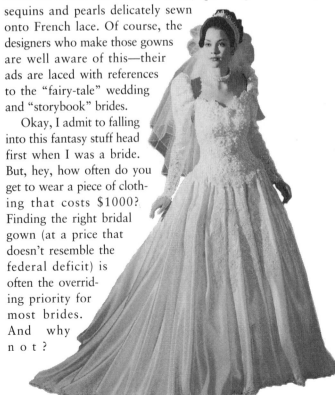

Okay, I admit to falling into this fantasy stuff head first when I was a bride. But, hey, how often do you get to wear a piece of clothing that costs $1000? Finding the right bridal gown (at a price that doesn't resemble the federal deficit) is often the overriding priority for most brides. And why not?

Bridal gown shopping is the ultimate battle between women and the evil apparel industry. This is the Olympics of shopping.

And, gee, wouldn't you have figured? Shopping for a bridal gown is perhaps the most perilous and tricky task in this journey we call wedding planning. You didn't expect this to be easy, did you?

The reasons for this degree of difficulty are complex. In this chapter, we explore the reasons why buying a bridal gown generates the biggest number of complaints from engaged couples. We'll teach you how to find the gown that's just right for you and how not to get ripped off doing it.

Where do brides buy bridal gowns? According to a magazine survey, 70% of all brides purchase a gown at a bridal shop, a specialty store that focuses on bridal and formal apparel. Another 12% purchase a dress from a department store, while 10% have a gown sewn by a professional or friend. The remainder wear a gown that was a family heirloom (2%), borrow or rent a dress (2%), or buy through a discount service or mail order (3%).

In this section, we will focus on buying a bridal gown from a traditional bridal shop. Of course, there are several little-known but quite fascinating alternatives to this route. We'll discuss them later in the chapter.

What Are You Buying?

 At the simplest level, you are buying a dress. But not any dress. This is a darn expensive dress. The average bridal gown costs $800 in most stores, no matter where you live. Many of the premium designer gowns sell for much more, topping $1000 and even $2000.

So what do you think you should get for $800? Well, before you answer this question, we ask you to shift your mind into BRIDAL MODE. That's because if you think in the REAL WORLD MODE you're going to be in for a shock. For example, if we gave you $800 and told you to buy a nice party or cocktail dress you'd expect a few things for that amount of money. Fine fabrics like silk? Sure. Quality construction with a lining and finished seams? Why not. How about sewn sequins and detailing? Hey, you'd expect that for $800! Right?

Well, BRIDAL MODE isn't like that. For $800, all you get is synthetic fabric, shoddy construction with unfinished seams and no lining. Want sequins, pearls and beads? Expect them to be just glued on, not sewn—especially for gowns that are under $600.

Frankly, we can't figure out why this is. Perhaps the entire bridal apparel industry (from the powerful designers to the lowly local bridal shop) think that when women get engaged they collectively lose all sense of reality. Like zombies, brides are supposed to walk into bridal shops and plunk down a cool $1000 for a gown they wouldn't even consider buying for $300 if they saw the same design at a department store.

As a side note, don't forget that the bridal gown is just the beginning. There are many "hidden costs" when buying a bridal gown—you'll also need undergarments, a slip, shoes and the ubiquitous headpiece and veil. If you think bridal gowns are overpriced, wait until you see the prices for accessories. The "average" headpiece and veil runs $150, while you can add another $350 for more accessories. Hence, the total ensemble may cost you $1335. Here's a break-down of extra costs:

HIDDEN COSTS WITH GOWNS CAN ADD UP
(Sample figures for a typical gown—and those necessary extras)

GOWN	$800
RUSH CHARGE	50
ALTERATIONS	65
PRESSING	30
DELIVERY TO CEREMONY	50
CRINOLINE/SLIP	45
BRA	30
HEADPIECE/VEIL	150
SHOES	60
JEWELRY	25
GLOVES/STOCKINGS	30
TOTAL	**$1335**

Wow! It's amazing how an $800 gown can turn into a $1335 total tab in a hurry. Of course, you don't have to pay that much. Order early (at least six months before the wedding) and you won't pay the rush charge. You can save big bucks by borrowing a crinoline/slip, forget the special delivery to the church (carry it yourself), and buy shoes, jewelry, and other accessories at discount stores. More on this later.

Unfortunately, you can also spend much more than those figures. The above figure for alterations is quite conservative—as you'll read in this chapter, you could get zapped for $100 or even $200 at some shops. Some "matching" headpieces and veils can cost over $200.

We should also note that most shops require a 50% deposit on all special orders. (We'll explain later why most gowns are special-ordered instead of bought off-the-rack.) That can be a sizeable financial hit several months before the wedding. The balance is due when the dress comes in.

Sources to Find a Bridal Shop

 Finding a bridal shop is easy. Finding a good bridal shop is somewhat more challenging. Beyond the basic sources, there are three important ways to locate local shops:

❦ *Bridal Magazines* The major bridal magazines are literally plastered with ads from apparel manufacturers. On the page next to the dress, you can often find a list of shops that carry the designer. Just look for your city and bingo! There will be at least one candidate for your search. Before you put much stock in magazines, however, read our article on them later in the chapter.

❦ *Friends* Ask everyone you know if they know someone who was recently married. Call several recent brides and drill them on their experiences. Any shops they recommend? Any shops they recommend you should avoid like the plague? Listen carefully to their advice—we know one couple who was repeatedly warned by friends not to buy at a particular shop. They bought anyway, and, wouldn't you know, they fell victim to a scam and lost $500.

❦ *The Better Business Bureau* Check to see if any shops you have heard about have a record of complaints. Any complaint (even if the company resolved it) is a big, red flag.

Games That Bridal Shops Play

(Not all bridal shops are guilty of the following dishonest practices. However, after visiting over 200 bridal shops, we have encountered several disturbing practices of which you should be aware.)

Once you decide which shop carries the type of gowns you want, the fun begins! It's time to hit the streets! Before you go, realize that once you step inside some bridal shops, you are entering the DARK AGES OF CONSUMERISM. For some reason, bridal shops exist in a time and space where their owners think they're exempt from such silly concepts as Honesty and Ethics. Let's take a look at the appalling tactics that some shops use to confuse you, the consumer.

1 MYSTERY GOWNS. Many bridal shops rip the tags out of their sample dresses to keep you from knowing who designed and manufactured the gown. In other cases, shop owners simply refuse to tell brides who made the dresses, even when the brides ask point blank. Why would they do this? We've interviewed many shop owners who basically

admit they do it to prevent price competition. Hey, they argue, if we tell you the designer, then you'll go down the street to our competitor and get the dress at a discount.

We say this is a bunch of bull. What the shops are trying to do is keep you ignorant. All designers are not equal, some offer better quality work than others. Keeping the designer from you is a sneaky way for them to pass off an inferior gown as "comparable" to a premium design.

What is most perplexing about this deceptive practice is the fact that most brides find out about the shop from a designer's ad in a bridal magazine. Designers spend millions trying to get brides to recognize their brand name and for what? To have their retailers tear out the tags is stupid, especially under the guise of stopping "price competition."

Not only is it stupid, it's also illegal. A federal law called the Textile Fiber Products Identification Act of 1960 requires all apparel (yes, even bridal) to be properly labeled. This must include the name of the manufacturer (or their "registered number" assigned by the Federal Trade Commission (202) 326-2222) as well as the fiber content and country of origin. Sadly, many bride shops openly and flagrantly violate this long-standing consumer law.

You'd be offended if you walked into a grocery store only to find all the labels torn off the food. We say you should be just as offended if a bridal shop does this too. If a shop doesn't clearly label their gowns (or refuses to identify the designer of the gown when asked), we suggest you go elsewhere.

SOLUTION: Find a few dresses you like in a bridal magazine. Then walk into the shops listed in the ads and ask to see those specific dresses. If the salespeople say they don't know who makes which gowns, don't believe them. Before you walk out, you may mention to the salesperson that they just lost a big sale.

2 SECRET CODES. We've visited many shops who secretly encode the tags on their dresses to hide the manufacturer and style number from you. The reason is the same as the above deceptive practice. Many shops don't want you to know what you're spending those big bucks for.

3 THE BIG FUSS. No matter what gowns you try on, the salesperson who helps you will invariably gush and say something like *"You're sooooo beautiful!"* Sometimes I wonder if I tried on a gown made out of potato sacks, whether the salesperson wouldn't say something like *"Wow! That natural look! It's so you!"*

As you might have guessed, most salespeople at bridal shops work on commission. Hence, it's to their advantage to get you to buy any gown, preferably an expensive one. Some salespeople go overboard, taking advantage of brides-to-be by playing on their emotions. For example, at one store we visited, the salespeople couldn't stop complimenting how wonderful one particularly expensive designer gown looked on me. One salesperson came up to me and asked if she could take my picture for "an album of all their brides." After the picture, the salespeople put the camera down and helped me back in the dressing room. That's when my fiance looked at the camera and noticed that it didn't have any film! Later we visited the same store again and saw no picture album. The whole "schtick" was a clever ploy to convince me to buy that dress. A word to the wise: don't get caught up in all the false flattery that will be heaped on you by the bridal shop.

SOLUTION: On your shopping trips, bring a trusted friend or relative (just one!) with you whose opinion you value—this ensures a more objective critique.

4 KILLER MARK-UPS. The profit for bridal shops just doesn't stop at the 100% mark-up they charge on gowns. Alterations are also a big profit center, averaging $50 to $200 per gown. Euphemistically called "custom fitting," alterations to make the gown fit perfectly are very expensive. One industry newsletter we saw recommended bridal shop owners triple the cost of the seamstress and pass that along to the brides. Hence, if the shop pays a seamstress $7 per hour to alter gowns, the charge to you, the consumer is $21 per hour—a bit greedy in our opinion.

Accessories are another big profit area. Shops sell everything from bras, shoes and slips to ring pillows, garter belts, and champagne glasses at steep mark-ups. Veils and headpieces are extraordinarily expensive.

5 FALSE DISCOUNTS. In what is a patently illegal practice, many shops mark their gowns over suggested retail and then offer you a "discount." Gee, thanks! For example, we visited one shop that was offering a 10% discount off all special-order gowns. One gown we saw had a price tag of $1100—we later learned the suggested retail for the gown was just $1000. Their big 10% discount knocked $110 off the gown, bringing the price down to $990. The real discount was just $10 off the real retail price—a puny 1%.

6 ELUSIVE EXCLUSIVES. Some bridal designers occasionally give one shop in a city an "exclusive" over certain dresses. These dresses are termed "confined," and you can't find them anywhere else in town. Or can you? Many bridal shops skirt these exclusive rules by a process called "trans-shipping."

You may run into "trans-shipping" on your visits to bridal shops. We visited several shops that told us they can order any gown we want, even if they don't carry it in their store. How do they do this? Let's assume BRIDAL SHOP 1 carries DRESSES A, B, and C. But you want a DRESS D. So SHOP 1 calls SHOP 2 (usually in a nearby city) who just happens to carry DRESS D. So, SHOP 2 places the order and then ships the dress to SHOP 1.

"Trans-shipping," which is not illegal per se but is in a grey area of interstate commerce law, occurs because most bridal shops can only carry and stock 10 to 12 lines of bridal apparel. But there are over 200 apparel designers out there, and odds are a customer may want a dress they don't carry. Instead of losing the order, the shop places the order through back-door channels. By the way, shops often add a small mark-up for the trouble of ordering a dress from another shop.

The use of exclusives in the bridal industry is quite controversial. Store owners love them since they limit competition and help stop discounting. The apparel designers, on the other hand, are divided. Some believe exclusives are the only way to control who resells their gowns. Others claim they can't make a profit by granting exclusives. Giving certain designs to just one shop in a city doesn't generate enough orders to make financial sense.

In fact, that's why we've noticed many designers talk with two tongues. While they flail against the evils of trans-shipping and discounting (keeping their retailers happy), the apparel designers then quietly sell to discounters. Others turn a blind eye to trans-shipping since, of course, they end up selling more dresses and making more profit.

The propaganda war has reached new heights lately, with traditional bridal shops displaying "authenticity" certificates that certify they are "authorized outlets." Bridal manufacturers are advertising in bridal magazines that only legitimate dealers will have these certificates. One flyer from a bridal shop we received said that if you don't buy from an authorized outlet, you will get inferior quality or a counterfeit gown.

Is this true? Of course not. In fact, that same shop that distributed the flyer also said they could get gowns that they do not regularly stock "from another source." Obviously, they are trans-shipping these gowns. Frankly, the duplicity of some of these bridal shops is disgusting.

What does this mean for you the consumer? Be careful of bridal shops who promise they can get in "any dress you want." Check with past client references and the Better Business Bureau to make sure the shop has fulfilled its previous promises.

Getting Started: How Far in Advance?

 Most brides are surprised when they learn how far in advance they must place an order for their gown. At the bare minimum you need at least three months. Ideally, you should order your gown any-where from five to nine months before your wedding. That's right, nine months!

Why do you need so much time? Well, the big factor is the kind of gown you want. Some gowns take as little as six weeks to order, while others can take up to six months. Later, we'll explain why it takes bridal apparel manufacturers so darn long to fill an order. But first, let's take a look at the five stages of buying a bridal gown:

1 SHOPPING. Hey, don't forget that you need time to look for the gown which is just right for you. Sure, you can do this in as little as one day, but most brides we have interviewed said they took two to three weeks. That's because it takes time to visit a handful of the area's best shops and more time to make a final decision.

2 ORDERING. Once you place your order, the shop sends it to the manufacturer. Some designers have six-week turnaround times. However, several "upper-end" designers can take as long as six months. A few manufacturers have quick delivery that can get you a gown in a couple of weeks, not months. That's why it's important you know the designer of the gown in order to make sure the gown will arrive in time for your wedding—see the reviews of designers at the end of this chapter for the scoop. Some manufacturers offer "rush service," but the extra fee for this may bust your budget.

3 ALTERATIONS. After the gown comes in, you must leave another month for alterations. Some shops may be able to do "rush" jobs but the quality may be rushed too. You may have several time-consuming "fittings," appointments with the seamstress where you inch closer and closer to getting the gown to fit just right.

4 PORTRAIT. In some areas, brides have a formal portrait taken before the wedding which is displayed at the reception. In order to leave enough time to view the proofs and get the final print framed, most photographers suggest doing the portrait four to six weeks before the wedding. That means the dress has to be altered and ready to go four to six weeks before your wedding.

5 SAFETY ZONE FOR MISTAKES. Yes, mistakes can happen, especially here. Apparel is most prone to problems since there are more people involved in this process than any other. Orders can be botched at several points between

the store and the manufacturer. Leaving time (perhaps two weeks) in your schedule to correct problems is prudent.

Whoa! That's a lot of time! The time guideline we recommend is six months. If you want an elaborate designer gown, allow for even more time. However, don't panic if your wedding is around the corner. Look for our TOP MONEY SAVING TIPS later in this chapter—many of these strategies can quickly unite you with a gown.

Step-by-step Shopping Strategies

 ✿ Step 1: After you've set the date, sit down with your fiance to talk about your wedding. The key decision is how formal you want the event. Now, the bridal magazines have all kinds of crazy rules to tell you what to wear for each formality degree but just remember this: your gown should reflect your ceremony and reception. The gown that is perfect for an intimate garden ceremony held in the afternoon probably won't work at a evening ceremony for 200 close friends at a big church with a sit-down dinner reception following.

✿ Step 2: Now that you have an idea of how formal your wedding is, look through those ads for bridal designers. Which gowns intrigue you? Which ones make you sick? Key on the elements of the dresses—the silhouettes, the necklines, waistlines, train length, amount of lace, etc.

✿ Step 3: Before you head out to local bridal shops, ask your ceremony site coordinator if there are any restrictions on the amount of skin you can show in the sanctuary. Some churches frown on low-cut, off-the-shoulder or strapless gowns. Determining what's appropriate before you fall in love with the "wrong" gown is prudent. Another note of caution: beware of sheath or mermaid-style gowns if you have to kneel during the ceremony. Most of these gowns don't have slits in the back, making kneeling next to impossible. One option is to have your seamstress add a slit in the back (look inside the gown to make sure a seam is there for the slit).

✿ Step 4: Listen to the advice of recently-married friends and acquaintances about local bridal shops. Their insights on selection, service and prices may be valuable. Using our other sources listed above, draw up a list of three to five stores that offer the gowns you want. Don't forget that a store's service (how you're treated when you come through the door) is almost as important as the selection of dresses.

❦ *Step 5:* In addition to the stores on your list, visit a store or two that sells expensive dresses. Why? This is the best way to educate yourself about quality bridal gowns. Expensive gowns (over $1000 or even $2000) feature quality construction, luxurious fabrics and exquisite detailing. Then, when you hit the discounters, warehouse stores and outlets, you can tell what's quality—and what's not. You won't be fooled by gowns marked "sale $490, originally $1000," when the fabric and construction indicate the original price should have been much less. Besides, trying on those fancy gowns is fun.

❦ *Step 6:* Back to reality. It's time to go shopping for real. Try to visit the stores on your list on any day other than a Saturday. Weekends at bridal shops are crazy—everyone tries to shop on Saturday. If you can go during the week (some stores are open in the evening), you'll find better service, less-crowded dressing rooms, etc. Call ahead—some shops require an appointment. Go with just one other person (your mom, a friend, even your fiance) whose opinion you value. Having more than one other person will give you too many opinions.

❦ *Step 7:* When you visit the shop, be prepared to answer a few questions. The first is probably the most critical: how much do you want to spend? We recommend lying here. Most salespeople will try to "up-sell" you slightly, so we recommend you under-estimate your price range by 10%. If you really have budgeted about $1000 for a gown (not including alterations, headpiece/veil and any accessories), tell them you want to spend $800 to $900. Undoubtedly, they'll show you a few dresses closer to $1000.

❦ *Step 8:* Next you'll be asked about your wedding date and how formal your wedding will be. We recommend fudging about your wedding date—push it forward about three to four weeks. For example, if you're real wedding date is June 18, tell the shop the "big day" is May 21. This insures that your gown will arrive (and any potential problems will be fixed) in time. The wedding date will also help determine whether you'll want long or short sleeves, for example. Also, they'll ask you what "style" of gown you prefer: Sheath or mermaid-style? Traditional floor-length skirt or tea length? High or low neckline? Long train or no train? Obviously, you won't know all the answers but try to give the salesperson an idea of your preferences.

❦ *Step 9:* Keep an open mind. Many dresses pictured in bridal magazines on those anorexic models look different in real life on real women. Try a few different styles, with a friend (your mom, a bridesmaid, etc.) taking notes on which gowns you like the best. Be careful of "gown overload:" trying on too many gowns in one day can confuse you, blending into a blur of lace and sequins. Our advice: don't try on more than five gowns at each shop. Besides you'll become exhausted.

❦ *Step 10:* Narrow down your choices to two or three gowns. Make an appointment with the same salesperson you talked with on your first visit. Now, it's decision time! Don't be rushed by anyone but also remember that time is of the essence—you need time for alterations, etc.

❦ *Step 11:* Congratulations! You've selected your bridal gown! Now, before you put down that hefty 50% deposit, ask the bridal shop the questions we list later in this chapter. Get measured (bust, waist, hips and from the base of your throat to the hemline) with a vinyl tape measure and ask to see the manufacturer's sizing chart. Given your measurements (and remember your bust measurement is not your bra size), select the gown size that corresponds to the largest of your measurements. Remember you can make a gown smaller but you can't expand it. It's important that you make the decision of what size to order—don't let the bridal shop make it for you. We'll explain why later in our PITFALLS section.

❦ *Step 12:* If you're unsure whether the shop is an authorized dealer for the gown you want, call the manufacturer (many designers' phone numbers are printed later in this chapter). Most manufacturers will tell you if the shop is a legitimate re-seller for their gowns. If the shop won't tell you the manufacturer of the gown, we suggest you go elsewhere. If the manufacturer tells you the shop is not an authorized dealer, the shop may be sewing counterfeit gowns or trans-shipping the gowns from another source. Ask the owner about this and if you don't get a straight answer, go elsewhere. Don't worry: you may be able to get the dress from another more honest shop even if the first shop claims they have an "exclusive."

An exception to this rule: many discount mail order and warehouse companies are not "official" authorized outlets, according to public statements by bridal manufactures. While the discounters often purchase gowns through legitimate channels, the designers don't want to admit that they're selling to them.

❦ *Step 13:* When you place an order, get a receipt with the price, color, size, manufacturer, style number, and most importantly, the promised delivery date. Also, listed on the ticket should be any extra special-order requests (some dresses can be ordered on a rush basis, with extra beading or length, different fabric and detailing, etc.). All these requests cost extra. If the store recommends a size for you, write on the ticket "Store recommends size." Then, if the gown comes in needing extensive (and expensive) alterations, you're in a better negotiating position. When you place your order, also get a written estimate on alterations. Be sure you ask about the store's refund policy, as well as any extra charges for pressing and so on.

❦ *Step 14:* One to two weeks after you place the order, call the bridal shop for a "confirmed shipping date." The shop receives this date from the manufacturer after it places the order.

REAL WEDDING TIP
Dialing for Deals

Does it pay to call around to get a good deal on a bridal gown? Recent bride Susan Zeller Smith of Layton, Utah says yes. "One way your book helped me was to suggest that to get a dress, I wasn't obligated to go to a bridal shop," Susan wrote. "For example, I found a Jessica McClintock dress I wanted for $375 in a bridal shop here in Utah. Then I went to a regular dress shop that I knew carried that brand. They could order it for me, charge me $375 and even had a seamstress lined up for alterations—but it would all take six weeks. Unfortunately, I only had four weeks (short engagement!)."

"So, I called the Jessica McClintock shop in San Diego, which I found by looking at ads in bridal magazines. The dress was in stock for $385. I would pay $10 shipping and handling, but no sales tax because it was an out-of-state sale. Then the sales clerk told me the store would match the lowest price I could find. So I did some calling around and found the dress for $300 at a local discount store in Utah. The San Diego shop matched that price! From finding and trying on the dress to actually having it in my hands was just 11 days. And I saved $75."

❦ *Step 15:* Starting two weeks before your dress is due in, call the bridal shop to confirm the date your dress will actually arrive. Delays at the factory (imported lace arriving late, a larger number of back-orders) can delay the delivery of your gown, as well as the bridesmaids'. Bridal shops are usually aware of such delays. Calling ahead will help avoid surprises.

❦ *Step 16:* Hooray! The dress has arrived! Now, inspect the dress carefully. Gowns have been known to come in with flaws, stains, tears—you name it. Don't rely on the bridal shop to inspect the dress for you (many let problems slip through the cracks). Also, confirm the size of the dress by actually measuring it. Incorrect sizing is a major problem with some manufacturers.

❦ *Step 17:* Alterations. Whether you have the shop or an outside seamstress alter the gown, give the alterations person a firm deadline. Be sure to confirm the experience level of the seamstress—how familiar are they with bridal fabric? How long have they been altering gowns? See our PITFALLS for more advice on alterations.

Questions to Ask a Bridal Shop

1 WHO IS THE MANUFACTURER OF THIS DRESS? As we previously mentioned, some shops try to hide this from you. Even though they have torn out the tags from the dress (in an illegal effort to keep you from comparison shopping), you can still ask them about who makes the dress. This is important for several reasons. First, you can determine if the store is an authorized dealer for the gown by calling the manufacturer. Second, you know what you are buying—some designers offer better quality than others. If the shop refuses to tell you, or if the salesperson says they just "don't know," go elsewhere.

2 HOW LONG WILL IT TAKE TO GET THE DRESS IN? A critical question since the delivery times for different manufacturers vary greatly. If you choose to fudge your wedding date (moving it forward a few weeks from the actual date), be careful here. If you move the date up too early, the shop may not be able to order the dress in time for the early date. In general, bridal gowns take anywhere from six weeks to six months to special order. Bridesmaids' gowns take about two to four months.

3 WHAT ARE YOUR PAYMENT POLICIES? Can you put the deposit on a credit card? This is a very important point as you'll learn in our next section. Also, confirm the

store's refund policy. Nearly all bridal shops have a "no refunds" policy on special-order dresses—even if the wedding is called off or there is a death in the family. Read the receipt (or contract) carefully before you sign.

4 CAN I HAVE A WRITTEN ESTIMATE FOR ALTERATIONS? Before you order, get this in writing. Remember that you do not have to use the store's in-house alterations department (even though they will strongly encourage you to). Quality alterations are extremely important—we've seen too many unskilled seamstresses (many at bridal shops) botch alterations. Whomever you decide to hire, try to meet the seamstress who will alter your gown. Ask them about their experience with bridal gowns. How long have they been doing this work? Have they ever worked with the fabric and lace on your dress before? If you detect any problems here or can't get a written estimate, consider hiring another seamstress.

5 WHAT FREE SERVICES ARE AVAILABLE? Some stores throw in a free "steaming" with all bridal gown orders. Other freebies might include free delivery and even ceremony coordination (especially when you place a large order with the shop). Some of these services might be offered quietly. Ask and ye shall receive.

Here's a little consumer tip that can protect you from getting ripped off by unscrupulous bridal shops: use your credit card (instead of cash or a check) to pay for your bridal gown. Most brides and grooms do not realize that a special federal consumer protection law protects all deposits and payments made with credit cards. The law, called Federal Regulation C, entitles consumers to receive refunds if the merchandise delivered doesn't live up to what's promised.

Specifically, the law says that if you have a problem with the quality of goods or services that you purchased with a credit card and you have tried in good faith to correct the problem with the merchant, you may not have to pay the bill. (As a side note, this only applies to purchases over $50 and if the purchase was made in your home state or within 100 miles of your mailing address).

So what does that mean for you? Well, let's suppose two brides put $500 deposits on the exact same dress at BRIDAL SHOP XYZ in their town. One bride puts the deposit on her MasterCard (or any credit card) and the other writes a check. Delivery will take four months (which is not an unusual amount of time).

Let us tell you that four months may not seem like a long time to you but it's an ETERNITY to retailers. Much can happen in four months. In fact, BRIDAL SHOP XYZ has now gone out of business. The owner of the shop has left town without a trace. So what's happened to our two brides? Well, the bride who put the deposit on her credit card will contact the bank that issued her card and, most likely, she will receive a refund.

And what happens to the other bride who paid with a check (or cash)? Her $500 is probably lost forever. Sure, she can sue the owner in small claims court—if she can find the owner. She can also report the incident (which is technically theft) to the local authorities. But, if the shop owner has left town, the bride may never see her money again.

Does this sound far-fetched? Well, it happens more often than you think. In one city we researched, for example, no less than ten bridal shops went out of business in just three years! While four closed "responsibly" (they stopped taking deposits and turned their special orders over to other shops in town), the other six bridal shops did not. Their owners took deposits until the day they closed and then quickly left town. We know dozens of brides who lost hundreds of dollars in deposits because they paid cash (or by check) instead of with a credit card.

In 1992, a couple who owned a chain of Detroit area bridal shops was indicated on 60 counts of fraud in a "bridal scam." Over 5000 brides were bilked out of $1 million in deposits when the shops failed to deliver dresses. And this isn't an isolated case: sources in the bridal industry tell us not a week goes by when there isn't a shop somewhere in the country that closes and takes brides' deposits.

According to several credit card-issuing banks we've talked to, deposits paid with credit cards for bridal apparel (or any wedding-related purchase) are protected by Federal Regulation C. Be aware that the rules apparently vary slightly with each issuing bank. One bank we talked to had a requirement that complaints have to be filed within 60 days of the purchase. The fact that a deposit isn't really a "purchase" clouds the issue somewhat. Another bank told us they would refund money (credit the account) to a bride under a scenario like the one above even if more than 60 days had elapsed from the date the deposit was processed.

What if you've already paid the bill? You still may be able to get a refund—contact your card-issuer for more info. What if the shop only takes cash or checks? Here's a sneaky solution: many credit cards also give you checks (which work like cash withdrawals) for purchases. Purchases with these credit card "checks" may be covered under the same law. Check with your bank first.

Now we are not telling you this to scare you. The odds of you getting ripped off by a dishonest bridal shop are not great, but . . . BE CAREFUL! This advice applies to other deposits too, not only for bridal apparel. If you can, don't pay for any other "wedding" deposits (the cake, flowers, photographer, etc.) with cash or a check. A WORD TO THE WISE: USE YOUR CREDIT CARD.

Top Money-saving Secrets

 Many of our top money-saving tips for bridal apparel involve alternatives to traditional bridal shops. The savings we calculate are based on a gown that retails for $1000.

1 RENT A GOWN. Since the mid 1980's, bridal apparel rental stores have opened in most major cities (look in the phone book under bridal shops). Rental prices for bridal gowns range from $75 for simple dresses to $600 for expensive designer gowns. That's right, you typically can rent one of those exquisite designer gowns dripping with pearls and lace that would retail for $1000 or $2000 for under $600. Most rental shops require a $100 to $200 deposit. The dresses, which are professionally cleaned after each rental, can be altered to fit. The only drawback to renting may be the search required to find a good rental shop—there are typically only one or two in each city. For example, while you'd expect to find a rental shop like Just Once in New York City (292 5th Ave., 212-465-0960), what about a smaller city like Kansas City? Even here we found a rental shop, An Alternative (800) 995-2338 or (816) 761-8686. The message: check your local Yellow Pages under "bridal shops" for possible sources or call the rental companies listed in Chapter 3. Total savings = $400 or more.

2 PURCHASE A GOWN THROUGH THE MAIL. Most brides don't realize they can order nationally-advertised gowns from bridal brokers at a substantial discount from retail. These brand-new gowns, discounted 20% to 30% off retail, are shipped directly to you, cutting out the middle-men. For more information on one of the most popular discounters, see our review of "Discount Bridal Service" later in this chapter. Another great mail-order source: JCPenney's bridal catalog (800) 527-8345 features affordable bridal

gowns from Sweetheart and Alfred Angelo for $175 to $495. Also available: bridesmaids gowns ($89 to $160), flower girl dresses, headpieces, shoes and other accessories. Total savings for a typical mail-order gown = $200 to $400.

3 CHECK THE CLASSIFIEDS. We've found some incredible bargains listed right in the Sunday classifieds. Sometimes weddings are cancelled or postponed. In other cases, recent brides who need extra cash are willing to part with their gowns. Most of these gowns are in excellent shape; some have never been worn before! Best of all: the prices we've noticed are often 50% or more off retail. Of course, you'll need to carefully inspect the gown before buying. Other items available through the classifieds: accessories like crinolines or full slips. Total possible savings = $500 or more.

4 CONSIDER "CUSTOM-DESIGNING." If you want a gown that costs over $1000, consider having a local seamstress create a copy of the original. We've seen several beautiful gowns that were custom-designed by talented seamstresses. Why is this a money-saving tip? Well, first a seamstress can often buy the fabric at wholesale (or at a discount from retail). Second, there are no costly alterations—your gown is made to fit. Certainly the labor costs for an expert seamstress can be substantial, but the results can be striking. Total savings here will vary but we priced one exquisite silk Jim Hjelm gown at $2700 retail which cost only $1400 to reproduce with a local seamstress.

5 HIT FILENE'S BASEMENT SALE. Can you buy a $3000 designer bridal gown for just $199? You can if you brave Filene's Basement sale in Boston and Chicago. Four times a year in Boston (and two times in Chicago), this sale prompts a stampede of brides who strip the racks of designer gowns in mere seconds. Call the stores directly for the latest schedule (Boston 617-542-2011, Chicago 312-553-1055) and read the box "The Running of the Brides" later in this chapter for more information on this amazing event.

6 SEW IT YOURSELF. If you have a flair for sewing (or know a good friend who does), consider making your gown yourself. Patterns for bridal gowns are readily available at local fabric shops. One fabric shop pointed out to us that the exact materials (fabric, lace, pattern) to make a popular designer dress would cost $225. The retail of this dress was $995—not counting an extra $100 for alterations. One note of caution: sewing with bridal fabric is challenging so be careful if you go this route. Total savings = $775, less your time and labor to sew the gown.

7 Buy a "sample" gown. Bridal shops often sell their "samples" throughout the year at substantial discounts from retail. Most gowns are marked down at least 50%, some even more. Since many shops sell most of their gowns by "special order," they need these "demonstrator" samples to entice orders. What happens when a gown is discontinued or they need more room for new styles? It's sale time! Check your local paper since some shops have big sample sales throughout the year. However, most shops have a rack of discounted "sample" gowns year-round. Before you use this tip, read our PITFALLS section for special tips on buying a sample gown. Total savings = $500 or more.

8 Wear your mom's dress or borrow a friend's gown. You'd be surprised how a seamstress can inexpensively restore a vintage gown. Even if you spend $100 to $200 to have the gown altered or jazzed up, this will be much less than buying a gown at retail. Borrowing a gown from a friend is another great money-saving option. Total savings = $800 or even more!

9 Order a bridesmaid's or less formal gown. Most brides don't realize that many bridesmaids' gowns can be ordered in white. For a less formal wedding, you can get a plain bridesmaid's gown for just $75 to $150. Beautiful, less-formal gowns (without trains, sequins, pearls, etc.) are available from ready-to-wear clothing designers like Jessica McClintock. Her stunning line of bridal dresses start at just $200 (ranging upward to $800).

10 Check out vintage clothing shops. A reader in Berkeley, CA shared with us a great bargain shopping tip: vintage clothing stores. In Berkeley, she found a beautiful 1950's wedding gown in excellent condition for just $200 at a local vintage clothing store. Most large cities have such stores; check your local phone book under "Clothes—Vintage."

11 Shop at bridal outlet stores. Scattered across the country are outlet stores for bridal designers and retailers that offer substantial savings. See the Best Buy section later in this chapter for more information.

12 Buy a consignment gown. These pre-owned gowns are often fantastic bargains. Many apparel consignment shops have popped up in major cities across the nation. In San Antonio, Texas, for example, we found not only one, but four consignment shops that carried bridal. Best of all, these shops often carry a wide assortment of

quality gowns by the top designers. One shop we visited had over 50 gowns, including one beautiful Priscilla of Boston gown with exquisitely beaded Venice lace. The gown, which originally retailed for $2000, was only $400! Or you could rent it for just $200! Now, that's a bargain.

If you want to sell your gown after your wedding, many shops accept consignments from across the country. Zazu (617) 527-2555 in Boston is a pioneer in the industry. If you're looking for a local consignment store, you can send a self addressed, stamped envelope to the Bridal Consignment Shop Network, c/o PJ's Closet, 432 Garrisonville Rd., Stafford, VA 22554. Another source: the National Association of Resale and Thrift Stores, Attention: Bridal Resources, 20331 Mack Ave., Grosse Pointe Woods, MI 48230 or call (800) 544-0751.

13 Swap the Fabric. Fallen in love with a silk gown but can't afford the silk price? You still might be able to afford that gown—just ask if the manufacturer offers the same style in a less-expensive fabric. For example, designer Carmi Couture (for a dealer near you, call 212-921-7658) offers a white Duchess satin sheath confection with jewel illusion neckline and Guipure lace bodice (style #3005). The price? $1400. If that's too much, you can request the same style in less-expensive Italian satin for $1100. That's a $300 savings for a simple fabric swap.

Biggest Myths about Bridal Gowns

 Myth #1 "*Considering how expensive those designer bridal gowns are, I assume they are being hand-crafted by skilled seamstresses.*"

Wrong. We spoke to a bridal apparel industry veteran who painted a very unflattering picture of how most bridal gowns are manufactured. First, the bridal manufacturer waits until they receive a certain number of orders for each size (that's why it takes so long to get a gown). Let's say they wait for 10 orders of size 8 gowns in a particular style. When the orders come in, they stack on a conveyer belt 10 layers of fabric, which are then cut by a laser. Later, machines sew the seams together. Even the lace added to the dress may have been machine-beaded at another location. Basically, that's why so many gowns look like disasters, with unfinished seams, no lining and shoddy construction. The assembly process has more to do with factory assembly lines than human beings lovingly hand-sewing the gowns. As a result, gowns are not custom-made to your measurements but rather are rough approximations which often require additional alterations (read: money).

The Running of the Brides
Snagging a Designer Gown for $199 at Filene's

There is probably no bridal event more famous in the U.S. than Filene's Basement sale. If you happen to be near Boston or Chicago when the sale is on and think you can survive the scene, this is definitely one event not to miss.

That's because Filene's sale features designer gowns that cost $1000, $2000 and even $3000—all marked down to an amazing $199. Yes, you read right. $199. As you might expect, bargains like this attract a crowd.

After interviewing several brides who braved the sale and got great deals, we'd like to offer our tips to making the most of Filene's Basement Bridal Sale.

1. *Plan in advance.* Filene's Basement does *not* regularly carry bridal gowns. Each year, they collect discontinued samples and other dresses from bankrupt shops and designers. When they've collected enough gowns, they hold the sale at only two locations: downtown Boston (617) 542-2011 and Chicago (312) 553-1055. In Boston, the sale usually is held four times a year—February, May/June, August and November. In Chicago, expect it in May and November. (Call the store directly for the latest schedule).

2. *Brace for bargains.* No matter what the original retail price, all gowns are marked at $199. Patricia Boudrot, Filene's spokesperson, told me she's seen one originally priced at $7000, although most would retail in the $1000 to $2000 range.

3. *Arrive early.* While the doors open at 8 am, brides start lining up as early as 5:30 am to 6 am. Several hundred brides will be in line by the time the doors open.

4. *Bring an entourage.* These gowns are heavy—some brides bring an entourage of friends and family to help them hold dresses. Of course, second opinions are nice too. In addition to bridal gowns, Filene's also sells bridesmaids, mothers-of-the-bride and other formal dresses at the sale.

5. *Dress appropriately.* Sneakers are a must. Forget your purse or let a friend carry it. While dressing rooms are avail-

Myth #2 "*I'm a rather contemporary person but when I visited a bridal shop, all I saw were boring, traditional gowns. Do I have to choose a gown that says "Hi! I'm young and innocent?"*

Getting married does not require you to lose all your

able, most brides just try on the dresses right there in the aisles. "Some women wear leotards or bodysuits," says Filene's spokesperson, "but others are in the underwear they plan to actually wear under the wedding gown—these women are not shy."

6. *Brace yourself.* This is not a sale for the meek—brides can get darn aggressive. Waiting brides have broken down the door at the entrance at least five times over the years in Boston. When the doors open, everyone rushes to the racks. All the gowns are gone in 32 to 46 seconds (this has been timed by more than a few amazed reporters, says Filene's.) In the feeding frenzy, fist-fights have broken out, although Filene's says security is on-hand to keep the event from becoming a melee.

7. *Grab anything.* Here's a bummer: gowns are not separated by size. Everything is mixed together. Hence, the best strategy would be to grab just about anything. Then let the bargaining begin.

8. *Be prepared to haggle.* At many sales, brides will trade with one another to find the style or size they want. That's why you should grab as many gowns as you can—more bargaining power. If you're a size 8 and you've grabbed a size 14, never put it back on the rack. Instead, trade it with another bride for a dress you like. You might have to barter several times before finding "the" dress.

9. *Mix and match.* Here's a smart strategy: mix and match different gowns. Some brides have had a seamstress combine pieces of two or more gowns they found at Filene's sale. Take the lace from one dress, combine it with the fabric and train from another and voila! A designer look at a fraction of the designer price. Remember the cost of embroidered lace and silk fabric today is far more than the $199 cost of each dress.

10. *Cut it down.* You may find the perfect gown at Filene's sale—except it's two sizes too big. Yet at these prices, you may be able to easily afford to have a seamstress cut it down to size. One bride had a size 14 re-made into a size 4.

fashion sense. Too often, the bridal apparel industry stereotypes all brides to fit certain molds. You must look like Cinderella or, if you're daring, perhaps Snow White. Well, we say, no Virginia, you don't have to look like TRADITIONAL BRIDE on your wedding day if that's not your style. Consider some snazzy alternatives. Watters and

Watters has several tailored suits and "informal" gowns that are striking sheaths with delicate portrait collars. In taffeta, satin and silk shantung, the gowns retail for $300 to $600. Another of our favorites is Jessica McClintock, whose cotton and linen suits are wonderfully sophisticated. Several other "ready-to-wear" women's apparel designers have entered the bridal market with splashy and contemporary gowns. Among the best are Scaasi and Carolina Herrera.

Myth #3 *"I know brides must always wear white but I've tried on several white gowns and they make me look like death warmed over. My mom says I have no other choice—it's white or nothing."*

Tell your mom you do have a choice. Almost all gowns also come in ivory (also called candlelight and, believe it or not, egg shell). But that's not all the color possibilities. Several gowns now are available in subtle blush colors like peach and pink. These creamy hues are simply breath-taking.

Helpful Hints

1 SHOPPING FOR A GOWN IS AN EXHAUSTING PROCESS. Take frequent breaks and don't try to squeeze too many shop visits into one day. Limit yourself to two to three shops, leaving time to think about which gown you like most.

2 SOMETIMES THE FIRST DRESS YOU TRY ON IS THE ONE YOU PICK. We're always surprised by the number of brides we've met who buy the first gown they tried on. Perhaps the first impression you get from that first gown is the one that most sticks in your mind.

Pitfalls to Avoid

Pitfall #1
BAIT AND SWITCH WITH ADVERTISED GOWNS.
"I fell in love with this dress in a bridal magazine. I called the local shop listed in the ad—they told me they didn't have that design, but had others 'just like it.' I was so furious . . . is this a scam or what?"

Well, it certainly isn't ethical. Believe or not, the designers do not always require their dealers to carry the advertised gown—even if the store is listed in the ad! While the shop may have other gowns by the same designer, the dress you fell in love with is sometimes nowhere to be found. Usually the shop comes up with some excuse (our favorite is "the designer decided not to cut that sample yet") and then subtly tries to "switch" you to a "similar design we have in stock." We urge the industry to stop this practice. Don't patronize shops who pull the "bait and switch" scam. And shame on the bridal magazines for allowing this charade to happen in the first place.

Another twist to this pitfall: stores who lie and say they have the advertised gown in stock. Once you arrive, the sales clerk announces that the sample "was just sold yesterday. Would you like to see other dresses?" The best way to avoid this is to call the store on the day you plan to visit. Confirm the dress is still there and get the name of person who verified this information over the phone. That way you can hold someone personally responsible if a bait and switch occurs.

Pitfall #2
OVER-SIZING TO MAKE EXTRA MONEY ON ALTERATIONS.

"I wear a size 6 in street clothes and I was rather surprised when the saleswoman at the bridal shop told me I needed to order a size 10. In fact, the sample gown was a 10 and it really didn't fit. What should I do about the size I order?"

First, understand that bridal sizes do not correspond to real-world sizes. However, a favorite ploy of dishonest bridal shops is to order a dress way too large for the bride. Then, when it comes in, guess what? It needs expensive alterations! Here are our tips on this very common deceptive practice:

❦ Don't pay attention to the sample gown. Most sample gowns are tried on so many times that they stretch—what once was a 10 may now be a 12 or even a 14!

❦ Instead, get measured with a vinyl tape measure. Needed measurements include bust, waist, hips, and from the base of the throat to the hemline. Don't let the bridal shop use a cloth measuring tape, since these can stretch over time and give inaccurate measurements.

❦ Ask to personally see the manufacturer's sizing chart. Each manufacturer has their own sizing chart that is sent to each bridal shop that carries their gowns. As you will see, just because you wear a size 8 in "street clothes" does not mean you will wear a size 8 in bridal gowns. Complicating this process is the fact there is no standard for bridal sizing—all manufacturers do their own sizing.

For example, a bride with the measurements of 36, 26, 38 (bust, waist, hips) would be a size 10 in a Bianchi, size 12 in an Ilissa, and a size 14 in a Mori Lee. According to a survey of 35 top manufacturers, this same bride would need to order a size 8 in 3% of the designers, a size 10 in 34% of the designers, a size 12 in 45% of the designers, or even a size 14 in 18% of the designers! Isn't this crazy?

❦ Given your measurements, pick a size that closely matches your largest measurement. Remember that gowns can only be altered in, not out. Make sure the size you pick is clearly marked on the sales receipt.

Brides encounter problems in this area when they let the shop pick the size for them. Instead of measuring you, they'll just guess what your size is (usually over-guessing). Other cases we've seen involve intentional fraud—the shop knowingly orders a size too large in order to make extra money on alterations. Be careful. If you accept the shop's "advice," write on the receipt that "Shop Recommends Size." If the dress comes in way too big or too small, you have more leverage in negotiating a solution.

Pitfall #3

MANUFACTURER GOOFS ON SIZING.

"I ordered four bridesmaids dresses from a local bridal shop. When they came in, they were all the wrong sizes—three

---

REAL WEDDING TIP
Stick to your guns

Even if you specify an exact size on the gown order form, you can still fall victim to sizing scams. A bride in Vermont was a case in point. The bridal shop told her she was a size 8. The bride insisted they order her a size 6, which was written on the sales slip. When the gown arrived, guess what size it was? An 8—the shop the claimed the manufacturer sent that size based on the bride's measurements. The bride bought this story and was zapped for an additional $240 to cut the gown down to a size 6 (her true size).

What's wrong with this picture? Manufacturers never see your measurements, unless you pay extra for a "custom cut." Obviously, the shop intentionally ordered the larger size OR tried to pawn off an in-stock sample in size 8. The lesson? Don't accept a gown that arrives in the wrong size. You have a contract with the store to deliver a particular size—if they fail to fulfill their end of the deal, insist on a complete refund.

were way too small and the other was floor length instead of tea length. The shop owner just shrugged her shoulders and told us their seamstress could fix the problem ...for a hefty charge. What should I do?"

First of all, the manufacturer is fully responsible for shipping the correct sizes. If the order is incorrect, the manufacturer should fix it free of charge. If there is not enough time before the wedding to send the dresses back, we believe the manufacturer should pay the bridal shop to alter the gowns to the correct size. The bride is definitely not at fault and should never be charged. In order to protect yourself from this pitfall, make sure all ordered bridal merchandise is inspected and measured when it comes in. Actually take a tape measure and make sure the gowns are the sizes that correspond to the sizing chart. We recommend this since many incorrectly-sized gowns are marked with tags that indicate the correct size. Sizing goofs are a common problem; we've seen numerous cases of gowns that came in too big or too small.

Compounding this rip-off are some shops that refuse to fix defective merchandise. Whether it's the wrong size or botched lace detailing, we've encountered some merchants who refuse to make good. Some claim "there's not enough time before the wedding to send the dress back." This points up the need to order a dress early.

How many dresses come in flawed? One major retailer who sells 10,000 bridal gowns a year told us that, shockingly, two out of every three dresses comes in with a flaw. In about half of those cases, the problem is minor and can be easily fixed. However, the other half include such serious problems as the wrong size or poor workmanship. These must be sent back to the manufacturer to correct.

Pitfall #4

THE BIG SWITCHEROO.

"My bridal gown came in yesterday and boy was I surprised! The lace and fabric looked nothing like the sample gown I tried on or even the magazine picture. What recourse do I have?"

"After four months of waiting, my special-order gown finally arrived. However, it looked suspiciously like the used sample I tried on four months ago. Have I been taken to the cleaners?"

This scam often appears in two flavors: the lace/fabric switcheroo and the "sample gown shell game." First, you must realize that many manufacturers reserve the right to change the lace, fabric and trim on any bridal gown. We've seen several cases where a manufacturer substituted a cheaper lace when they ran out of the more expensive lace. If you're unhappy with the substitutions, ask the bridal shop to go to bat for you. Reputable bridal shops may be able to negotiate a solution (free alterations, a partial refund, etc.) with the manufacturer. If time permits, the gown may be sent back to the manufacturer to make it correct. (Note: many manufactures can ship overnight a correct dress—don't let the shop bully you into thinking you need more time).

We urge all bridal manufacturers to deliver what they promise. If they can't, the bride should be notified and given the opportunity to cancel the order. Substituting lace, fabric or detailing is a deceptive practice and should be stopped.

What about the "sample gown shell game"? This is when a store promises to order a brand new gown, but instead tries to pawn off the used sample dress you originally tried on. The bottom line: you are duped into paying full price for a used gown—clearly an unlawful deceptive trade practice. We've heard reports that this insidious scam is rampant at some shops in Chicago and Detroit, though it can happen anywhere.

Here are some rather ingenious ways to spot this rip-off, as submitted by our readers. First, take a needle and red thread with you to the bridal shop. While you're in the dressing room, sew this thread inside the sample dress in an inconspicuous location. If the shop tries the scam, you can spot the used "sample" by the thread.

Another protection is to take a picture of the gown. But most shops don't allow pictures, you say? Sneak a small camera in your purse and snap a few pictures in the dressing room, after the salesperson leaves. The pictures will help you remember all the details and styling of the sample dress—just in case the shop tries to substitute that used sample or a different gown altogether. One bridal shop employee tipped us off to this scam, saying they often substituted cheaper dresses on brides since they could never remember what they ordered several months ago!

Pitfall #5
WHOOPS! WE FORGOT TO PLACE THE ORDER!

"I ordered a gown from a bridal shop four months ago and was notified yesterday that the shop forgot to place my order! I couldn't believe it! And now they won't give me a refund, instead suggesting I buy a gown out of their stock. What should I do?"

Contact your attorney. When a shop fails to place an order, they are breaking a valid contract and should give you a refund. A pitch to buy a sample gown is terrible. Unfortunately, we have heard of several cases in which bridal shops just forgot to place the order. They simply shrug their shoulders and say "we're sorry!"

Protect yourself by dealing with a reputable shop (find one using the sources we list earlier in this chapter). When you place an order, get a promised delivery date. A few weeks after the purchase, call the bridal shop to confirm the shipping date (they receive this from the manufacturer). The more communication you have with your shop the more likely you will get your gown.

Pitfall #6
BOTCHED ALTERATIONS.

"My bridesmaids gowns came in three weeks ago and they were beautiful! However, when we picked them up after alterations, we couldn't believe our eyes! Those same gowns were a disaster, poorly altered and sewn! How could we have prevented this?"

Bridal shops love to pitch their "expert alterations" service to brides as the only alterative for their gowns. In realty, their "expert seamstress" is sometimes a person they hired last week for $5 per hour who has only altered her daughter's prom gown. No wonder this is one of the biggest problem areas consumers have with bridal shops.

The main problem is the skill level needed to alter bridal gowns. The fabric is slippery and intricately-beaded gowns can make even the most simple jobs challenging. Some bridal shops ask for these problems by hiring inexperienced seamstresses who then botch the alterations.

You can prevent this problem by asking to meet the seamstress before you do the alterations. Ask them about their experience with bridal gowns. Ask to see their work area. If it looks like a sweatshop or if you sense the seamstress is unqualified, get the gown altered somewhere else. Many communities have "free-lance" seamstresses who do excellent work at much more affordable rates. One note of caution: don't skimp here. You want the best alterations money can buy.

Pitfall #7
SAMPLE GOWNS MAY NOT BE BARGAINS.

"I don't have enough time to order a gown before my wedding. I was thinking of buying a sample gown. Are there any things I should watch out for?"

Sample gowns may be a terrific buy or a terrible nightmare. As we explained earlier in this chapter, sample gowns (just like demonstrator models) are cleared out periodically to make room for new styles. Many are marked 50% (or more) off the retail price. The big pitfall here: most sample gowns are in less than great shape. That's because most have been tried on dozens (if not hundreds) of times by different shoppers. Sample gowns may be dirty, stained (especially from makeup) and beaten up. We've seen several that have beads missing and lace that is falling off. Furthermore, the gowns are stretched out and often in no way resemble their original size.

Of course, the condition of sample gowns varies greatly from store to store—some simply take better care of their merchandise. If you go this route, go over the dress with a fine tooth comb. If the shop agrees to clean the gown, get a written guarantee that the purchase is contingent on your approval of the gown after the cleaning. Cleaning a bridal gown is tricky since some dry-cleaning chemicals can discolor the glue used to affix beads/detailing. An inexperienced cleaner can destroy a bridal gown.

Pitfall #8
SALON-STYLE SHOPS.

"I went to a bridal salon where they kept all the gowns in the back. They told me they'd bring out the gowns they thought I would like. Is this kosher?"

We're not big fans of bridal shops that operate "salon-style." In most cases, these shops keep all their gowns out of sight and then ask you for your likes, dislikes, and price ranges. Unless you know exactly what you want, salons can be trying. First of all, the salesperson brings out what she thinks you want to see. We've been to several of these salons and they've yet to figure out what I want. Instead, they tend to bring out what they want to sell (i.e., an expensively-priced gown). We suggest you shop at stores that allow you to see the merchandise. While you can't get a whole picture of what a gown looks like hanging on a hanger, you can tell which detailing (necklines, bodices, beading) you like and have a better feel for prices.

Pitfall #9
HOTEL SALES, FLY-BY-NIGHT COUNTERFEITERS,
AND "UNAUTHORIZED RETAILERS."

"I saw an ad in our paper for a big sale of bridal gowns at a local hotel. They offered large discounts and unbelievable prices. Are these guys for real?"

Well, yes and no. Most of these bridal gown sales at hotels are sponsored by liquidators who are looking to dump merchandise from bankrupt bridal stores. Some of these guys are less than reputable, promising all kinds of service only to leave town quickly after they collect their money. The merchandise for sale is mostly sample gowns. Particularly a problem on the East and West coasts, hotel bridal gown sales are often too good to be true.

Another problem is counterfeit gowns. We have seen reports that several disreputable bridal shops sold brides gowns which were cheap knock-offs of designer gowns. The brides thought they were getting designer originals. You can prevent this problem by calling the manufacturer of the gown to confirm the shop is a legitimate dealer.

A different twist on this scam are shops selling gowns bought on the "grey market." In the past few years, "buying offices" have sprung up to supply gowns to bridal shops who want to skirt the industry's "minimum purchase" requirements. In a couple of cases, we've seen brides stung by these shops, when the gowns they ordered never arrived. Such bridal shops will tell you it takes an incredibly long time (say, six months) to order in a gown that typically takes only 12 weeks. While there are exceptions to this rule (Discount Bridal Service is a reputable discounter that we review later in the chapter), many of these "unauthorized" shops are nothing but trouble.

Pitfall #10

RIP-OFF CHARGES FOR LARGE SIZES, PETITES AND RUSH ORDERS.

"Okay, I'm not one of those anorexic models you see in the magazines. However, when I visited a bridal shop, all they had were size 10 dresses to try on! Then, they told me they charge extra for 'large sizes!' Is this salt in the wound or what?"

Yes, the bridal industry slaps brides who need a large size with a "penalty fee" that can be as much as $50 to $200 or more. But don't feel too singled out, there are also extra charges for petites. The industry claims the extra costs come from "special cuttings" and "increased fabric costs," but we haven't bought that line. Another rip-off: rush charges. Even if your wedding is still three months away, some designers still insist on "rush fees" to get you the dress on time. However, just because the manufacturers can't figure out how to sew a gown in less than three months, doesn't mean you should pay a premium. One solution: if you're a petite, order a regular size dress and have it altered. Our sources say it just isn't worth it to shell out the extra charges to get a petite.

Pitfall #11

DECEPTIVE DISCONTINUATIONS.

"I saw a great gown in a bridal shop last week. Yesterday, they called me to tell me my dress has been discontinued, BUT if I placed my order by Friday, they could still get my gown. Is this legitimate?"

Probably not. This is a common tactic by some dishonest bridal shops that try to pressure brides into quick decisions. Now while it is true that some gowns are discontinued every season, shops can't order a gown after they've been notified of its discontinued status. Hence, they're pulling your leg, trying to get a sale. If you doubt a shop's veracity, call another shop that also carries that same manufacturer. Or call your local Discount Bridal Service Representative.

Pitfall #12
SHOPS THAT HOLD BACK ORDERS.

"I ordered a bridal gown that the shop said would take three months to get in. Four months later, I have no gown and just excuses from the shop. When I ask for a confirmation that they placed the order, I get stonewalled. While my wedding is still two months away, I'm worried."

And you should be! This is another common scam perpetrated by some shops. Instead of immediately placing the order with the manufacturer, they hold on to it. Why? Well, financially-strapped stores may be tempted to use your money to pay other bills—ordering the gown immediately means having to pay the invoice that much faster. How common is this problem? Even Vincent Piccione, president of Alfred Angelo, recently acknowledged how widespread the tactic is. "A major problem that concerns us is retailers who hold on to orders. This is one practice that should be eliminated, thereby putting an end to the root cause of so many horror stories that plague the industry," Piccione said in an industry trade journal.

A parallel scam is the "involuntary lay-away" rip-off. In this case, the bridal shop claims it will take much longer than reality to get in a special-order dress. Most designers fill orders within three or four months, with six being the maximum. Yet, some of our readers report shops who claim it will take *eight or ten months* to get in their dress. What's happening? Perhaps the shop is using your money to pay their electric bill or other expenses—and plans to order your dress a few months down the line. In a sense, this is like a "involuntary lay-away" plan, where the shop holds your money for several months longer than necessary.

How can you avoid this problem? First, put the deposit on a credit card. Ask the bridal shop for a confirmation that the order is placed—most manufactures provide this paperwork. On the order ticket, write "the shop promises to provide an order confirmation or a confirmed shipping date (from the manufacturer) within two weeks." If the shop fails to do so, cancel the order and go elsewhere. Be suspicious of retailers who claim they need more than six months to deliver a bridal gown.

Pitfall #13
IT AIN'T OVER IF IT'S OVER.

"My fiance and I fell on hard financial times and had to postpone our wedding. The problem is I had already ordered a gown. When I contacted the shop, they told me I couldn't cancel the order. Help!"

Most (if not all) bridal shops have "no refund, no cancellation" policies on special-order bridal gowns. Wedding called off? Death in the family? It doesn't matter—you're still on the hook to buy the dress. That means the shop can also take you to court to force you to pay the balance due on the dress.

If you're merely postponing your wedding, ask the shop if you can get "store credit." At least you might be able to use this in the future, or sell the credit to a friend.

Reviews of Selected Bridal Manufacturers

Here is a look at some of the best manufacturers of bridal gowns. Since there are over 200 manufacturers of bridal apparel, we don't have the space to review everyone. Instead, we decided to concentrate on those who are the best and most visible. Our rating system (the key is given below) is based on our extensive research into bridal apparel. In the past six years, we have visited over 200 bridal shops and tried on hundreds of gowns from dozens of manufacturers. The ratings reflect our opinion of the manufacturer's offerings, creativity, prices and quality at the time of this writing. Remember that styles and prices are constantly changing. **Please note: these manufacturers do not sell gowns directly to consumers. We have included phone numbers to call at the end of each review to help you locate a local store or dealer that carries each designer.**

In the last few years, competition in the bridal gown business grew even more intense. A decline in the number of weddings, coupled with an increase in popularity of less-expensive, more sophisticated designs has fueled a virtual price war. Designers are tripping over each other to roll out lower-price gowns. Full-price retailers are battling bridal "warehouses," mail-order discounters and other off-price competitors. What does this mean for you, the bride? Happy days—better-quality gowns at lower prices. Here's a wrap-up of who we think are the best of the best designers.

The Ratings

★★★★   EXCELLENT — *our top pick!*
  ★★★   GOOD — *above average quality, prices and creativity.*
    ★★   FAIR — *could stand some improvement.*
      ★   POOR — *yuck! Could stand major improvement.*

REAL WEDDING TIP
Looking for a large size?

 A reader in Albuquerque, New Mexico called us with this frustrating story—she fell in love with a gown, only to learn the dress' manufacturer doesn't offer large sizes. In fact, less than half of the bridal designers we researched carry "large" or "women" sizes (that is, sizes larger than 20). Most charge an extra fee, which ranges from $20 to $200. Here's a list of designers who offer larger sizes: Alfred Angelo (including the Michele Vincent line), Bridal Originals, Bonny, Bridals by Justine, Country Elegance, Eden, Impression, Jasmine, Jessica McClintock, Joelle, Lili, Mary's, Mori Lee, Mon Cherie, Moonlight, Private Label by G, Sweetheart, T.C. Originals, Timeless Tradition, Victoria's Bridal Collection, Vow & Vogue. (For more information, see the designer's individual review in this section).

Alfred Angelo ★★ One of the country's largest bridal designers, Angelo offers just about something for everyone. Most gowns are in the $300 to $700 range, but a few "couture" gowns top $1000. One typical gown we saw was a doupioni silk design with a high wedding band collar, fitted bodice with hand-beaded re-embroidered lace, full skirt and chapel train. Price: $550. While some of Angelo's upper-end gowns (such as the Michele Piccione and Christian Dior lines) have been favorably compared to Bianchi's elegance, others are less impressive—you get what you pay for with Angelo. Large sizes are available (18-20 are $20 extra and 38 to 44 are 10% more). Only selected styles are available in petites. The biggest news with Alfred Angelo is their new outlet store in Florida—see the Spotlight: Best Buy "Bridal Outlets" later in this chapter for more info. One negative that tempers our recommendation of Alfred Angelo: we find some of the company's marketing practices (such as requiring dealers to sign agreements not to rent their dresses) to be distasteful. See the box at the end of the next chapter for more on this story. Call (800) 528-3589 or (407) 241-7755 to find a local dealer.

Ange D' Amour ★★ This small designer is described by insiders as a "sleeper line with very good value." Most run $600 to $1100 and have moderate amounts of beading and lace. One interesting design that caught our eye was a "Venice lace mini-dress with detachable train" for $750. Only sizes 4 to 20 are available. Call (800) 288-3888 to find a local dealer.

Bianchi ★★½ Bianchi, the Boston juggernaut that sells 50,000 bridal gowns a year, is one of the industry's preeminent powers. Bianchi is one of those designers that does something for everyone. From plain to ornate, Bianchi's beautiful, hand-sewn gowns have prices that range from $850 to $3100. Many brides we met said they chose a Bianchi because that's what their mothers wore at their weddings. A design that caught our eye was a "princess sheath" in silk shantung with empire bodice covered in Guipure lace. Price: $1178. Sizes go up to 24, with some petites available. Call (800) 669-2346 to find a local dealer.

Bonny ★★★ A small, import line with little exposure, yet we've been impressed with their quality. For example, the beads and sequins are sewn on—for gowns that retail for $440 to $850, that's unusual. Bonny has one of the best ivory fabrics in the business and features gowns that are ornate but not overdone. They even have five silk designs that retail for under $800. Bonny's sister line is Sabrina, a lower-priced collection that comes in only four sizes. Sabrina gowns retail for about $450, with quick delivery available. Another Bonny line, "Essence by Esther," features more ornate designs with prices around $800. A nice touch for Bonny: this line is one of the few that has sizes up to 44 (for $30 to $60 extra). Call (714) 961-8884 to find a local dealer.

Bridal Originals ★★ A good "middle of the road" designer, Bridal Originals offers a wide selection of gowns without ignoring the informal and second-time bride. The majority of the line is moderately styled (some call it plain vanilla). Retailing for $430 to $880, most Bridal Original gowns average $600 and are widely available. One interesting design was a heavily beaded and sequined, mermaid-style gown. This lavish dress had floral appliques as well. Sizes up to 30 are available—Bridal Originals is one of the few designers that encourages stores to carry large-size samples. Bridesmaids ($100 to $200) are very traditional and basic. One plus: Bridal Originals has extensive mother-of-the-bride and flower girl collections. Call (800) 876-GOWN or (312) 467-6140 to find a local dealer.

Carmi Couture ★★★½ "Have it your way" must be the theme at Carmi Couture Collection, an up and coming designer. Many dress designs are available in different fabric choices, beaded or unbeaded, with train or without, hem lace or no lace. This flexibility was most impressive. For example, one style featured a Guipure lace bodice, off-the-shoulder cap sleeves, full inverted pleated skirt, and cathedral train with an obi bow. In silk shantung, the gown was

$1300. Can't afford that? How about the same dress in polyester-shantung for $1050. All in all, prices ranged from $790 to $2200. A small drawback: only sizes 4 to 20 are available (with an extra $100 charge for sizes 18 and 20). A separate line of dresses is available in petite sizes only. We were most impressed with Carmi's lush fabrics and creative laces. Availability is still somewhat limited, but the designer has recently expanded the number of stores carrying its gowns. Call (212) 921-7658 to find a local dealer.

Carolina Herrera ★★★ The Porsche of bridal designers, Herrera first came to prominence with a Kennedy family wedding. "Understated elegance" is how we would describe these pricey designs, which have a contemporary European feel. Herrera may be the most creative of bridal designers currently on the market. Availability of these gowns is limited to tony salons and shops. One design we liked was a summery, white organza dress with daisies on the bodice and sleeves, jewel neckline and drop waist. Price: $2400, quite pricey considering the short, chapel-length train. Call (212) 575-0557 to find a local dealer.

Christos ★★ We've dropped our rating of this small designer from the last edition. While Christos' dresses still feature lush fabric and beautiful detailing, the styling of recent designs has been disappointing—an off-the-shoulder, A-line dress with sparse detailing is typical of the line's lackluster showing in past seasons. Despite the sky-high prices that top $2000 and even $3000, and the limited availability (mostly in department stores and fancy bridal salons), Christos still has its fans in some areas, especially Texas. Call (212) 921-0025 to find a local dealer.

Country Elegance by Susan Lane ★★★½ For second-time brides or theme weddings, our pick would be a dress by Country Elegance. Designer Susan Lane has crafted a fascinating line of period-inspired dresses. Designs include Victorian-inspired motifs with high-neck lines and overlay collars in Alencon lace. Other dresses echo the 20's, 30's and 50's fashions. For example, the "Amanda" style is an ivory lace over satin dress with bateau neckline and drop-waist flowing into an ankle length skirt. Price: $410. All the gowns feature delicate laces and tiny flower appliques that are quite impressive. Prices range from $220 to $730, with most designs about $400. Gorgeous colors are available, including antique ivories, rose beiges, and pale blushes. With little or no trains, these mainly informal gowns are a hit with second-time brides. Another plus: Country Elegance's beautiful flower girl dresses are winners, if not somewhat pricey at about $150. If we had to criticize anything about Country Elegance, it would have to be their limited size options. Bridal gown sizes only go up to 16 and tend to run small. About a half dozen styles are available in the 18 to 24 size range (for a whopping $100 to $140 extra). Another important note: one reader called us to say that the fabric on her "rose beige" dress changed color slightly when pressed. Call (818) 765-1551 to find a local dealer.

Demetrios/Ilissa ★★½ No designer typified the last decade's wedding excesses better than Demetrios. Their over-encrusted designs were everywhere, even inspiring the birth of an entire bridal magazine. Yet this designer's star has faded somewhat in the last few years. While Demetrios has tried to adjust to the more casual 90's with toned-down dresses, he just hasn't quite come to grips with the "less is more" demanded by today's bride. A typical example: Demetrios is still churning out gowns like style #1793—a strapless sheath covered top to bottom in Venice lace and pearls. Quite pricey at $1390. On the bright side, Demetrios' line is so huge (14 collections featuring a whopping 200 styles) there probably is something here for everyone. Prices range from $590 to $3900. The only drawback with Demetrios/Ilissa: sizes only go from 4 to 20 (sizes 18 to 20 are $60 extra). Also, a bridal shop owner we spoke to complained that the designer's deliveries are erratic—some dresses arrive in a couple of weeks, while others take six months. The quality and workmanship can be variable as well. As a result, we've lowered Demetrios' rating slightly from the last edition of this book. Call (212) 967-5222 to find a local dealer.

Diamond Collection ★★★ With its trend-setting designs, Diamond Collection's highly-stylized and distinctive gowns are a favorite with the haute couture set. Clearly one of the most innovative manufacturers in the market, Diamond is designed by Robert Legere, Ron Lovece, and Randy Fenoli. Big this year at Diamond are overstuffed tulle skirts, giving many of their designs a Glenda the Good Witch feel. One typical style from designer Fenoli was a retro creation with halter-style neckline, rhinestone-studded Venice lace bodice and full tulle skirt for $1960. In contrast, Lovece offers more understated looks—we liked his silk-satin princess-style design with fabric roses adorning the neckline. Price: $2600. Want a matching veil? It will set you back another $500. As you can tell, Diamond's dress prices aren't for the faint of heart, ranging from $1390 to $3580. Only sizes 4 to 20 can be ordered, with sizes 18 and 20 running an extra $100. Limited availability—mostly in tony bridal shops. Call (212) 302-0210 to find a local dealer.

Eden ★★★★ What a wonderful line! Eden has one of the largest selection of gowns in the $400 to $500 range. If you like Jim Hjelm dresses but can't afford Jim Hjelm prices, Eden has knocked off some of his designs for $790 to $1590. One stand-out gown that caught our eye was a silk shantung design for $600 with hand-beaded embroidered lace, sweetheart neckline, pouff sleeves and basque waist with bow in back. Petites are available, as are large sizes (24 to 32) for $200 extra. A recent addition from this designer is their "value collection," eight styles that retail for *under* $400. Eden also offers a big selection of informals as well. "They ship fast and ship right," says one of our sources. "Eden is headed for glory!" And we agree. Call (818) 441-8715 to find a local dealer.

Eva Haynal Forsyth ★★★ This tony designer is mainly available at department store bridal salons. Several of their latest designs feature exquisite gold embroidery and detailing. Scaasi, the famous ready-to-wear designer, also designs for Eva. For example, one Eva dress was a silver brocade gown with a white mink, portrait collar and silver rhinestone buttons. Price: $3000. Others dresses range from $1500 to a whopping $4100, in sizes 4 to 18. Call (212) 302-7710 or (804) 971-3853 to find a local dealer.

Eve of Milady ★★½ Extremely ornate and traditional, Eve must be doing something right: her designs are often copied by the smaller designers. Mainly available at upscale bridal shops, Eve's line doesn't change much from year to year, but it's still a crowd pleaser. Prices start at $750 (for the less-expensive Boutique line) and range up to $3300 for "Couture" gowns. Typical of the Couture line was a stunning sheath with all-over, floral-inspired lace accented with rhinestones. Bridesmaids are no bargain either—running $190 to $260. Eve strikes a balance between the over-embroidered look and the stark, no detail designs prevalent at other upper-end designers—this season's dresses use luxurious lace and fabric to set them apart from the competition. One bummer: Eve is one of the few designers that actually charges more for ivory fabric, a $100 extra fee. Sizes 4 to 20 are available, with another $100 charge for sizes 18 and 20. Call (212) 302-0050 to find a local dealer.

Fink ★★½ Fink is a small line that doesn't advertise much in the bridal magazines. Nonetheless, the designs may be worth the effort to search out. Styling is above average, yet still fairly traditional. One of our favorite designs from Fink is an Italian satin sheath with removable, wrap-around train, bodice and hemline with Alencon lace and off-the-shoulder net sleeves. Price: $1150. Shipping is slow but worth the wait, our sources say. Prices run $500 to $1200. Add another 10% for sizes 18 and 20. Sizes 4 to 20 are available. Call (212) 921-5683 to find a local dealer.

Galina ★★★½ One of our picks for best bridal designers, Galina pioneered many of the hot bridal looks of the past decade. Fine fabrics are the trademark of Galina, whose dresses tend to be elegantly detailed with simple trains and hemlines. A pleasant surprise is Galina's budget-priced line, called "Galina Bouquet." These gowns range from $700 to $1100, while the regular Galina gowns retail for $1200 to $3000. Another plus: Galina doesn't shy away from color, making some of the most beautiful pale pink gowns available on the market. One Galina Bouquet gown that caught our attention featured a white ribbon lace bodice, scoop neckline, and organza skirt with triple-ribbon edging. Price: $770. In fact, we thought many of the Bouquet dresses were best buys. Sizes go up to 20, with an extra $100 to $150 charge for sizes 18 and 20. Call (212) 564-1020 to find a local dealer.

Impression ★★½ Don't judge this designer by their lackluster ads. What the ads don't show is the opulent lace and wonderful fabrics. The designs are very traditional, with classic lines and detailing. Impression's dresses range from $450 to $850. Sizes 2 to 30 are available, with sizes larger than 16 running an extra $30 to $70. Call (800) BRIDAL-1 to find a local dealer.

Jasmine ★★★★ Here's a hot line that's a very good value. Jasmine's innovative detailing and well-priced gowns are winning many fans. The Haute Couture line is quite stylish—nice use of lace and beading, without being too gaudy. The Jasmine Collection's dresses are more simple with traditional necklines and silhouettes. The fabric in this line isn't as luxurious as the Haute Couture collection. One stand-out we liked was a silk shantung Haute Couture design with off-the-shoulder neckline and beaded appliques adorning the front and back bodice. Cascading lace appliques on the skirt finish the look. Price: $1000. Overall, Jasmine gowns range from $570 to $1200. Large sizes up to 44 are available for an additional $60 to $100. Call (708) 519-7778 to find a local dealer.

Jessica McClintock ★★★★ This ready-to-wear designer has won a lot of fans with her well-designed and priced bridal apparel. Based in San Francisco, McClintock's designs are fresh and innovative, described as "very feminine." Several sheath and strapless looks are stand-outs, as were several silk creations we viewed. The informals are fantastic, offering the most choices in this category next to Susan Lane. Few can beat McClintock's prices considering the quality: most dresses cost between $180 and $760. Bridesmaids' gowns (with fabrics such as cotton, silk and velvet, ranging from $104 to $300) are also impressive. The designer also has 11 affordable flower girl dresses for $56 to $92. For the prices and quality, McClintock is a definite best buy. Most dresses are available in sizes 4 to 16, although a few are available up to 24. McClintock has 14 stores in nine states, plus a large number of dealers. For even more savings, check out their bridal outlet stores—more information on that later. Delivery usually takes less than a month, much faster than other bridal designers. We should note that

The Catalog Chase

With all the designer phone numbers listed in this chapter, you might think that you can call and get a catalog, right? Wrong. Most bridal dress designers do not send out catalogs to consumers—and some can be downright hostile on the phone when you ask. Instead, designers dole out glossy four-color catalogs to bridal shops, hoping they'll use them as sales tools.

Fat chance. Most shops horde the catalogs and reprints of ads from bridal magazines, afraid that if they pass them out, their customers would use them to comparison shop competitors. Interestingly enough, several shops debated this topic in a recent issue of *Vows*, a trade magazine. "(Catalogs are) just putting a tool in (the bride's) hands to price shop you to death," an Ohio bridal shop owner said. "I think catalogs are wonderful," said a Wisconsin dress shop manager, who uses them as a resource—not for brides, mind you, but for her *salespeople*. She added: "I don't think they should be finding their way into the hands of consumers."

Of course, not everyone has such an anti-consumer attitude. "I don't worry that the bride is going to shop around," said another shop owner who does hand out the catalogs. "We know they are going to shop around. I feel that if they have something with our name on it, they are going to remember us." And even shops who refuse to give out catalogs will relent and give them to customers—that is, *after* a deposit is placed. Another exception to the catalog chase: bridesmaids dresses catalogs. Most shops will hand these out so you can show an out-of-town bridesmaid a picture of the dress.

McClintock has cut back advertising lately—hence you may want to send for her bridal catalog by mailing a check for $6 to Jessica McClintock, 1400 16th St., San Francisco, CA, 94103. Call (800) 333-5301 or (415) 495-3030 to find a local dealer.

Jim Hjelm ★★★★ Hjelm produces classic silhouettes with exquisite beading and lace detailing. Quality is impeccable; prices range from $650 to $2750. Hjelm's lower-price collection, "Visions," features seven styles that are good buys—one white silk shantung dress with ribbon lace, off-the-shoulder scalloped neckline, long-fitted sleeves, and full gathered skirt with chapel train was just $950. Sizes 4 to 20 are available, with sizes 18 to 20 running $150 extra. While Jim Hjelm's "Private Collection" (read: expensive) gowns are more fashion-forward in styling, the designer plays it safe with the lower-price gowns. Hjelm's bridesmaids designs could use an overhaul; most are dull and expensive, running from $170 to $230. Call (212) 764-6960 to find a local dealer.

Joelle ★★½ Joelle's designer, Zurc, has spiced up this collection with some outstanding dresses. From sheaths with cap sleeves and wrap-around trains, to tulle-skirted designs with lace cut-out sleeves and delicate detailing, Joelle seems to be on a roll. One new design that got our eye was a Marie Antoinette-inspired style complete with three-quarter ruffled sleeves. All you need is a powdered wig and shazam! Instant theme wedding. The bridesmaids are also quite stylish this year, with two-piece suits and wrap-around tulip skirts ($156 to $250). Bridal gown prices are moderate, ranging from $340 to $1300. Sizes run 4 to 20, with some styles in sizes 38 to 42 (for an extra $30 to $80). Call (212) 736-8811 to find a local dealer.

Laura Ashley Here's a sad story of one designer who lost their focus. Laura Ashley made a splash in the 1980's with a line of wedding dresses perfect for a garden wedding. The simple, informal designs made of cotton had equally simple price tags—most were under $500. Then, Ashley blew it; as their gowns became popular, they raised prices so high that some gowns topped $1500 in recent years. While you might spend $400 for a simple dress with no train, shelling out over $1000 bucks for the same look seemed a bit silly. Simple bridesmaids dresses were equally pricey, approaching $250. At the same time Laura Ashley was raising prices, other bridal designers were slashing theirs and introducing low-cost dresses that knocked-off Ashley's simple designs. As a result of Ashley's big miscalculation, sales plummeted. What happened? The company was forced to discontinue the entire bridal line in 1995.

Lili ★★½ This California-based importer claims to be the fastest growing bridal designer in the U.S. Unfortunately, some of this growth caught up with the company recently when they had to discontinue several styles because of import quota problems. Nonetheless, we found Lili to be one of the best buys for brides. Nearly all of these ornate, hand-beaded gowns retail for $424 to $750. Lili also brags about quick delivery (as little as one week in some cases), since it stocks many styles in their warehouse. New this year at Lili is their "Kensington Collection," several all-silk designs with simple accents. All of their gowns are hand-beaded—an unusual sight in this price range. We just hope that they are able to overcome their growing pains in future seasons. Sizes 4 to 20 are available; a few styles are also in larger sizes up to 28. Call (800) 258-7944 to find a local dealer.

Marisa ★★★★ Especially popular among southern brides, Marisa is a small line of some very unusual dresses. Nothing is "run of the mill" here. Marisa's young designer does original designs, not copies. The unique lace treatments and plain skirts give these dresses a different look— the focus is on the upper-half of the dress, not the bottom. Stunning rose Guipure lace highlighted one silk shantung dress that was our favorite; it had off-the-shoulder cap sleeves, sweetheart neckline and a chapel-length train. Price: $1100. Overall, Marisa's gowns are expensive, with most designs running $990 to $1900. Sizes range from 4 to 20, with sizes 18 and 20 are $100 extra. Even though the dresses are pricey, each does have a built-in petticoat and excellent craftsmanship. One note of caution about Marisa: just because you see one of their dresses in a magazine, don't assume it's available on the market. In a recent season, we noticed two separate cases of Marisa advertising a gown in a major bridal magazine, only to not put the dresses into production. Call (212) 944-0022 to find a local dealer.

Mary's ★★ Mary's by P.C. Mary's Inc. is a Texas-based importer that offers basic styles that are middle-of-the-road in quality. Recently, the designer has offered dresses that range from "ruffle explosions" to the over-encrusted lace look, similar to Demetrios. Mary's offers several sheath designs, including one satin dress with shirred portrait neckline and a double-bowed back for $440. The designer has eliminated many of the expensive designs from past seasons—prices now range from $340 to $840 with sizes 4 to 30. Sizes 18 to 30 are an extra $30 to $50. Call (713) 933-9678 to find a local dealer.

Mon Cheri ★★★½ Don't look for this import designer's ads in the bridal magazines—Mon Cheri rarely advertises. Instead, the designer concentrates on lower prices for brides. Mon Cheri's strategy is to knock-off the best dress designs from other manufacturers, although lately they've experimented with some original creations. The line includes five separate collections, including "Pure Silk" gowns that retail for an incredibly affordable $700. We were also impressed by the new Mon Cheri Couture collection, all-silk gowns that are elegant knocks of upper-end designers like Eva Forsyth in the $750 to $1000 range. Overall, Mon Cheri's prices start at $380 and most are in the $600 to $800 range. They even have two all-cotton designs. We liked one cotton brocade gown with triple wrap sleeves trimmed with fabric flowers. A steal for $658. Veils are also a good deal, running $60 to $150. "The designs are fantastic copies of expensive designers and the prices hard to beat," one source old us. Large sizes (18 to 20 and 38 to 44) are only a $20 to $60 up-charge—very reasonable. Call (609) 530-1900 to find a local dealer.

Moonlight ★★★ We've upped the rating of this designer, reflecting a rise in their quality and reliability. Designer Carol Hai turns out gowns with big doses of flair and drama. You won't find many simple skirts and plain bodices here. Instead, check out the satin sheath with huge shoulder bows that might knock over a bridesmaid who gets too close during the photo session. If that's too much, you may like Moonlight's new silk gowns with more toned-down accents. They're also a great value—these silk designs run $710 to $1190. Overall, Moonlight's prices range from $550 to $1500. Quality is very good (the same plant that produces Jasmine gowns also churns out Moonlight). Sizes run 4 to 44, with sizes 38 to 44 costing an extra $80 to $120. Call (708) 884-7199 to find a local dealer.

Mori Lee/Regency ★★ Here's a hot import designer who continues to wow industry insiders with their affordable gowns. Designer Madeline Gardner has created some unique styles, with quality and craftsmanship that rivals domestic designers. Mori Lee offers three collections, starting with the "Boutique" line that's in the affordable, under $550 range. Their regular Mori Lee line and the "Regency by Madeline Gardner" collection run $450 to $930. A satin mermaid style with Battenberg cut-out lace is $700, for example. A few designs are available in large sizes (up to 42) for $80 extra. While Mori Lee is a "best buy" for value, their deliveries are another story. Insiders call them "horrendous," with some dresses taking four weeks to get in and others six months. "If you want a bridesmaids dress, you better have six months and an iron stomach," says one source. Mori Lee will hopefully fix these problems with a new plant they've purchased in Pennsylvania, which will produce bridesmaids in the $96 to $140 range (a good value). Call (212) 947-3490 to find a local dealer.

Paula Varsalona ★★ This small designer from Kansas City is famous for doing unique and original designs. One dress design we liked was a white-on-white swirl pattern with giant, leg-o-mutton sleeves and strategically scattered seed pearls. Occasionally, all that creativity misses the mark—Varsalona wins our award for the most ridiculous bridal design. Her sequined jump-suit with detachable tulle over-skirt is a flop, in our opinion. For all those brides who want to wear a pant suit to their wedding, this design can be had for a mere $1995. Overall, Varsalona's prices range up to $4860. New this year is a smart-looking bridesmaids collection, with prices running $184 to $260. Call (212) 221-5600 to find a local dealer.

Priscilla of Boston ★★★½ Boston-based Priscilla has a fresh look this year, with over 80 new designs. New owner and designer Patricia Kaneb (who bought the company in 1993) has attempted to turn around the ailing design house that fell on hard times in the '80's when many department store boutiques closed. Kaneb, a 33-year-old Boston University MBA, has added a couture line with six designs that cost as much as (you might want to sit down before you read this) $9000. If that's too rich, Priscilla's regular dresses are a more down-to-earth $780 to $3600. A typical example: check out the silk, off-the-shoulder dress with Lyon lace for $1900. Most of Priscilla's gowns have classic lines and delicate lace—don't expect lots of dangling beads and flashy sequins. Sizes run 2 to 20; Priscilla is one of the few designers that has an entire petite collection. Call (617) 242-2677 to find a local dealer.

Private Label by G/Ginza Collection ★★★ This designer offers gowns in the very affordable under $500 range. Even more remarkable is the quality—every gown is hand-beaded! No glue! While Ginza gowns range from $310 to $690, Private Label by G is somewhat more expensive, running from $500 to $800. Most of the gowns are copies of more expensive designers like Eve of Milady and feature lace cut-outs on the trains. For example, one traditionally styled gown featured a heart-shaped cut-out adorned with drop-pearls above the cathedral-length train. More beading accented the V-necked satin bodice. Price: $730. Both Ginza and Private Label have sizes up to 42 but no petites. Large sizes (38, 40, 42) are an extra $100. Call (800) 654-7375 to find a local dealer.

St. Pucchi ★★½ Wow is about all we can say about this Texas-based designer. 100% pure silk, these top-of-the-line gowns are individually hand-cut and hand-embroidered—the detailing is just incredible! Completely lined (with sewn in bra cups and petticoats), St. Pucchi's has several collections with prices that are not for the faint of wallet—the gowns start at $1090. One gown we saw had lace cut-work on the sleeves, bodice and train. If you're looking for a gown that's heavily beaded, nobody beats St. Pucchi for their flash and panache. On the down side, delivery is slow, taking three to five months. Sizes go up to 20 (with a 20% up-charge for sizes 18 and 20). One positive development: St. Pucchi has recently released a line of lower-priced gowns called "St. Pucchi Classique." These retail for $800 to $1400. Call (214) 631-4039 to find a local dealer.

Sweetheart ★★ Here's a very traditional designer that has an occasional flash of style. Most gowns are between $400 and $850. We were impressed with some of their new silk designs—one Doupioni silk dress featured a beaded Alencon lace bodice, sprinkled with pale pink rosebuds. Short pouff sleeves and full train completed the look for $700. One plus: Sweetheart has a large selection of informals. Another advantage is their delivery time—since the designer keeps most sizes (4-44) in stock, delivery is relatively quick. Call (212) 868-7536 to find a local dealer.

Venus ★★½ California-based Venus has backed off the glitz with their new designs. Most feature classic lines and do away with the over-done beading look. A new silk line with nine styles was most impressive, with prices starting at $600. Overall, Venus' dresses range from $300 to $1200. In addition to Venus, the company also markets the Pallas Athena collection, a less-ornate (and less-expensive) line of dresses. Informals are available for as little as $160. Call (800) OH-VENUS or (818) 285-6528 to find a local dealer.

Vera Wang ★★★ She's been described as the "Giorgio Armani" of the bridal world. She's designed dresses for some big-time celebrities, including Mariah Carey's wedding gown and Nancy Kerrigan's outfit at the Olympics. Most of all, she's Vera Wang, the hottest bridal designer on the planet. Wang's trademark are unusual fabrics like crepe silks and special touches like sheer stretch netting. All this "elegant simplicity" doesn't come cheap—Wang gowns start at $1800 and go to $4000. The average dress runs $2800. And those are the off-the-rack designs—if you want a custom design, prepare to shell out at least $10,000. At those prices, we can't give her our top rating, no matter how creative the dresses are. Available at Wang's New York "Bridal House" as well as several department stores nationwide (call 212-628-3400).

Victoria's Bridal Collection ★★★ "Very traditional" describes this California-based designer's dresses, which range from $400 to $1400. A typical example: a V-necked ball-gown with beaded, Venice-lace, satin-rose cluster accents, and a double-bow back for $558. Victoria's best fabric is a matte satin, a more elegant look than the shiny stuff. Both petite and large sizes are available. Call (714) 258-8714 for a local dealer.

Vow & Vogue ★★★½ This designer has wowed brides with a collection of unbelievably affordable gowns. For example, we noticed one silk design with sophisticated lace-covered bodice, matte satin skirt and delicate beading for a mere $620. In fact, Vow & Vogue's line of "Silk Sensation" dresses range from just $400 to $720—now, that's a deal. Sizes range from 4 to 26, with an extra $20 to $50 for large sizes. Call (909) 598-0528 to find a local dealer.

Wallentin ★★ Texas-based Wallentin is a designer with two different collections: the expensive and the very expensive. On the upper end, the Wallentin Collection includes pricey confections that range from $1260 up to an incredible $4080 (time to mortgage the house). For that money, you get intricate beading and exquisite lace cut-outs similar to St. Pucchi in style. In the less-pricey, Camelot Collection, expect gowns in the $500 to $1400 range. One style featured embroidered and beaded Battenberg cut-outs, gathered puff sleeves and a very large back bow for $800. While we liked Wallentin, their ads don't do justice to their gowns. We wished we could see more detail in the dresses. Sizes run 4 to 20. Call (800) 925-5954, (214) 721-7049 to find a local dealer.

Spotlight: Best Buy #1

Discount Bridal Service
(Over 300 representatives nationwide)
(800) 874-8794

Discount Bridal Service (DBS) is a mail-order company that offers 20% to 30% discounts on almost all nationally-advertised bridal apparel. Hold it! How can that be, you ask?

Well, DBS has found an interesting way to get you those same fancy designer gowns without the fancy designer price tag. Here's how they do it: DBS has a central headquarters in Baltimore, Maryland and a network of over 300 representatives in major cities. The reps don't have typical bridal shops with all the high overhead and bloated inventory expenses. By cutting out expensive overhead, DBS passes the savings along to brides in the form of sizeable discounts.

For example, we priced one fancy designer gown dripping with lace and pearls at a retail of $2390. Then we called the local DBS rep in our city and found that she could order the very same dress for just $1700! Wow! That's a savings of $690 or nearly 30%! Other bridal gowns we priced were available at 20% to 25% discounts, with great deals on bridesmaids, headpieces/veils, flower girl and mother of the bride dresses as well!

So what's the catch, you say? Well, you do have to pay for shipping, freight and insurance on all orders...but that came to just $30 extra on the gown we priced. Another slight disadvantage: DBS requires all orders to be paid in advance. Also, some dresses take more time than normal to order—up to six months in some cases

When you order a gown from DBS, the merchandise is directly shipped to your home address after being inspected at their headquarters. If the gown needs alterations, DBS reps can usually refer you to one of several local seamstresses. Another big plus for DBS: while most bridal shops carry just 10 to 12 bridal apparel lines, DBS can order from over 100 different manufacturers.

So what do regular bridal shops think of DBS? Well, most of their comments are unprintable here. Basically, many bridal shops are mad as all heck that brides can get gowns at such big discounts. Bridal shops are also angry that consumers come into their shop to try on their gowns and then go to DBS to buy. Of course, all this is just sour grapes—if shops provided good service and lower prices, there would be no reason to order from DBS.

Other bridal shops question the authenticity of the company, wondering how they can order those same designer quality gowns. Surprisingly, this is a good example of the behind-the-scenes struggle between retailers and manufacturers over discounting. While everyone (except the brides) complains about discounting, many of the manufacturers are quietly selling to discounters like DBS.

Anyway, we like DBS and recommend the company highly. Perhaps the biggest challenge to ordering a gown from the company is identifying the exact dress. With many shops coding and concealing the identity of the gowns, the best solution may be to find a picture of the same gown in a bridal magazine. Since many gowns are advertised at one point in their life, DBS can nail down the exact manufacturer and style by just knowing the magazine issue and page number.

Here are a few other "frequently asked questions" about this mail-order service we hear from brides:

❦ *Does DBS take credit cards?* Until recently, the answer was no—you had to pay in full with either cash or check. This was obviously a major negative, in our opinion. As this book went to press, however, the company announced a plan to have all their dealers take credit cards soon. As of this writing, only a handful of dealers processed credit card payments, but we're hopeful this number will increase in the near future.

❦ *I called the designer and they said they don't sell to DBS. What gives?* Some designers are telling the truth—and others aren't. It's true that DBS buys some of its gowns through "third-party sources" (such as another bridal shop who carries the line). In other cases, designers sell directly to DBS, but deny it in public. Why? They don't want to offend their full-price dealers. Yet, the bridal industry is a very small cottage business—everyone knows what everyone else is doing. So, the designers' denials ring false to us. Anyway, it doesn't matter to you—DBS sells first-quality, name-brand gowns, not copies or clones. We wouldn't recommend any company in this book that sells counterfeit merchandise.

❦ *Does it take longer to order a gown from DBS?* Yes, sometimes. However, this varies from designer to designer, even gown to gown. The best bet is to call and ask. What causes this delay? One reason is DBS' quality assurance program; all gowns are first shipped from the manufacturer to their Baltimore, Maryland headquarters for inspection. After it passes, it's shipped on to you—this extra step can add time. Even if you have to pay a rush charge from DBS, it still may be less than the price at a local shop. Compare prices to make sure you're getting the best deal from any source.

As a side note, DBS representatives often offer discounts on wedding invitations and other accessories. Even if you decide not to order a gown from DBS, they may be able to save you money on another aspect of your wedding. For the DBS representative in your town, call toll-free (800) 874-8794. If you want a designer bridal gown but don't have a designer bank account, Discount Bridal Service may be the answer.

Spotlight: Best Buy #2

Kleinfelds
(718) 833-1100

Kleinfelds, 8202 5th Ave., Brooklyn, NY claims to be the largest bridal retailer in the country, if not the world. And all that buying power translates into lower prices on their giant selection of bridal apparel. While the store claims it isn't a "discount" store, their prices are often 10% to 25% below retail.

What if you don't live in or near New York? Well, you can order gowns by phone. Just fax them a magazine picture of the gown, along with your measurements. Kleinfelds will then special-order the gown and have it shipped to your home address. The company even takes credit cards, a big plus in our opinion. Delivery takes about three to six months.

If you can't get to Kleinfelds, it's possible that Kleinfelds will be coming to a location near you. In 1995, the company joined forces with Saks Fifth Avenue to roll out "Wedding Dress" boutiques. Located inside Saks Fifth Avenue's department stores, these Kleinfelds outposts carry an "edited" selection of gowns (about 200 styles). While the prices are the same as at the original Kleinfelds store, the alterations charges may vary. At this writing, there are two Wedding Dress boutiques open in Saks (in New York and Atlanta), with more slated for California and Florida.

In business since 1942, Kleinfelds even has an entire building dedicated to bridesmaids and "special occasion" dresses for moms and guests. The "bridal attendants" store is about two blocks from their main location, at 8209 3rd Ave. in Brooklyn (718) 238-1500.

What do our readers think of Kleinfelds? The reviews are decidedly mixed. One bride called to rave about their mail-order service, claiming she saved 20% over retail. Others aren't so generous about the store itself. One bride panned the store's selection of sample dresses which were in "terrible condition," she said. "The salespeople were also very pushy." Other brides complain about appointments running two hours late, designer tags torn out of dresses and general rude treatment. "This is a very New York experience," one bride summed up. "Terrible service but great deals."

Spotlight: Best Buy #3

Bridal Outlets & Discount Warehouses

If the sixties were the "we" decade and seventies were the "me" decade, then the nineties will probably be known as the "never buy retail" decade. Popping up all across the country are Outlet Malls where you can get designer goods at non-designer prices. Can't find what you're looking for there? Well, visit any of the warehouse clubs and buy something in bulk for a steal.

But can you get such a deal on a bridal dress? The answer is yes, if you're lucky enough to live in a city with a bridal outlet store or warehouse. Here's the scoop.

Bridal Warehouses. Frankly, most bridal designers would rather die than be caught "discounting" their past-seasons gowns to brides. Instead of selling these goods to brides directly, they'd rather dump them to a "liquidator" who would quietly dispose of them without much fuss.

In the past, these liquidators would ply the country like nomads, setting up "special sales" in hotel ballrooms. ONE DAY ONLY their ads would scream, attracting flocks of brides who would pursue the used samples at the local Holiday Inn.

When the recession of the early 90's hit, the liquidators had a flash of inspiration—why not set up a "warehouse" where brides could buy these gowns? If it works for office supplies and electronics, why not bridal?

Suddenly, they began popping up like weeds. **David's Bridal** (formally David's Warehouse) was probably the first. David's has 25 stores as far north as Boston and as far west as Phoenix (call 800-399-2743 or 610-896-2111 for a store near you). The average warehouse stocks 1300 bridal gowns, in sizes 2 to 24. All gowns are off-the-rack, no special orders.

Even regular bridal retailers have gotten into the act, figuring if you can't beat 'em, join 'em. Hence the BridesMart chain in Texas (the largest in the state) has set up several bridal warehouses in Houston.

What are all these "warehouses" selling? Many stock hundreds of "past season" (read: old) bridal gowns. Our readers report the condition of the dresses varies between "excellent" and "trashed." While some dresses are last season's closeouts, others are used samples bought from bankrupt bridal stores. David's sells private-label gowns made overseas under such names as Oleg Cassini and Gloria Vanderbilt.

Of course, the advantage is you can quickly get a gown. Many warehouses stock a wide variety of sizes—if you find what you're looking for, you can walk out that same day with a dress. No waiting months for a "special order" to arrive.

Critics point out that the deals aren't as good as they seem. At one bridal warehouse, we heard reports of inflated suggested-retail prices. For example, the warehouse was claiming that a $300 gown had a "suggested retail price" of $900. Sewn in Taiwan, this gown probably would have retailed for no more than $400 or $500. Hence, the deals aren't as sweet as they may seem. Furthermore, the quality of these clone knock-offs gowns is certainly not the same as designer originals.

A bride in Columbus called us with a similar complaint about a David's Bridal outlet in Ohio. She found one dress with a "suggested" retail price if $900. While David's regular price was $625, it was marked down to $450 during a grand opening sale. Was this a good deal? Not so fast, says the bride. She swears she saw the exact same dress (an Alfred Angelo design) in another shop for just $525. So, while it was marked below the competition, it was far from a 50% savings off the so-called retail price.

Given all the caveats, should you visit the neighborhood bridal warehouse? Sure, why not. Just do some shopping in advance at other bridal shops so you are more aware of quality and price. Don't think you're getting a big bargain just because the store has the word "warehouse" in its name.

Bridal Outlets While most famous bridal designers do not have outlets, there are a few exceptions.

Jessica McClintock, for example, has not one but FIVE outlets for her popular line of bridal apparel. The flagship outlet store is the Gunne Sax outlet in San Francisco (415) 495-3326, which not only has 20,000 dresses discounted 20% to 70%, but includes a fabric outlet too. Also in California, the "La Petite Factory" (909) 982-1866 in Mont Clair and "Sutter Place" in Huntington Beach (714) 841-7124 are Jessica McClintock outlets under assumed names. If you live in the East, check out the Jessica McClintock outlets in Reading, PA (610) 478-0810 or Central Valley, NY in Woodbury Commons (914) 928-7474. All outlet stores carry past-season styles at a 20% to 70% savings.

Laura Ashley fans will probably be thrilled to hear that the designer has five outlets, in Secaucus, New Jersey (201) 863-3066, Woodbridge, Virginia (703) 494-3124, Myrtle Beach, South Carolina (803) 236-4244, Freeport, Maine (207) 865-3300 and Orlando, Florida (407) 351-2785. We strongly urge you to call before you make the trip—not all of the outlets have bridesmaids and the selection changes frequently. When they are available, the savings can be as much as 60% off retail.

Alfred Angelo sells discontinued styles and over-stock samples at an outlet store in Sawgrass Mills Mall near Ft. Lauderdale, Florida (305) 846-9198. Prices are about 50% off retail, with bridal gowns ranging from $149 to $629. All sales are "cash and carry" (there are no special orders). The outlet also sells bridesmaids dresses.

JCPenney (214) 431-0226 has several bridal outlets in a few states. Our readers have praised the selection and prices

Gown Preservation
The dirty little secret of the bridal dress industry

Bridal gowns in dress shops take an incredible amount of abuse. Make-up stains, filthy hemlines, lace that gets dirty—repeated try-ons can turn the most beautiful white gown into a mess.

So, if a bridal gown gets stained, do dress shops send it out to one of those expensive, national gown cleaners? Or even a local dry cleaner? Nope, here's the surprising secret: most bridal shops just pop that dirty gown into a washing machine in the back of the store.

You read right—many dress shops simply wash bridal gowns in a regular washing machine to remove dirt, make-up stains and other signs of wear and tear. Now, we find this highly ironic since many of these same shops pitch their customers to use very expensive, nationwide "gown preservation" companies that charge $100, $200 or more to "preserve" their gown. In a business where "custom-ordered" gowns require $150 in alterations and accessories like veils are grossly overpriced, this is probably the final insult to brides who have traversed the wedding industry—the gown preservation scam.

Just what do these gown preservation companies do for all this money? Well, just ask recent bride Shelley Brown-Parish of Hampton Falls, NH. On the advice of the bridal shop where she bought the gown, she paid $250 to Nationwide Gown Cleaning Service of Flushing, NY to clean and preserve her $3800 Scassi wedding gown. The allegedly clean gown was returned to her in a sealed box, along with a notice saying if the box was opened, the company would not guarantee the gown.

Four years later, Brown decided to sell the gown and took it to a local consignment shop. When the box was opened, she was horrified. "The entire gown had changed color from white to ivory," she said, noting it had "large yellow stains all over the dress, blue ball-point pen marks on the front and on the train, and also had blood stains where the gown had been fastened to the tissue in the preservation box." Nationwide Gown Cleaning (which also goes under the names Continental Gown Cleaning and Prestige Gown Cleaning) said they'd re-clean the gown and have it back to her in two weeks.

One year later, there was still no gown.

After complaining to the Better Business Bureau and bringing her story to the *Boston Globe*, the company still refused to return her dress. So, she sued them. After a local TV station picked up the chase, she finally got the gown back, which was *still* dirty and now smelled of cigarette smoke! The dress is now so famous it was featured on a recent NBC's "Leeza" show on wedding scams as an example of what can go wrong with these gown preservation companies.

So what lessons does this have for other brides?

First, we think this whole "gown preservation box" scheme is a rip-off. According to the National Association of Resale and Thrift Shops, over 80% of bridal gowns brought into re-sale shops to be consigned in their original, unopened, sealed boxes are found to be dirty. These national gown preservation companies are duping brides into thinking their gowns are being preserved when evidence shows they're not even being *cleaned*. Here's our advice for brides who want to preserve their gowns:

1. Don't. If you're saving the dress for your daughter, you're assuming the dress will fit her, not have yellowed or gone out of style. That's a slim shot at best.

2. We recommend consigning your dress at a local re-sale shop as soon as possible after the wedding. Why? Styles change and dresses start to age quickly. Take the money and put it towards a savings account for your first child.

3. Clean and preserve it yourself. Most bridal gowns are made of synthetic fabrics (satin, taffeta, organza and tulle) that can be cleaned in a washing machine. Cold water, a gentle cycle and a pure detergent (no fabric softeners or bleach) is best. Some bridal shop owners first spray the inside and outside of the dress with Shout or Spray 'N Wash. Hang dry on a plastic hanger. Note: before washing, you should first test the beading or pearls. Place one bead/pearl in cold water for 10 minutes and see if it disintegrates (some designers use very cheap pearls). If it passes the test, you can clean the gown at home.

4. After the dress is clean, wrap it in a clean and dry, white cotton sheet. If you want to stuff it with tissue paper, make sure it's acid free paper (available from local arts supplies or craft stores or call the Container Store at 1-800-733-3532). Put it in an acid-free box (also available from the source above) and store it in a cool dry place—no attics or basements.

5. If this sounds too daunting, take it to a reputable, local (and we stress the word *local*) dry cleaner. Look over the cleaned dress in natural light before leaving the store. Why a local cleaner? You have much more control over the situation when the owner is right there than dealing with a long-distance company. Be sure to check references and the Better Business Bureau to see if the cleaner has a good record. Another tip: if the gown is expensive (over $500), insist that the shop only release the gown when you show a photo ID.

One final caveat—even if you do all the above steps and use that acid-free box, there is no guarantee that the dress won't yellow. Whether you pop that dress in the Maytag or send it to an expensive gown preservation company, there is still a good chance it will yellow.

for both bridal gowns and bridesmaids dresses. Call your local JCPenney store for outlet locations near you.

Arizona brides can find deals on bridal gowns at **Affordable Dreams** in Phoenix (602) 279-4933. This shop sells first-quality over-runs from several famous designers at 50% to 70% off.

Dallas-based **St. Pucchi** is one of the few "couture" designers with an outlet. Pucchi's "wholesale warehouse" (214) 631-4039, located in a commercial district near downtown, fails the "truth in advertising" test. While it is a warehouse, everything is not priced at wholesale.

True, there is a back room with 100+ samples which range in condition from "brand new" to "torn to shreds." Mostly sizes 10's, the dresses from Pucchi's lower-priced Classique line ran $50 to $1500, about 45% to 75% off retail. A slim selection of mangled headpieces and single bridesmaids' dresses were shoved in one corner.

The biggest disappointment was the fact that a whole room of "special order" (read: new) dresses were not discounted. These dresses ranged from $950 to $4700 and delivery takes three months.

It really torques us to walk into a "wholesale warehouse" only to find the nicest merchandise is priced at regular retail—a lesson for outlet shoppers everywhere. Add on top of this the warehouse's non-existent service and you're suppose to pay full price for this? Pucchi's "outlet" is for hard-core fans only—if you can find a sample that's not too trashed, it may be a good deal. But if you're not a size 10 and don't have time to make repeat visits, you may want to skip this one. One interesting note: it appears that the gowns we saw had tags indicating the true style number—a boon for discount mail-order shoppers.

Mention the address **"1385 Broadway"** to any New York City bride and you're likely to get a smile. That address is home to the "bridal building" a collection of showrooms and sales offices of the country's best known bridal designers. Here's the reason brides are flocking to that address: many of these showrooms are open to the public on Saturdays and pass along big discounts to brides. That's right—the same designers who rail against discounting are themselves quietly discounting at 1385 Broadway.

We recently visited the non-descript office building and were impressed at the deals. When you enter the building, you're handed a list of which floors are open that Saturday. (This apparently changes from week to week). After a crowded elevator ride (hey, this is New York), we arrived at the first open floor. We visited several showrooms and came away with the following impressions: designers are selling not only used samples but also are taking special orders for new gowns. Discounts for samples were up to 50%, while special orders were an amazing 20% to 25% off.

Why do the designers do this? One insider told us it's the only way the designers can keep their best salespeople happy—the commissions from "Saturday sales" are a big salary boost.

Service varied widely from showroom to showroom—in some cases staffers were relatively friendly (for New York). Other showrooms had little or no service and the attitudes of some salespeople needed adjusting.

Alterations is another issue—some showrooms include alterations in the price, while others charge exorbitant fees. One designer was charging a flat $200 fee for alterations, no matter what needs to be done.

So is it a good deal? Yes, with some cautions. Critics contend that the prices on some gowns at 1385 Broadway are lower at places like Kleinfelds in Brooklyn (see the "Best Buy" earlier in this chapter). So, like any so-called "discount" option, make sure you shop around first to educate yourself on quality and price.

Don't forget to factor in the price of parking and tolls ($15 a trip) for not only the initial visit but also any follow-up alteration fittings. Selection and which showrooms are open will vary from week to week—it's really a gamble to find the right dress. Our sources say the best pickings are after the twice yearly bridal markets in April and September. Lots of samples are available at these times, but special orders are taken all year round. So, if you live near New York, you may want to venture into the jungle and check out the bridal building.

Bridal Magazines: Friend or Foe?

One of the first things you probably did after you got engaged was trot down to your local newsstand and pick up a copy of a bridal magazine. Hoping to find answers to wedding questions, you thumb through all the glossy advertisements.

But what kind of advice are these magazines giving consumers? And who's side are they on anyway? The short answer is: not yours. And the advice is silly at best. For example, in a special section titled "A Lavish Wedding For Less," *Bride's* magazine reveals that "the fewer prints you choose for your photo album, the less you'll pay." No kidding.

Of course, *Modern Bride* magazine is just as absurd. In an article titled, "50 ways to Stretch Your Wedding Dollars," the rocket scientists at *Modern Bride* suggest "hiring a professional wedding planner." Later, they advise "stick to your budget.

Headpieces and Veils

If you think bridal gowns are overpriced, you haven't seen anything yet! Wait until you see the price tags on headpieces and veils! You may have to be revived with smelling salts. That's because hefty markups on these items regularly push the prices of headpieces/veils over $150 and even $300.

Now let's look at what you are actually buying here. Let's see, we have a headpiece frame which costs about $5 in fabric stores. Then you add some lace, pearls and beads. Top it off with veiling which costs $2 to $5 per yard at most fabric stores. Sure, the labor involved to assemble these things isn't cheap, but we still don't comprehend how this all adds up to $200.

Our best advice on headpieces and veils is to consider going "custom" here. If you have a relative who can sew, here is where they can help you. Another option is resale/consignment shops that sell headpieces and veils for about $100 or less. Don't forget that you can rent a headpiece and veil at rental shops for a fraction of retail prices. One rental shop we visited had over 20 styles that rented for $25 to $30 each. Wow!

By the way, on your visit to most bridal shops, you're going to be strongly encouraged to purchase a wide range of accessories, from lingerie to shoes. See our "Etcetera" Chapter for more details.

If you want a more expensive dress, cut back in another area." Sure.

Even that arbiter of New England taste and blue light specials, Martha Stewart, isn't immune to passing out misleading information to engaged couples. In a recent wedding issue of her namesake magazine, she claims that "samples allow a bride to select a style; (then) each dress is custom-made to fit the bride." Be sure to send Martha your alterations bill when that custom-made dress needs some nips and tucks.

Of course, suspiciously missing in all these articles are any real tips on saving money on such items as the bridal gown. Why, you might ask? Just take a look at these magazines—the majority of their advertising comes from bridal designers. And those designers would prefer you buy a dress at full retail. Forget about renting or discount sources.

In a 1992 article in the *Wall Street Journal*, *Bride's* magazine admitted to blocking adds from companies that discount or rent dresses. Rather sexist from a magazine that takes plenty of ads for guys tux rentals, eh?

"*Bride's* has NEVER accepted these ads," the publisher said in a letter to full-price retailers, reprinted in the *Journal*. "[We] believe that these can only hurt your business." And the magazine's.

Clone Gowns: Is Your Gown a Knock-off?

Here's an ominous new trend in bridal fashion: clone gowns. Yes, it's happened with computers and now it's coming to a bridal shop near you!

So, what is a "clone" gown? As you might expect from the name, these gowns are knock-offs of designers originals. Most are made in Taiwan and then are imported into the U.S. We've noticed a flood of these gowns in the past year or so—one import company has even opened up a retail shop in Houston, Texas that sells nothing but clone gowns.

Many "traditional" bridal shops have also jumped on the clone gown bandwagon. Why? Clone gowns are cheaper for the store to buy. Does that mean they are passing along the savings to consumers? Don't bet on it—our sources indicate stores are taking larger mark-ups on clone gowns. This helps boost profit margins that have been sagging due to competition from discounters.

For example, we found one clone gown in a bridal shop for $900. We were shocked to find the gown's true cost was just $275.

What is the down-side with clone gowns? Fixing problems with special orders is one challenge. Since the gowns are imported, it may take longer to fix snafus. Also, most clone gowns are marketed by import companies with only skeletal U.S. operations. Legitimate designers (even those that manufacture in the Orient) have U.S. sales offices and warehouses. If a problem develops, they can get a replacement gown much quicker.

Of course, buying a clone gown off-the-rack will avoid such problems. But, how can you spot a "clone gown"? Typically, they have obscure names and are never advertised in bridal magazines. If you must special-order, ask the store for information on the manufacturer—where are they located? Can you call them to confirm their customer service commitment? The store should readily give you information on a designer/manufacturer—it's your guarantee that the store is on the up and up. If they balk, then walk.

Accessories & Other Outrageously Priced Extras

If you thought the bridal gown was expensive by itself, wait till you see the prices on "bridal accessories:" headpieces/veils, petticoats, lingerie, shoes, garters, gloves, stockings, jewelry are all available from your local friendly bridal shop at mark-ups that are quite obscene.

And, amazingly, the bridal industry makes no bones about the fat profits it fleeces from brides and grooms on these items. According to *Vows: The Bridal & Wedding Business Journal*, "Accessories are an important, lucrative part of the bridal business." One executive of a hosiery company advises shops to "go ahead and get the garters, the gloves and stockings for the entire bridal party—they're easy add-on sales. The mark-up on them is usually 100 percent and that's quite easy to achieve."

And some shops don't stop at 100%. *Glamour Magazine* interviewed one furious bride who was suckered into buying a $28 bra at a bridal shop. The boutique owner told her she must wear that bra. When she got home, she discovered that the manufacturer's price tag said $22. Hence the bridal shop had taken an $11 bra (at wholesale) and marked it up to $28—a tidy 155% mark-up. What a racket!

Of course, the accessories don't stop at the bride. Ring pillows, cake tops, guest books and attendants gifts are items you must have, says the bridal shop. Just listen to what wedding guru Beverly Clark (who, by the way, has her own collection of bridal accessories that she hawks) advises to bridal retailers in *Vows*: "Each time the wedding entourage enters your store, you have an opportunity to increase your overall dollar volume, in excess of $300 per party." And here's the kicker: "In this economy," Clark said, "you [the bridal retailer] have to get every dollar out of the bride." Isn't that nice? And people wonder why the bridal industry gets such a bad rap?

Avoiding the big rip-offs in this category is tricky. Nearly a third of all brides fall victim to sales hype and buy accessories at bridal shops. While brides try on gowns, owners of bridal shops often sneak out those bras, jewelry, hosiery and other do-dads. There may be subtle and not-so-subtle pressure to buy the "whole outfit." We say resist the pressure and shop around. For example, those $70 shoes at bridal shops (which *Glamour Magazine* says are "usually made of poor-quality, dyed-to-match satin") may be much cheaper at chain shoe stores. Those stores also offer a wider selection, too. One bride told us she found white leather pumps for just $22 at a department store end-of-summer sale. She added some beaded clip-ons ($4 to $10 each) from a shoe store and had a great look for less than *half* the bridal shop price.

Forget the jewelry at bridal shops. Much of it is fake and grossly over-priced—sometimes two to three times the retail prices of other stores. Other, non-bridal stores are likely to have better prices. The same goes for gloves, lingerie, guest books and more. The best shops will rent slips and petticoats for a fraction of retail prices.

And don't think the bridal industry has forgotten about the groom either. One of the biggest profit areas in formal-wear rental has nothing to do with the tuxedo—it's the shoes that are the money-makers. Yes, we're talking about those cheesy, plastic black shoes that bridal shops and tux places buy for $14 each. The shops turn around and rent them for $10 a pop—since the shoes can be rented out 20 times or more, each pair can reap revenues of $200! According to *Vows*, the magazine conservatively estimated the profit from shoe rental at a fat 55%. "That is over three times the profit that most operators enjoy on a tuxedo rental." And the key word in that sentence is enjoy. Our advice: skip the shoes and buy a nice pair of black shoes. Since you'll wear them again and again, in the long run, you'll probably come out ahead.

Alterations

One of the best euphemisms in the bridal business is what the shops refer to as "custom fitting." Whether called by this name or another more common moniker (alterations), there's no denying that this is a high expense area.

After shelling out $500 to $1000 (or more) on a gown, many brides are surprised to learn that their gown requires "custom-fitting" (read: more money). That's because few gowns are made to your measurements—most are made on assembly lines to correspond to a standard size. This may be close to your measurements. Close, but not close enough.

Remember the survey we quoted earlier in the chapter, when we revealed the same bride would be a different size in different designer's gowns? Well, the other news from that survey is that 60% of the time, the bride will need additional alterations. Er, "custom-fitting."

So, what's a fair price for a little tuck here and there? For that answer, we looked at another survey, this one by Bridal Information Resource, an industry newsletter. In 1991, the publisher surveyed 130 bridal shops to determine "average" cost for such common alterations as a bridal gown hem and bridesmaids dress alterations.

For example, the survey revealed that an average bridal gown requires $62 in alterations—some shops charge as little as $30 and others over $125. A hem for the gown averaged $28, with prices from $20 to over $100.

Bridesmaids dresses didn't escape the needle either. The bridesmaid is socked with additional $17 in alterations, with some shops charging a whopping $50 or more. A simple hem for a bridesmaids dress can run $10 to $30.

Here's the biggest rip-off: shops that raise the price of alterations for more expensive gowns for no reason at all. According to an article in *Vows: The Bridal Business Journal*, "shops that have a higher price point, charge more for alterations. These more expensive dresses are not more difficult to alter, nor do they fit badly. It's a matter of what the market will bear."

Wow! Can you believe it? Just consider it a little gift from the bridal industry—for those of you who purchase expensive (i.e., anything over $500) dresses, you get the privilege of being overcharged on alterations.

So, how can you avoid these problems? First, realize that some shops offer alterations for free. Of course, you can also take your gown to an independent seamstress (local fabric stores often have recommendations). This avoids the bridal shop altogether and, in some cases, may be the best route.

Chapter 3

Apparel for the Wedding Party

Y es, there are bridesmaids gowns out there that don't look hideous! We'll tell you in this chapter who are the best bridesmaids gown designers and give you several surprisingly affordable alternatives. We'll also give you valuable tips on tuxedos for the guys.

Bridesmaids' Gowns

What Are You Buying?

Perhaps nothing symbolizes what's wrong with the "wedding industry" more than the bridesmaid's gown. Have you seen any of these abominations to fashion? Cheap polyester fabric, ugly colors, absurd detailing like gargantuan puff sleeves—it seems like a bridesmaid's gown can transform any woman into a taffeta nightmare. What's most appalling about bridesmaids' gowns is that they are actually designed that way! No kidding!

We're not sure why bridesmaids' gowns are designed as "throw-away" gowns and disposable dresses, meant to be worn for only one day. One thing we are sure of is their high prices; even the low-end gowns sell for $100 to $150. That's too much money to "throw away" in our opinion. To get a gown of any quality that would actually look half decent, bridesmaids might have to shell out nearly $200 or $300—and that doesn't even include expensive alterations.

The most hilarious part of this travesty is the suggestion by bridal shops that (are you ready for this?) most of their bridesmaids' gowns can be worn again as formals! Yea, right. How many New Year's Eve parties have you been to where women wore bridesmaids' gowns? Please, we wish these bridal shop owners would stop saying such dribble. Ninety-nine percent of all bridesmaids' gowns are banished to the back of the closet within hours of the wedding.

Anyway, your bridesmaids have to wear something to your wedding. So here's our suggestions.

Our Recommendations for Bridesmaids' Gowns

❦ Buy the cheapest bridesmaids' gowns you can stomach. Some of the basic styles sell for about $90. The nicest thing you can do for your bridesmaids who are on a tight budget is not burden them with paying for a $180 gown that they can only wear once.

❦ Consider an alternative to typical bridesmaids' gowns. Yes, there are several beautiful gowns your bridesmaids could actually wear again. As you might expect, these gowns are designed not by bridal designers, but by "ready-to-wear" manufacturers. Check out a department store for possibilities. One bride told us she found beautiful silk dresses at Talbot's (call 800-225-8204 for a catalog or store near you) for just $90 to $168.

Money-saving Secrets

 1 PACKAGE DISCOUNTS. If you order your gown from a bridal shop, they may offer a discount if you also order all the bridesmaids' dresses from that store. This discount can range from 10% to 20%. Sometimes this is negotiable, so ask.

2 CONSIDER ALTERNATIVE SOURCES. Resale/consignment shops often carry matching bridesmaids' gowns at attractive prices in a range of sizes. Rental stores rent bridesmaids' gowns at a fraction of retail prices. At the end of this section, we'll pass along the names of several rental stores across the country.

3 CALL DISCOUNT BRIDAL SERVICE. With savings of up to 40% and dresses that are shipped directly to each bridesmaids, you can't go wrong. For more details, see a review of DBS in Chapter 2.

Getting Started: How Far In Advance?

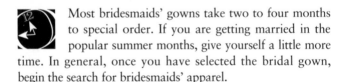 Most bridesmaids' gowns take two to four months to special order. If you are getting married in the popular summer months, give yourself a little more time. In general, once you have selected the bridal gown, begin the search for bridesmaids' apparel.

Step-by-step Shopping Strategies

❦ *Step 1:* After buying your bridal gown (and hence deciding on the setting and formality of your wedding), start the search for bridesmaids' gowns.

Shopping for bridesmaids' before you find your gown will only distract you.

❦ *Step 2:* Take into account your bridesmaids' ability to pay for the dress. (Traditionally, the bridesmaid pays for her gown plus alterations.) Are your bridesmaids starving college students or corporate lawyers earning $75,000 a year? Obviously, this is a big factor in your decision.

❦ *Step 3:* Given the financial condition of your attendants, start the shopping process. Follow much the same steps as for finding a bridal gown. Look at fabrics, finishes, and styles.

❦ *Step 4:* When you decide on a gown, announce your decision to the bridesmaids. Make sure each bridesmaid is individually measured and receives a written receipt that specifies the manufacturer, style number, size and delivery date.

❦ *Step 5:* Be sure to leave two weeks or more for alterations. Get written cost estimates on the alterations before the order is placed.

Helpful Hint

DON'T GO SHOPPING WITH MORE THAN ONE BRIDESMAID. If you want to make the process of shopping for bridesmaids' gowns go as smooth as possible, just take along one friend. Too many bridesmaids (each with their own opinions and tastes) will only complicate the decision. Make the decision and announce it to the other bridesmaids.

Pitfall to Avoid

Pitfall #1
DISINTEGRATING BRIDESMAIDS DRESSES.

"I ordered five bridesmaids dresses from a major manufacturer. When they came in, I was shocked! Every single dress was defective. All of the dresses came out of the boxes with threads hanging from every seam and the seams all pulled and puckered. The buttons and loops on the back of the dresses fell apart when the girls tried to button them. These had to be sewn on four of the five dresses one half hour before I was to be married. The most appalling defect of all was the lace on the front of one of the dresses. It was sewn on crooked and had to be taken off and reattached by a professional dressmaker. While my maid of honor was up at the altar next to me, we could actually hear her dress popping apart."

Yes, it's no wonder why the bridesmaids dress is the biggest joke in the fashion business. The quality and workmanship on many of these dresses can be described in one word—abysmal. And it's not just on the cheap dresses—the ones described above cost $130 each, according to the bride. The best advice we can give is to order early. Leaving enough time will enable the shop to fix the problems. Another idea is to by-pass the standard bridesmaid dress entirely. Select dresses at a department store or from a catalog and laugh at the bridal industry.

Pitfall #2
CLASHING COLOR MOTIFS.

"I was a bridesmaid in a wedding recently. The bride picked out lovely peach bridesmaids' gowns. Unfortunately, the church was all decorated in bright red—all her pictures looked like 'Night of the Clashing Circus Clowns!' It wasn't pretty."

Be careful when you select the bridesmaids' gowns to take into account the decor of your ceremony site. Many of your wedding pictures will have the ceremony site as a backdrop. Try to pick a color that not only pleases you but also doesn't clash with the decor of your ceremony site.

Pitfall #3
DUPED BY DOUPIONI.

"My bridesmaids ordered five dresses made of Doupioni silk. What a disaster! The dresses looked like the girls had slept in them and we couldn't iron those wrinkles out!"

Doupioni silk is one of those hip fabrics for bridesmaids dresses that doesn't actually live up to its billing. While the sample dress you first try on may look fine, the actual dresses may have flaws like slubs, dark threads, wrinkles and more. Designers say these "flaws add to the character of the fabric and are part of its natural beauty." Nice try. We think the designers are trying to pass off low-quality silks on an unsuspecting public. You don't pay that much money for dresses that look like they've been slept in. Our best advice is to ask the shop to see a recently arrived order of dresses from that manufacturer—that way you can see what you'll be getting. Or just avoid Doupioni silk dresses altogether.

Reviews of Selected Bridesmaids Designers

Obviously, there are many manufacturers of bridesmaids' gowns. Frankly, most of the bridesmaids' gowns we have seen are hideous. So we are not going to waste your time by writing about the worst. Instead, here are reviews of some of the best and most visible manufacturers. Just like our rating system for bridal gowns, these reviews are based on our personal experience with these gowns. Our opinions reflect hands-on inspections.

So, what's new in the bridesmaids world? Well, the good news is more designers are producing more stylish dresses. Encouraged by the phenomenal success of Watters and Watters, designers are attempting more sophisticated designs. Instead of tailored suits, the current trend with bridesmaids is more of an evening-gown look with floor-length skirts. Here's a round-up of what's new.

The Ratings

★★★★ EXCELLENT — *our top pick!*
  ★★★ GOOD — *above average quality, prices and creativity.*
    ★★ FAIR — *could stand some improvement.*
      ★ POOR — *yuck! Could stand major improvement.*

Alfred Angelo ★★ Described by one bridal industry veteran as "disposable dresses," Alfred Angelo's bridesmaids' gowns are underwhelming in our opinion. Typical designs feature big puff sleeves, hip-enhancing peplums and cutesy bow accents—all in such fabrics colors as fuchsia and "lipstick." Prices range from $85 to $280. On the bright side, Angelo has added a line of classic silk dresses and couture-inspired designs. For example, the new velvet and French satin pant suit ($184) is a winner, as is the two-piece Doupioni silk creation ($200). If you're in a hurry, Angelo has four styles in sizes 4 to 44 that are available for immediate delivery. Call (800) 528-3589 or (407) 241-7755 to find a local dealer.

Alyce Designs ★½ If you like basic, traditional bridesmaid dresses, check out Alyce Designs. With prices ranging from $126 to $300, this Illinois-based designer churns out styles like #1575—a two-piece taffeta design with full skirt and puff sleeves ($138). When the designer attempts to get creative, it misses the mark. Just check out the burgundy sheath with black velvet accent, which looks like an out take from the *Star Trek* costume closet. Sizes 2 to 24 are available. Call (708) 966-9200 for a local dealer.

Bianchi ★★★ While more of a small player in the bridesmaids market, Bianchi is a trend-setter when it comes to designs. The designer's use of tapestry fabrics helped spark a fad that was copied by other designers. This season we liked a "spruce velvet sheath," featuring a scalloped neckline and sleeves for $179.50. Other dresses were on the pricey side too, ranging from $140 to $260. Call (800) 669-2346 for a local dealer.

Bill Levkoff ★★½ Considered higher quality than other designers, Bill Levkoff offers good value for the money. Designer Veronica Cifone was trained at Galina and is very plugged into the latest trends. While some designs are incredibly boring (the "typical bridesmaid" taffeta with puff sleeves), others are more creative. New this year are several understated satin and crepe designs, as well as several strapless options. For example, one Forest green chiffon gown ($220) featured a shirred portrait collar and rhinestone pin. With a look leaning toward evening wear/cocktail dresses, Levkoff is heavy on the use of sheer fabrics this season. Basically, this line has something for everyone—from two-piece suits to your standard bridesmaids look. Prices range from $102 to $250 with sizes on some styles up to 42 (but no petites). Call (800) LEV-KOFF to find a local dealer.

Champagne Formals ★★ This small line focuses on simple designs at affordable prices. One stand-out dress from Champagne was a tulip-skirted crepe and satin design in ivory for $135. The quintessential bridesmaids dress (puff sleeves, tea-length skirt, back bow in teal taffeta) will run $115. We appreciate the fact that Champagne prints the retail prices in their ads. Call (212) 302-9162 for a local dealer.

Currie Bonner ★★★ With three retail stores in Atlanta, Charlotte, and Dallas, Currie Bonner is a custom-manufacturer of bridesmaids' dresses. A wide assortment of fabrics are available, from the ordinary (taffeta and satin) to the exotic (linen, velvet and shantung). Styles are quite impressive, including some drop-waisted designs, several dresses with ruffles and others with full skirts and fitted bodices. What if you don't live near those cities listed above? Well, you can order from their mail-order catalog (call 1-800-409-9997 for a copy) which features a sampling of their bridesmaids dresses. Prices, which vary depending on the fabric and style chosen, range from $135 for the simplest plain taffeta design to $300 for a silk gown. Call (800) 409-9997 or (404) 231-5441 for more information.

Dessy Creations ★★½ "Classic sophistication" is how we'd describe the bridesmaids designs by Dessy. Most dresses are simple with sparse or no detailing. Check out the black velvet sheath with Alencon lace neckline for $260. All in all, prices for Dessy dresses range from $92 to $270. New this year at Dessy is a small line of informal bridal gowns that run $190 to $470. Another addition from this designer: one maternity style for your pregnant bridesmaids.

Currie Bonner lets you mix and match different skirts and tops for a unique bridesmaids look. These dresses combine a damask skirt and wide portrait collar top for $222.

Only sizes 4 to 20 are available. And, finally, here's a little secret the bridal industry doesn't want you to know— Dessy makes bridesmaids dresses for David's Bridal (the discount warehouse chain profiled in the last chapter) under the brand name Oleg Cassini. Call (800) 52-DESSY to be connected to a local dealer. Call (212) 354-5808 to speak to their corporate headquarters.

Jordan ★½ Known for their basic, "bread and butter" bridesmaids designs, Jordan's dresses go for $130 to $230. Very basic accents: bow bustles, puff sleeves—you get the idea. The colors are quite conservative too (rose, teal, royal blue). New this year is a line of sexier, more revealing gowns. For example, one crepe dress ($158) with a chiffon collar featured a slit in the skirt that went all the way up to . . . well, use your imagination. If you're in a hurry, Jordan offers "jet service" for quick delivery. Six styles are available for fast shipping, for an additional $6 to $40 charge. Sizes up to 42 are offered. Jordan is available nearly everywhere. Call (212) 921-5560 for a local dealer.

New Image ★★½ New Image seems to be suffering from the "conservative" disease this year. Compared to previous seasons, this line seems to be lacking in pizzazz. Sheer netting and "mushroom" pleats are in, as are brooches and satin edging. One sophisticated design was a navy blue dress with velvet collar, accented by sheer net yoke and long sleeves. Price: $230. Other dresses ranged from $150 to $250. Sizes 4 to 22. Call (800) 421-IMAGE for a local dealer.

Watters and Watters ★★★★ This young, Dallas-based designer continues on a roll. Perhaps the hottest brides-maid's designer in the country, Watters and Watters seems to be working from a simple concept: design a nice-looking dress that doesn't look like a bridesmaid. More like well-tailored suits and elegant evening gowns than cheap polyester horrors, WW still keeps a feminine look with beautiful detailing and colors. New this year is an emphasis on rich fabrics like velvets, chiffons, crepes—and gone are the frilly touches like lace collars and rhinestone buttons. If we had to complain about anything with Watters and Watters, it would have to be their prices—bridesmaids are an expensive $200 to $320. On the upside, the designer has expanded their line of informal bridal dresses, which run $284 to $560. Sizes 2 to 24 are available. If you're plugged into the Internet, check out WW's home page on the Web to see their latest catalog. The address is http://wwi.computek.net/. Call (214) 991-6994 for a local dealer.

Spotlight: Best Buy #1

Local shops rent bridal gowns and bridesmaids dresses

Despite the best efforts by the bridal magazines and design-ers to kill off dress rental shops, there are a handful of places you can actually rent a bridesmaids dress.

Formals Etc. has not one but six stores in Louisiana that rent bridal gowns (for $200 to $275) and bridesmaids dresses ($65). Call (318) 640-3766 to find a location near you.

In Boston, Teresa's Gowns (617) 233-8737 rents wedding gowns ($100 and up) and bridesmaids ($50). If you live in Kansas City, check out An Alternative (800) 995-2338 or (816) 761-8686. New Jersey brides can rent bridal gowns and mother of the bride dresses at Expecting Elegance (201) 947-8300.

In general, one of the best places to look for a dress rental shop is your local phone book; most advertise under the heading "Bridal Shops."

Tuxedos

Nowhere are the wedding etiquette rules sillier than for men's formal wear. For example, they say you MUST wear a black tux with tails for a formal wedding after six in the evening. If you don't, the vengeful WEDDING GODS will strike you down, ostracize your family and charge obscene amounts of money to your credit cards.

Now if your wedding is before six you can wear grey or white short coats . . . but not if the moon is full. And, of course, you must follow the omnipotent "formality" rules that dictate proper dress for weddings that are very formal, just plain formal, semi-formal, pseudo-formal and the dreaded para-formal. Just kidding.

We believe all this is nonsense. The grooms and groomsmen should wear whatever they believe is appropriate. Who cares what time of day the wedding is? If your wedding is an informal ceremony in a local civic rose garden, you don't have to wear a tuxedo. We know we might incur the wrath of Emily Post for saying this, but hey do what you want to do. If you look good in a double-breasted tux, wear that. If you don't, look for another style. You get the idea.

What Are You Buying?

 Actually, most grooms and groomsmen rent formal wear for weddings. Imagine what would happen if the men had to shell out the same kind of money that bridesmaids spend on those horrendously ugly bridesmaids' gowns. There would be mass revolts and street rioting. Fortunately, for national security's sake, most men's formal wear is rented. Typically, the groomsmen are financially responsible for their tuxedo rentals, so basically you and your fiance's only expense is the groom's tux. Here are the three basic options for men's formal wear:

1 RENT. When you rent a tux, you get just about everything: jacket, pants, cummerbund, shirt, tie, cuff links, and, of course, shirt studs (little jewelry that covers your buttons and makes you look rich). Notice what's missing? If you answered "shoes" give yourself extra points. While most tuxes rent for $50 to $90, the shoes are often $10 to $15 extra. Of course, it's more expensive in major metropolitan areas (like New York City, where tux rentals can top $125 and shoes go for $20). A small deposit/damage waiver ($10 to $20) is required to reserve a tux. There are three types of places to find formal wear rentals:

❦ *Chain stores.* Large formal wear franchised chains (a la McDonald's) are located across the U.S. They basically offer the same styles and brand names. Service can range from helpful to dreadful. Most of these chains don't carry any stock at their stores—a central warehouse is used to dispense the tuxedos. Hence, it's difficult to decide which style is best for you by just looking at the mannequins. To try on a particular style, you must ask the shop for a "trial fitting." For no charge, most shops will bring in a style in your size. The only disadvantage is that this requires a second visit to the shop, rather inconvenient for those of you who lead busy lives.

❦ *Bridal Shops.* More and more bridal shops are now getting into the business of renting tuxes. However, instead of stocking tuxes at their store, they use a service which supplies them with rentals. Hence, the way you pick a tuxedo is to look through a book with pictures of tuxedo-clad soap stars awash in testosterone. Thrilling. Personally, we'd rather look at the mannequins. Anyway, on the up side, the bridal shops may cut you a deal if you buy the bridal and bridesmaids' gowns from them. On the down side, while bridal shop employees may know a lot about bridal gowns, they may know diddly-squat about men's formal wear.

How the Bridal Designers Block

In the last chapter, we talked about how bridal magazines block ads from companies that want to rent bridal and bridesmaids dresses to women. By locking these rental firms out of the only national advertising vehicle that reaches brides, the magazines have worked to shut the door on dress rentals.

But that's not the whole story. Several bridal manufacturers have taken public and not-so-public steps to stop dress rental. Such actions have aroused the attention of the Federal Trade Commission, whose Dallas office has launched an investigation into the practices of certain designers.

Our investigation into the tactics of one of the largest bridal designers, Alfred Angelo, revealed some surprising information. As one of the top three bridal dressmakers, Angelo's designs are available in hundreds of shops. Angelo recently sent a "marketing statement" to each of its dealers, requiring them to agree in writing that they will "not rent Alfred Angelo Dream Maker dresses to consumers." Stores that do face "immediate termination of your account."

We asked the company about this practice. Bernard Toll, Angelo's public relations liaison, told us that "we do this for obvious reasons. Alfred Angelo dresses are not designed to withstand multiple wearings, countless alterations which leave telltale needle marks and legally required cleanings. Each Alfred Angelo dress is produced to make just one bride's dreams become a lovely reality on her wedding day."

Now, this is a curious argument. Angelo is essentially arguing that their dresses are of such poor quality that they won't "withstand repeated wearings." Considering the average bridesmaids dress costs $150, we find this to be appalling. Angelo's arguments seem to give credence to the perception that the industry designs

❦ *Independent shops.* Occasionally, we find an independent tuxedo rental shop, one that is not affiliated with a national chain. We often are impressed by the quality of service at these outlets. Furthermore, independent shops may carry a wider selection of styles and designers. You can also find some great deals. For example, Tux Express in Scottsdale, Arizona (602) 991-6655 rents designer-brand tuxes for $29 to $59, far below the prices of the chains.

2 BUY. If you expect to need a tuxedo again for a fancy party or corporate banquet, it may pay to buy. That's because most tuxedos cost $200 to $400 to purchase. Considering rental fees of $50 to $100, it may pay to purchase.

Rental of Bridesmaids Dresses

"disposable dresses" of such inferior craftsmanship you can't be expected to wear them more than one day.

The bridal industry says that women "don't want to rent dresses. They'd rather buy." However the actions of the magazines and dress designers indicate quite the opposite—they're trying to stifle the consumer demand for a needed service for purely selfish reasons: women buy $500 million worth of bridesmaids dresses each year. Rental of these dresses would half this business and force the designers to make dresses that don't disintegrate after one wearing. By renting bridesmaids dresses alone, women could save $250 million each year.

It is our opinion that designers who block stores from renting dresses are guilty of restraint of trade. We hope the FTC's investigation of these practices reaches a similar conclusion.

On another related issue, we also noted that Angelo promises stores that it will "not sell discontinued merchandise to the large bridal outlet warehouses." However, Angelo operates a separate company called "Bridal Placements of Boca," which sells discontinued merchandise to shops. While the company denies it, insiders say Bridal Placements sells Angelo gowns to bridal warehouses. In fact, we called several bridal warehouses and every one told us they carry Alfred Angelo dresses. While Bernard Toll told us that Angelo "will not knowingly sell to bridal discount warehouses," it's obvious someone is supplying these outlets with gowns. One warehouse even told us we could special order a brand new Alfred Angelo dress at a discounted price.

If you disagree with Angelo's policies on rental dresses and discount stores, we urge you to write Alfred Angelo's president, Vincent Piccione, at 791 Park of Commerce Blvd., Boca Raton, FL 33487.

3 GO WITH YOUR OWN SUIT. Especially for less formal weddings, having the groom and groomsmen wear dark suits is perfectly acceptable. There is no law saying you must wear a tuxedo for your wedding.

Spotlight: Best Buy

Gingiss Formalwear

Probably our most favorite formal wear chain is Gingiss Formalwear. Perhaps what we like most about Gingiss is the fact you can try on tuxedos right in their store on your first visit. Hey, what a concept! Most Gingiss stores keeps their stock on the premises, enabling you to try on several styles in your size.

You get to see how the tuxedo looks on you, not on a mannequin or a model in a catalog. Furthermore, you don't have to make a second trip back to the store for a trial fitting—you can look at the styles, try on a few top choices and make your decision all in one shot.

We should note that there are few exceptions to this rule. While most stores have tuxedos in stock, a few cities have stores who use a central warehouse. For example, in Los Angeles, a bride told us she was charged a $20 fee by a local Gingiss to get in a style for her groom to try on. The non-refundable fee could be applied toward a tuxedo rental. We didn't like this extra charge, so we'd recommend calling your local Gingiss to see what their policy is.

On the bright side, Gingiss' mail-in measurement program for out-of-town groomsmen is excellent. With over 250 stores in 34 states, Gingiss enables out-of-town groomsmen to go to the Gingiss in their city, see the actual tux and get measured. Sure, other chains have mail-in measurement programs but Gingiss seems more organized.

Gingiss' prices are moderate, ranging from $50 to $90. There are discounts for group orders; the Gingiss in our town gives the groom's tux rental free with five other rentals. Check for specials from Gingiss, especially in January.

One interesting piece of news from the Gingiss camp was their recent buy-out of Tuxedo Junction, a 31-store chain based in Buffalo, NY. Tuxedo Junction manufactured its own line of tuxedos, shirts and shoes, and Gingiss now plans to market these as their own "in-house" brand. Unfortunately, Gingiss does not plan to pass on the savings from manufacturing its own products to consumers in the form of lower rental rates. Gingiss President Michael Corrao told *Vows Magazine* that "the intent . . . [is] to provide unique styles, greater selection, a more directed product, without a compromise on price."

Despite this development, we still like Gingiss and pick the company as one of the very best formal wear chains in the U.S. For a local dealer, call 708-620-9050.

Reviews of Selected Tux Designers

After Six ★★   Vests in flashy fabrics highlight After Six's tuxedos this season. Subtle textures and weaves complement the rather traditional designs.

Alexander Julian ★★★   This designer is using wider lapels and longer jackets to differentiate his tuxes from the pack this season. Also unique: vests in such patterns as "window-pane" plaid and gold matte satin. You'll find many Julian tuxes at Gingiss; call (800) 847-8600 or (718) 361-6262 for a dealer near you that carries this designer.

Demetrios ★★½   The famous bridal gown designer has branched into the tux business with six styles. The Beatle-esque "Olympia" sports a four-button single-breasted coat with 60's styling—this attempt at haute couture missed the mark, in our opinion. On the other end, Demetrios has a winner with the Santurni, a very traditional two-button shawl-collar tux. Call (212) 967-5222 for a dealer near you.

Lord West ★★   Referring to itself as "All-American Formalwear," Lord West does very traditional styles. In addition to a line of tuxes sporting its name, Lord West is also the distributor for Pierre Cardin tuxedos. Among its more silly designs is the "Team NFL" tuxes, with black vests printed with your favorite team logo. Finally, what the world really needs—formalwear for the sports nut.

Oscar De La Renta ★★½   The "Dimension" collection from this well-known designer aims for something different—double lapels in several coat styles, for example. Also innovative is the "Allure" tuxes with a patterned black satin lapel/vest combination. Call (800) 351-6767 for a dealer near you.

Perry Ellis ★★½   A muted, dark-green plaid tux is the most adventurous designs from Perry Ellis this year. Nonetheless, most of the tuxes in this line are quite traditional, with an even mix of double-breasted and single-breasted options.

Ralph Lauren ★★   The plaid bedding and housewares from this well-known designer have crept into his tuxedo line. Most notably, check out the Scottish-inspired, Black-watch plaid tuxedo. While this works in a plaid vest with black coat and pants style, it misses the mark when the plaid pattern adorns the pants.

Raffinati ★★★ Beyond the traditional styles, Raffinati also goes out on a limb with some stylish, European-inspired looks. Our favorite is the "Mirage," a black tux featuring a collarless shawl lapel. Also hip this year at Raffinati is the no-bow-tie look—shirts that have stand-up collar and sewn-in black band. Call (800) 351-6767 for a dealer near you.

If you don't see a phone listed for a designer reviewed above, call a local formalwear store in your area for availability.

Our Top Money-Saving Secrets for Tuxedos

 1 PACKAGE DISCOUNTS. Almost all tuxedo places offer a free tux rental with the rental of five or six tuxedos. In some cases, tux shops distribute coupons good for $10 or more off each rental. Be sure to ask about group discounts if the shop "forgets" to tell you about them.

2 SKIP THE RENTAL SHOES. Why? Those cheap rental shoes can be awfully uncomfortable. Instead, wear your own black dress shoes if you have them and save $10.

Getting Started: How Far in Advance?

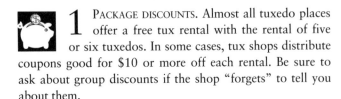 Boy, this varies greatly from area to area. In small towns, or for less popular months, you can shop one to two months before the wedding. However, you may need to reserve your tuxedos three to four months before the wedding in larger cities or for popular summer wedding months. If you have out-of-town groomsmen, you may want to leave extra time to get their measurements in.

Helpful Hint

LIE TO THE GROOMSMEN. We got this tip from one frustrated groom who found his groomsmen procrastinated getting measured for their tuxedos. The tardy groomsmen got measured just days before the wedding, frustrating everyone from the engaged couple to the tux shop. So, he recommended that other grooms lie about when the measurements have to be in. For example, tell them they must get measured six weeks before the wedding even though the real deadline is just one month before. That way the procrastinators won't upset the schedule if they are slightly late.

The Bonehead Award for Bad Customer Service

Bridesmaids designer Dessy is the winner of our first annual "Bonehead Award for Bad Customer Service" in the bridal industry for their frustrating 800-number referral system. Brides who call the 800-number listed in Dessy's ads (800) 52-DESSY are automatically connected to a local dealer who carries their dresses. The only problem? It doesn't work in some areas of the country. Also, brides calling the number to find other info about Dessy have been frustrated with being routed to a bridal shop, where clueless sales clerks are stumped with even the easiest question. Our suggestion to fix this mess— first, Dessy's ads should warn you about this referral phone system. Also, you should have a choice to be connected to either to a local dealer or to corporate headquarters (which can only be reached by calling 212-354-5808).

Trends

❦ *Vests.* Say good-bye to cummerbunds. Vests have taken the tux market by storm this season—some designers are even showing vests in subtle colors and weaves.

❦ *Plaids.* Muted plaids have shown up on ties, cummerbunds and vests as designers have sought to replace the teal and fuchsia satin looks of the past with more toned-down sophistication. Some tux makers have even gone out on a limb with plaid coats and pants, although the jury is still out on this trend.

❦ *Banded collar shirts.* You've seen them at the Oscars. Now, they've arrived at your local formalwear shop—the bow-tie-less look of the banded collar shirt (also called Mandarin-style).

❦ *Wider lapels.* Eeek! It's a return to the 70's. Some tuxes now sport wider lapels. We hope powder blue coats and ruffled shirts won't be coming next.

Chapter 4

Ceremony Sites

Did you realize how much rental fees vary from site to site? In this chapter, we'll show you a group of often-overlooked wedding ceremony sites that are extremely affordable—plus we'll give you six important questions to ask a ceremony site coordinator.

Selecting a site for your ceremony first requires a decision on the type of ceremony you want. We basically divide ceremonies into two categories: religious and civil.

1 RELIGIOUS CEREMONIES. Religious ceremonies (75% of all weddings), of course, are most likely held in a house of worship. Requirements for religious ceremonies vary greatly from one denomination to another. Pre-marriage counseling is required by some religions; others forbid interfaith marriages. Often the rules are established by the church or temple's local priest, minister, pastor or rabbi. Call your local house of worship for guidelines and requirements.

2 CIVIL CEREMONIES. About one-fourth of all weddings are civil ceremonies. Legal requirements vary from state to state, but usually a judge or other officiant presides over the ceremony. Customs and traditions vary greatly from region to region of the country. For example, we spoke to one hotel catering manager who worked in both Boston, Massachusetts and Austin, Texas. In Boston, she told us nearly 75% of couples had a civil ceremony on site at the hotel. Just the opposite was true in Texas where most weddings are held in a church with only the reception following at the hotel.

Religious vs. Civil: It's All a Matter of State

Interestingly enough, the split between civil and religious ceremonies varies greatly from state to state. According to federal government statistics, the state with the largest number of religious wedding ceremonies is West Virginia. In that state, a whopping 97% of all weddings are religious ceremonies. On the other end of the spectrum, South Carolina leads the nation in civil ceremonies (54% of all weddings).

So what happened to Nevada, where the large number of Las Vegas weddings probably would rank that state #1 in civil ceremonies? Well, Nevada was omitted from this study for reasons unknown. Other omitted states include Ohio and Iowa (both of which do not record the type of ceremony) and Arkansas, Oklahoma, Texas, New Mexico, Arizona, Washington, and North Dakota.

HERE ARE HOW SOME OF THE OTHER STATES STACK UP:

States with a high number of civil ceremonies: South Carolina (54%), Florida (45%) New Hampshire (40%), Hawaii (36%), New York (35%). Other states with higher than average numbers of civil ceremonies include Maine, Georgia and Virginia.

States with a high number of religious ceremonies: West Virginia (97%), Missouri (91%), Nebraska (84.2%), Michigan (83.9%), Pennsylvania (83.7%), Idaho (83.5%), California (83.1%).

What Are You Buying?

 When you book a ceremony site, you are not only purchasing use of the site for the wedding but also for time to set-up and tear-down the decorations. Now we say purchasing because many sites charge fees to use the facilities for a wedding. One bride we spoke to was surprised that the church they belonged to charged her over $600 in fees for her wedding. Of course, these fees often go to reimburse church staff and to pay expenses like utilities, clean-up, etc. Unfortunately, some churches use weddings to subsidize other less-profitable operations. Anyway, the fees vary widely from site to site but the charges tend to be more in larger cities.

What if you are not a member of a church but you want a church wedding? Well, a few churches allow non-members to use their facilities for weddings . . . but with a few catches. First, the fees are normally higher. Secondly, members get first shot at dates so non-members may not be able to book a wedding until, say, three months in advance. Obviously, this is a roll of the dice.

Sources to Find a Great Ceremony Site

 There are several great sources to use to find ceremony sites.

❧ *Local Visitors/Tourism Bureaus.* Many have a guide to local facilities that are available for weddings and receptions. Your

LOSING THEIR RELIGION

Think you're the only one who's frustrated with the seemingly ridiculous policies of your local church? The following is a copy of a letter recent bride Lisa Olson Kirsch of Salem, Massachusetts sent to the Salem Ministerial Association, complaining about the church practices in her area.

"During recent wedding planning, I have been shocked by local churches' insensitive and self-serving policies. I've heard horror stories about weddings being bumped at the last minute by 'regular' church members, as well as long lists of mandates stipulating where photographers may stand and what types of equipment they and the guests may use. You cannot select your own minster or, for that matter, your own organist. You can indicate your music preferences from a small, pre-approved list of traditional songs, but the final decision is left to their discretion and you can think again if you hope to have meaningful, contemporary music or taped selections.

While churches often emphatically state that their building is their 'home' and 'not for rent,' they all seem to have ready a pre-printed fee schedule with very specific and commercial-like rates. The list goes on and on. I understand the intent of the churches may be to protect their facility and the credibility of the ceremony, but the way they go about it seems less than Christian-like and disregards the unique qualities and contributions that should make each wedding memorable and personalized. It's a disgrace that deserves thoughtful reconsideration by each church and it's members."

local Chamber of Commerce or Historical Society office may also have more leads.

❦ *Local parks departments.* Most city and county parks and historical areas are administered by a parks department. Ask them which sites are most popular for wedding ceremonies.

❦ *For historic sites, check out the book* Places *at your local library.* This directory lists historical and other interesting places (many of which are available for rent) across the country. Published by Tenth House Enterprises, call (212) 737-7536 for more information.

Getting Started: How Far in Advance?

Especially for popular wedding months, start your search for a ceremony site as soon as you have selected the date. Prime dates can book up to a year in advance—you know, there are only so many Saturdays in

June. However, be aware that popular months vary by region. For example, in the South, December is a particularly popular month. In Arizona, and many areas of the desert Southwest, the spring months (such as May) are almost as popular as the hot summer months. The following chart lists the most and least popular months for weddings by state.

Be aware that religious restrictions may rule out certain times of the year. For example, Catholics and Greek Orthodox avoid marrying during Lent in March. Jews don't have weddings during the High Holy Days (usually in September or October).

Top Money-saving Secrets

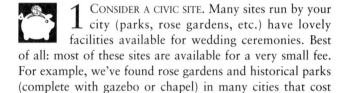

1 Consider a civic site. Many sites run by your city (parks, rose gardens, etc.) have lovely facilities available for wedding ceremonies. Best of all: most of these sites are available for a very small fee. For example, we've found rose gardens and historical parks (complete with gazebo or chapel) in many cities that cost under $100. The down side: their affordability often makes these sites very popular.

2 Call around to different sites. You wouldn't believe how widely fees vary from facility to facility.

3 Consider becoming a member. Many churches charge less for weddings of members than non-members. If you are planning to settle down in the town where your wedding is, consider joining the church where you'll be married.

4 Ask about any discounts. For example, some churches and synagogues offer discounts on wedding invitations as a fund raiser.

Questions to Ask of a Ceremony Site/Officiant

1 Do you have my wedding date available? Yes, it's an obvious question, but probably the most important one. Many brides forget there are many other brides competing for the same slots on a Saturday afternoon.

2 What are the restrictions, set-up times and clean-up requirements? Boy, this is an important question. Many sites have written rules about this stuff. One local church we know has so many rules and guidelines for weddings that they filled up a 72-page book! Make sure you are fully aware of these details to avoid any surprises.

Most/Least Popular Months

STATE	Most Popular	Least Popular
New England:		
Maine	July, August, June	Jan., Feb., Mar.
New Hampshire	July, August, June	Feb., Mar., Jan.
Vermont	July, August, June	Mar., Feb., Jan.
Massachusetts	June, Oct., Sept.	Jan., Feb., Mar.
Rhode Island	Sept., June, Oct.	Jan., Feb., Mar.
Connecticut	June, Oct., Sept.	Jan., Feb., Mar.
Middle Atlantic:		
New York	June, August, July	Feb., Jan., Mar.
New Jersey	Oct., June, May	Feb., Jan., Mar.
Pennsylvania	June, Oct, Sept.	Jan., Feb., Mar.
East North Central:		
Ohio	June, July, August	Jan., Feb., Mar.
Indiana	June, July, August	Jan., Feb., Mar.
Illinois	June, August, Sept.	Feb., Jan., April
Michigan	August, June, July	Jan., Feb., Mar.
Wisconsin	June, August, July	Jan., Feb., Mar.
West North Central:		
Minnesota	June, August, Sept.	Jan., Feb., Mar.
Iowa	June, August, July	Jan., Feb., Mar.
Missouri	June, July, August	Jan., Feb., Mar.
North Dakota	June, July, August	Jan., Mar., Feb.
South Dakota	June, August, July	Feb., Jan., Mar.
Nebraska	June, August, July	Jan., Feb., Mar.
Kansas	June, July, May	Feb., Jan., Mar.
South Atlantic:		
Delaware	June, May, August	Jan., Feb., Mar.
Maryland	June, May, July	Feb., Jan., Mar.
Wash. D.C.	June, Sept., August	Feb., Mar., Jan.
Virginia	June, July, August	Jan., Feb., Mar.
West Virginia	June, July, August	Jan., Feb., Mar.
North Carolina	June, July, August	Jan., Mar., Feb.
South Carolina	July, June, August	Jan, Feb., Mar.
Georgia	June, July, Dec.	Jan., Feb., Mar.
Florida	Dec., June, July	Jan., Nov., Feb.

for Weddings by State

STATE	Most Popular	Least Popular
East South Central:		
Kentucky	June, July, May	Jan., Feb., Mar.
Tennessee	June, July, August	Jan., Feb., Mar.
Alabama	June, July, August	Jan., Feb., Mar.
Mississippi	June, July, Dec.	Jan., Feb., Mar.
West South Central:		
Arkansas	June, July, August	Jan., Feb., Oct.
Louisiana	June, July, Dec.	Jan., Feb., Mar.
Oklahoma	June, May, August	Jan., Oct., Nov.
Texas	June, July, Sept.	Jan., Feb., Nov.
Mountain:		
Montana	June, July, August	Jan., Feb., Mar.
Idaho	August, July, June	Jan., Feb., Mar.
Wyoming	August, June, July	Jan., Mar., Feb.
Colorado	June, August, Sept.	Jan., April, Feb.
New Mexico	May, June, August	Jan., Nov., Oct.
Arizona	June, May, Dec.	Feb., Oct., Jan.
Utah	August, June, Sept.	Jan., Feb., April
Nevada	July, June, April	Jan., Feb., Mar.
Pacific:		
Washington	August, June, July	Jan., Feb., Nov.
Oregon	August, June, July	Jan., Feb., Nov.
California	June, August, Sept.	Jan., Feb., Mar.
Alaska	August, July, June	Jan., Mar., Nov.
Hawaii	Dec., July, August	Jan., Feb., Mar.
US (TOTAL)	**June, August, July**	**Jan., Feb., Mar.**

Note: Months are listed in order of popularity. For example, "July, August, June" means that July is the #1 month, followed by August and so on. The least popular month is listed first, followed by the second least popular and so on.

Source: US Dept. of Health and Human Resources.

3 WHO WILL BE MY CONTACT AT THE SITE? In order to prevent miscommunications, make sure you find out who is
the wedding coordinator. This person will be an invaluable
referral source of other wedding services.

4 WHAT IS THE EXPECTED HONORARIUM, DONATION OR FEE
PAID TO THE CHURCH/OFFICIANT? WHEN IS THIS NORMALLY
PAID?

5 WHAT KIND OF EQUIPMENT MUST BE RENTED FOR MY WED-
DING? Don't assume that something in the sanctuary or at
the site is included in your rental of the facility.

6 IS ANY PRE-WEDDING COUNSELING REQUIRED? Some churches require couples to attend pre-wedding counseling.
Others require the couple to promise to raise their children in
that religion. Before you are asked to make any commitments,
ask the site coordinator about this matter.

7 FOR OFFICIANTS, ARE THERE ANY TRAVEL CHARGES,
REHEARSAL FEES, OR OTHER COSTS? DO YOU OFFER DIFFER-
ENT CEREMONY OPTIONS? If you're planning a wedding in a
non-religious site (hotel, home, etc.), you may want to confirm these details.

Chapter 5

Wedding Flowers

H ey, getting flowers for your wedding should be easy, right? Well...maybe. But the average floral bill for a wedding can top $1000—so some of the 16 money-saving tips we discovered for wedding flowers may come in handy. Some may even surprise you! We also cut through the "floral speak" and give you seven floral "best buys."

What Are You Buying?

Besides the flowers themselves, you are buying a decorating consultant. Not only is the florist's knowledge of flowers important but also their understanding of colors and contrasts. Florists must be able to come up with a floral motif to best complement the bride, the bridal gown, the bridesmaids' colors, the ceremony and the reception. To synthesize these elements and the "feel of the wedding" (a formal sit-down dinner versus an informal barbecue) takes talent. Lots of it.

Your tastes and desires are key here, and a florist who understands a couple's individuality is the best choice. There are three basic categories of flowers that you are buying:

❦ **Personal Flowers.** The bride's and bridesmaids' bouquets, corsages for the mothers and house party, and boutonnieres for the men.

❦ **Ceremony Site Flowers.** Altar flowers and/or aisle arrangements (ribbons, candles, pew markers).

❦ **Reception Site Flowers.** Guest book table, table centerpieces (including a head table, buffet table and individual guests tables) and the cake table. Other floral expense areas may include the rehearsal dinner and any other pre-wedding parties.

AVERAGE TOTAL COSTS: About $800 covers the total floral bill at most weddings, according to industry estimates. In the largest cities (such as New York or LA), the flower budget can easily zoom past $1000 or even $2000 for lavish affairs. Deposits range from nothing (the exception) to as much as 50% of the estimated bill. Many ask for $50 to $100 to reserve the date. The balance is usually due one to two weeks before the wedding (because many florists must order the flowers in advance from their suppliers).

Sources to Find an Affordable Wedding Florist

 Since there are three general types of florists out there, we thought it might be helpful to explain the differences, then detail where to find the one that will work best for you:

1 CASH 'N CARRY. These shops basically specialize in providing an arrangement for Mother's Day, or a friend's birthday. They usually don't do many weddings and may not have as much experience with such a special event.

2 FULL SERVICE. Weddings, funerals, wire service arrangements, special events are within a full service florist's repertoire. A majority of florists fit in this category, although some are better than others at weddings.

3 SPECIALISTS. Some florists specialize in one aspect of the floral business. Obviously, those who specialize in weddings are your best bet. Those that don't may have little incentive to do a good job since they don't target that market anyway. Don't assume that your neighborhood florist, who has done great arrangements for you at Christmas and other times, will be best for your wedding.

Where to Find Florists Who are Wedding Specialists

❦ *Ceremony site coordinators.* Ask the person who coordinates (or books) weddings at your church, synagogue, etc. for florist recommendations. This is a great source since they often see florists' work up close and personal. They also know the florists who have been late to set up and those who have not provided the freshest flowers or best service. If your ceremony site coordinator doesn't have any recommendations, call around to a few popular churches in your area. Odds are you'll turn up some valuable referrals.

❦ *Photographers.* Many have opinions as to which florists offer the best service and which don't. However, their contact with florists is limited to the final product at the wedding— their opinions could be somewhat biased.

❧ *If you plan to produce your own arrangements* or have a friend do it, look under the Yellow Page heading of "Florists-Wholesale" for supplies. Some wholesalers refuse to sell to the public while others don't have such restrictions.

Top Money-saving Secrets

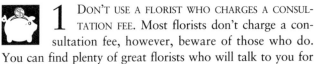

1 DON'T USE A FLORIST WHO CHARGES A CONSULTATION FEE. Most florists don't charge a consultation fee, however, beware of those who do. You can find plenty of great florists who will talk to you for free; don't spend time with the few that charge such fees.

2 CHOOSE A WEDDING DATE THAT IS NOT NEAR A HOLIDAY. As you may well realize, all roses are outrageously priced in February thanks to Valentine's Day. So if you want roses, don't plan on a wedding at that time. Also, December is an expensive time to buy fresh flowers since the supply is limited and the demand from Christmas and other events is high. On the other hand, brides have found Christmas weddings are less expensive for ceremony flowers since the church may already be decorated.

3 SEASONAL AND REGIONAL FLOWERS CAN BE GREAT BARGAINS. For example, in California, certain orchids and other tropical flowers grown locally may be available at affordable prices. Also, seasonality often affects floral prices. For example, tulips are abundant from December through February and as such are fairly inexpensive. If you want them in July, however, they will be extremely expensive if they are available at all.

4 AVOID EXOTIC FLOWERS. What is considered an exotic flower may vary from region to region. For example, in the Southwest, lilies of the valley (see picture) are very expensive and difficult to find. Yet in the northern part of the U.S., where they are common, they may be very reasonable. Exotic flowers such as pricey orchids from Hawaii are usually expensive no matter where you live.

5 INSTEAD OF BIG (AND EXPENSIVE) BOUQUETS, CARRY A SINGLE FLOWER. This is extremely elegant especially with long stem varieties like calla lilies and roses. If you want to carry a bouquet, consider having the bridesmaids carry single flowers.

6 USE SILK FLOWERS to replace expensive, fresh varieties. Even dried flowers may be affordable alternatives. All-silk arrangements may not be much less expensive if you have them made by a florist—their charge for labor may be expensive no matter what type of flower they use. However, you can save money doing it yourself or substituting silk exotics (like orchids) for real ones.

7 LIMIT THE NUMBER OF ATTENDANTS. This is just basic math: the more attendants, the more flowers, the higher the final cost.

8 SPEND YOUR MONEY WHERE PEOPLE WILL SEE IT. Most wedding ceremonies are relatively short (about 30 minutes) therefore your guests will be spending most of their time at your reception. We suggest that you spend money on flowers at the reception rather than at the ceremony. You'll be able to enjoy them more at the reception and so will your guests. At the typical wedding, ceremony site flowers are the biggest expense, but you see them for the shortest amount of time!

9 IF THERE IS ANOTHER WEDDING SCHEDULED for the same day at your ceremony site, share the floral arrangements with the other bride! Splitting the cost here could be a major savings. Use neutral hues like whites and creams to avoid any color clashes.

10 BALLOONS CAN BE AN AFFORDABLE OPTION FOR RECEPTION SITE DECORATION. For example, we priced balloon table centerpieces at about $18 each. To get the kind of height and volume that balloons provide, you would need to spend two to three times that amount on fresh flowers. We recommend balloons for reception sites with high ceilings since the height of most balloon arrangements can make small rooms look crowded.

11 RENTING PLANTS AND OTHER GREENERY AS FILLER. A great money-saving option, this may save you from buying tons of flowers for a reception or ceremony site that needs lots of decoration. Examples of places to use greenery are chuppahs and trellises.

12 RE-USE SOME OF THE ARRANGEMENTS AND BOUQUETS. The bridesmaid's bouquets can be used to decorate the cake and guest book tables. Some altar arrangements can be moved to the reception site (although there may be a delivery fee).

13 CONSIDER ARRANGING THE FLOWERS YOURSELF OR HAVING A FRIEND ARRANGE THEM. This option is available only for those who feel confident in their skills at flower arranging. Many wholesale florists can supply all the necessary accessories for flower arranging. Silk flowers are also available from wholesalers in your area and can be arranged by you or a friend. Craft magazines are great places to find ideas on arranging flowers. The savings from this option may be as much as 50%.

14 SCALE-DOWN THE PEW DECORATIONS AT THE CEREMONY. Consider using just greenery or bows instead of fresh flowers. Some brides have eliminated this decoration altogether. Another option: craft stores will teach you how to make the bows yourself.

15 PICK THE GENERAL COLOR SCHEME AND LET YOUR FLORIST BUY THE MOST AFFORDABLE FLOWERS AVAILABLE THE WEEK OF YOUR WEDDING. Obviously, you must feel very confident in your florist to go this route. Specifically rule out any flowers you don't want but try to remain flexible. This tip is a money-saver since your florist may be able to purchase certain in-season varieties at substantially lower prices.

16 CALL A LOCAL HORTICULTURAL SCHOOL. A bride in Ohio wrote to us with this great tip—she found that the students at a local horticultural school would arrange the flowers

---

REAL WEDDING TIP:
Beware the Surprise Consulting Fee

 A reader in Richardson, TX gave a florist a $100 deposit to hold the date for her wedding. The florist said she could work within the bride's specified budget, promising to mail a detailed proposal in short order.

Two weeks later, the proposal comes in—at *twice* the amount bride had budgeted. Obviously, the bride wasn't very happy. When she told the florist she was going elsewhere for flowers, the florist said she was keeping the $100, calling it a "consulting fee." To make matters worse, she had the gall to send the bride another bill for $62, for "additional labor" to prepare the proposal.

What's the lesson? Whenever you give a deposit, make sure you get a written receipt that states any refund/cancellation policies. Even better: put it on a credit card. Then, if the florist decides your refundable deposit is now non-refundable, you can go to your credit card company to dispute the charge. While it may be tempting to place deposits to hold dates, make sure your get written documentation spelling out the refund policies first.

for her wedding for free. She paid for the flowers (only $200) and they did all the labor—a great deal! Check the local phone book for any schools in your area. Another idea: craft stores and community colleges often have classes in flower-arranging. If you don't have time to take a class, see if the students will take on your wedding as a class project.

Spotlight: Best Buys

For some lovely yet affordable flowers that won't bust your budget, we've compiled a short list of flowers that can be used to fill out arrangements. Be aware that certain flowers may be more affordable in various regions of the U.S. Ask your florist for local recommendations. Also, seasonality may affect the prices of certain flowers.

❦ *Gerbera Daisies.* These giant-sized versions of common daisies make wonderful and colorful bridesmaids' bouquets. They also have long stems and can be used successfully in table and altar arrangements. They come in incredible colors from plain white to deep fuchsia. Pastels are also available.

❦ *Stattice.* A fabulous filler flower for bridal bouquets, these bunches of tiny white or purple blossoms are reasonably-priced options. Other fillers that are inexpensive include Queen Anne's Lace and Stock.

❦ *Alstroemeria Lilies.* These are miniature lilies that come in over 20 different shades. Some flowers are even multi-colored. Because they are small, they look best in bouquets, hairpieces, on wedding cakes or in table arrangements.

❦ *Carnations.* Ah, the old standby. These are a great pick for altar arrangements since they stand out without great expense. They come in every color variety, but we don't recommend the dyed ones—stick to natural colors. Some varieties are also available as miniatures if you want to add them to table arrangements or bouquets. These are very "heat-hardy" too for those of you in hot climates.

❦ *Chrysanthemums.* More commonly referred to as mums, these flowers are also great filler for altar arrangements. They add oodles of volume to your arrangements without costing a great deal. These flowers are available in a wide range of colors from white to bronze. Some even look like simple daisies in pinks, yellows and white.

❦ *Gladiolus.* These long-stalked flowers are covered in bright blooms. They look especially nice in altar or buffet arrangements to add height. Individual blooms can be used as glamelias (ask your florist for an example). Colors range from white to pink to deep, true red.

❦ *Freesia.* Another small delicate flower with a pleasing scent, freesia can be used as a wonderful substitute for the more expensive stephanotis. They come in white, yellow, pink, orange, lavender, and red.

Getting Started: How Far in Advance?

Book a florist up to six months in advance of your wedding. In larger cities, some florists may even require more time. For most towns, however, many florists consider three to six months notice adequate. Realize that you can put down a small deposit further in advance and then talk specifics at a later date.

Biggest Myths about Wedding Flowers

Myth #1 *"My mother insists that we have lots and lots of flowers at my wedding. Is this really necessary?"*

Bridal magazines often tell us we should have flowers dripping from the ceiling and crawling along the floor. Some florists feed this perception by suggesting superfluous floral items like "cake knife corsages" (believe it or not, a special flower wrapped with a bow around the knife you cut the cake with), "hairpiece flowers" and arrangements for the gift table. We are not making this stuff up. Does the gift table really need a floral arrangement?

Emily Post even recommends flowers or greenery to decorate the area where your receiving line stands. How silly! Florists must see brides as an endless money pit. We hate to tread on those floral traditionalists but remember that the next day, all those flowers will be dead.

Myth #2 *"I figured on spending only about $100 on my wedding flowers. Given the cost of arrangements I've sent friends, I assume this is a good estimate."*

Most flowers are cheap. Most florists aren't. What you are paying for is the florist's talent, skill and overhead. The manual labor needed to create beautiful bouquets and arrangements (not to mention delivering them) is what costs big money. We should note that some exotic flowers (orchids, etc.) are pricey exceptions: they virtually guarantee an astronomically high floral bill.

Step-by-step Shopping Strategies

 Step 1: First, you must have the time, place and apparel selected before you can get an accurate bid from a florist. The bridal gown is crucial—everything flows from this design element. The colors of the bridesmaids gowns are also important.

Step 2: Choose two to three florists from the sources above to visit. Make an appointment with each and leave about one hour's time to discuss the details.

Step 3: Be sure to bring swatches of the bridesmaids apparel and a picture of the bridal gown you have selected. A magazine ad or rough sketch will suffice. Give this to the florist so they'll remember what the dress looks like when they actually make the bouquet. Also, it will be helpful to bring any pictures of flowers/designs you like.

Step 4: Look through actual photographs of their previous work. Don't settle for FTD design books or floral magazines. Identify flowers and designs that fit your wedding's style—unadorned wedding gowns can be set-off by a lush bride's bouquet. Similarly, a simple bouquet may better compliment an ornate bridal dress. See if the florist attempts to understand your tastes and desires instead of merely telling you what you must have.

Step 5: Get a written proposal specifying exact flowers to be used. Each item (brides bouquet, corsages, etc.) should be priced individually.

Step 6: Pick your top florist choice and ask to visit one of their weddings during set-up. On your visit, check to see if they are on-time and organized. Also, look to see how fresh the flowers are. Do you find the designs pleasing (keeping in mind that the other bride's taste may be different from your own)?

❦ *Step 7*: If you believe an on-site meeting at your ceremony or reception site is necessary, now is the time. Finalize the details.

❦ *Step 8*: Get a written contract that spells out the date, set-up time, place, and specific flowers and designs to be created. Specific details (if you want open roses, for example) need to be spelled out clearly. As you get closer to your wedding, there may be some modifications (more corsages, etc.). Make sure you have the florist write down any changes—send written notes to verify the alterations.

❦ *Step 9*: If you're having a large or complex wedding, a pre-wedding floral check-up may be necessary. Here you'll meet with the florist about one to two weeks prior to the date to iron out any last minute details/changes, etc.

Questions to Ask a Florist

 1 IS MY DATE AVAILABLE? If it is, check to see if a deposit is necessary to hold the date. Also ask if there is any consultation fee.

2 DO YOU HAVE ACTUAL PHOTOGRAPHS OR SAMPLES of your past work? It's important to see the work of your florist, not the airbrushed photos from an FTD book. There is no better way to see if their style complements your tastes and to see just how skilled they are.

3 DO YOU OFFER ANY SILK OR DRIED FLOWER ARRANGEMENTS? This may be important to you if you want to save your bouquet or want an unusual look for a table center-piece. Sometimes these two options may be less expensive than fresh flowers, especially for some exotics like orchids.

A dried rose topiary centerpiece.

4 IS THERE A DELIVERY OR SET-UP FEE? Watch out—this can be a substantial extra charge. Most florist will charge you some set-up fee especially if you have either complex flower arrangements or a site that is a long distance from their shop. If the charge is high, consider finding a florist closer to the site or cut back on the complicated decorations.

5 HOW MANY WEDDINGS DO YOU DO IN A DAY? The biggest problem with some florists is that they become "overex-

tended"—trying to do too many weddings in one day. A florist can probably do up to two or three weddings a day if they are held at different times and/or they have plenty of help. If their schedule looks crowded for your wedding date, however, they may arrive late or deliver the wrong flowers. Look for someone focused on your wedding.

6 ARE YOU FAMILIAR WITH MY CEREMONY SITE LOCATION? If not, will you visit it with me? It may be a good idea to introduce your florist to the ceremony or reception site if they've never seen it. Ask if there is any charge for this on-site visit.

7 WHAT RENTAL ITEMS DO YOU HAVE? How are they priced? Some things you may want to rent include candelabrum, aisle standards, or urns. We prefer florists who don't over-charge on rentals. One way to find out is to compare prices with a local rental store. A common mark-up for florists is about 10% for their time to coordinate this detail. If you would prefer to rent the items yourself because you can get a better price, be sure you have the time to take care of it.

8 CAN I ATTEND ONE OF YOUR WEDDINGS DURING SET-UP FOR A LOOK AT YOUR DESIGNS? Here is another way to determine how professional and talented your florist is. You'll need to visit during set-up and leave before the wedding party arrives. Look for timeliness, freshness and beauty of the flowers and how well the florist and staff work together.

9 WHAT TIME WILL YOU BE AT MY CEREMONY/RECEPTION SITES TO SET-UP MY WEDDING? Confirm this time constantly throughout your planning. Many florists set-up weddings a couple hours in advance. If this is the case with your wedding, be sure the temperature at the site is not too hot or too cold for the flowers—you want them to look fresh at wedding time.

10 WILL YOU MERELY DROP OFF MY FLOWERS OR STAY THROUGH THE CEREMONY? The degree of service here differs dramatically from florist to florist. Some just drop off the flowers at the ceremony and leave, while others stay to pin on corsages, make sure nothing is missing, etc. There may be an extra fee ($50) for this service—for large weddings, however, this may be a worth while investment.

Helpful Hints

1 PUT YOUR DEPOSIT AND BALANCE ON A CREDIT CARD. We have heard countless stories of couples who hired a florist to do their flowers only to have the wrong flowers delivered. Or worse, the florist went out of business. Although these are rare occurrences, its best to be safe. Payments on credit cards are protected by special consumer protection laws. See the Apparel chapter for more details.

2 KEEP AN OPEN MIND. Instead of setting your heart on a particular design or flower, let your florist come up with some suggestions. Because florists works with flowers so closely, they may be aware of some options that are really terrific. Especially with regards to colors, listen to your florist's ideas and look at some of their past work before you make up your mind. You might be surprised!

3 CONFIRM ANY RESTRICTIONS ON FLOWERS/DECORATIONS. Some churches prohibit candles and still others "request" that you donate the altar arrangement to the church. Reception sites may also have similar rules, especially regarding the throwing of rice or birdseed.

Pitfalls to Avoid

Pitfall #1
"FTD COOKIE-CUTTER" WEDDINGS
"I met with a florist for my wedding and was extremely disappointed. All they showed me were boring FTD design books. The few real photos I saw featured bouquets that all looked the same."

Some florists try to make every wedding fit a "cookie cutter" mold. Instead of keying on the individuality involved, they merely suggest stiff, formulated designs that are uninspired at best and dreadful at worst. We find "cash and carry" florists most guilty of this offense—they simply don't care enough about weddings to try harder.

Pitfall #2
PLASTIC BOUQUET HOLDERS
"We attended a fancy wedding last weekend and were surprised at the bouquets. The beautiful flowers were stuck in cheap, plastic holders that just looked out of place!"

Plastic bouquet holders have become a crutch for many lazy florists. Instead of hand-tying and hand-wrapping the bouquets, some florists simply stick the flowers into floral foam inside plastic holders. Besides looking cheap, poorly-inserted flowers can actually drop out of the plastic holder!

Some florists insist plastic holders are necessary since they provide a water source for delicate flowers. If your florist uses plastic holders for this purpose, insist the plastic be covered with green floral tape or pretty ribbon. Better yet, choose a florist that hand ties and hand wraps the bouquets. A small tube of water can be attached to delicate flowers needing moisture.

Pitfall #3
HEAT-SENSITIVE FLOWERS.

"My friend got married last summer in an outdoor ceremony. Unfortunately, the heat caused many of the flowers to wilt and even turn brown."

The fragrant, yet fragile gardenia.

If you live where it will be hot during your wedding, watch out for heat-sensitivity. Some flowers with this problem include stephanotis and gardenias. Ask your florist for flowers that can withstand the heat and still look fresh. As a side note, we heard from one florist who uses an "anti-transpirant" spray such as Bloomlife Plastic Wax or Crowning Glory. These products seal in the moisture so flowers don't wilt as fast.

Trends

❧ *Old-fashioned posy bouquets.* These are round, smaller bouquets of tightly arranged blooms. This trend echoes the Victorian tradition of carrying small bouquets on outings.

❧ *Single flower bouquets.* It's just roses. Or just orchids. These mono-chromatic bouquets have few or no accent flowers.

❧ *New growing techniques have produced some unique hybrid flowers.* One neat example of this is the posy calla lily. A much smaller version of the huge white blooms, this one comes in burgundy, electric yellow, white, pink, and gold. For the smaller bride who wants to carry calla lilies, here's an option that won't overwhelm.

❧ *Wedding floral specialists.* We've noticed an upswing in the number of florists who are concentrating solely on weddings. Some will even come to your home for a consultation or make appointments with you after work.

Unique Ideas

1 HOLD THE RICE. The traditional rice throw at the newly-weds has been declared "environmentally-incorrect" (bird eat the rice; birds die). So, couples have been replacing the rice with flower petals, potpourri and even colorful streamers. Another idea: balloon releases make a dramatic exit for the bride and groom.

2 CONSIDER USING FRUITS AND VEGETABLES OR DRIED FLOWERS TO DECORATE YOUR RECEPTION TABLES. These will fit themes such as a fall wedding (gourds and pumpkins with fall leaves) or a Victorian style wedding. We've even heard of dessert being used as a centerpiece: piles of strawberries with silver bowls of chocolate sauce and powdered sugar on mirrors. Mmmmm.

Spotlight: Roses

Roses are still by far the most requested flowers in wedding arrangements and bouquets across the U.S. Without exception, every bridal consultant we talked to mentioned roses as popular wedding flowers in their city. With this in mind, you might appreciate a little extra information on roses.

Types of Roses

"Where do florists get roses? Will they look like roses at the grocery store? How can I be sure to get the best quality?"

Florists buy roses from wholesalers. Wholesalers buy them from a variety of sources. California is the largest producer of roses for the U.S., but roses also come from Colombia (Visa roses) and Mexico (Vega roses). Holland and France also export some varieties. Some of the best roses are Vegas, whose blossoms tend to be bigger than California roses and better shaped than Visas. Each florist has his or her own preference on which kind you should buy.

Roses also come in a variety of qualities, similar to eggs at the grocery store. California roses, for example, come in Select (the best), Extra Fancy (middle quality) and Fancy (cheap). Most of what you see in grocery stores are Fancy. Few professional florists sell Fancy roses, but it is difficult to determine yourself which grade your florist buys. If you are concerned about the quality, ask the florist which grade is used. Hopefully, they'll say Select. Select roses will be more expensive, but the quality will be better.

Color Options

"I requested bridal white roses from my florist for my bridal bouquet, but the bouquet I saw on my wedding day looked pinkish rather than white. Was my florist substituting the wrong flowers?"

Definitely not. One thing brides should understand about colors in the floral business is that they can be very deceiving. For example, a red rose isn't actually a true red. And a bridal white rose isn't really all-white. A bridal white rose, one of the most common roses for weddings, is actually a creamy white rose with a pink or peach tinged center. Many bridal white roses together in a bouquet may give the illusion of more pink than you intended. So you see how misleading names can be.

Here are some examples of other popular wedding roses:

❦ *Champaign*
A creamy, antique ivory colored rose.

❦ *Candia*
Creamy white with dark pink edges to the petals. This would be a truly unusual look.

❦ *Darling*
A creamy peach rose suitable for a touch of color in the bride's or bridesmaids' bouquets.

❦ *Bridal Pink*
These are definitely all-pink roses. Many brides assume they will be soft pink, but they are actually quite a bit brighter.

❦ *Delores*
This is a soft pink rose.

❦ *Jacaranda or Purvey*
A hot pink rose; perfect with the jewel tones of bridesmaids' dresses.

❦ *Lady Diana*
Named after the Princess of Wales, these are pale peach roses. They are beautiful for bridal work and may even look pinkish rather than peach against a pink background.

❦ *Sonia*
A brighter peach rose with a little more vibrant color than the Lady Di.

❦ *Jacqueline Kennedy*
One of the few true red roses but tends to be rather small.

❦ *Madame Delbard*
This is a French rose with a rich velvety red color. It opens well but can be expensive.

❧ *Sterling Silver*

Also called an *Elizabeth Taylor*, the color is a lovely lavender. It tends to have a small blossom so you may need more of these blooms than you think.

❧ *Ranunculus*

These flowers aren't actually roses, but they do look a lot like a fully open rose. They make a very inexpensive alternative to roses especially since they are available in February and March, the time of year when roses are most expensive. They come in reds, pinks, and yellows.

One interesting final note on roses: colors have little or nothing to do with prices. You might expect more unusual hues (lavender, for example) to cost more but in reality the wholesale price is often the same.

Spotlight: Do-it-yourself Supplies

Michaels Arts and Crafts Stores
(214) 580-8242

One of the best sources for silk flowers and wedding supplies in the U.S. has got to be Michaels Arts and Crafts stores. With over 400 stores across the country, Michaels provides not only a large number of attractive, affordable silk flowers, but they also have in-store arrangers who can help put your wedding flowers together.

Michaels sells all the supplies necessary to design your own bouquets and arrangements, but if you prefer to use their staff to help you, they do provide a very reasonable alternative to retail florist shops. For example, when we visited a Michaels store, the floral department told us most silk bouquets range from $25 to $65. Wow! This is a great savings when compared with the average fresh bouquets from a retail florist—which can range from $75 to $200 and more.

Michaels stores also carry other accessories for do-it-yourself brides. They have supplies with which to make veils and headpieces, wedding cakes, your own favors and other wedding items. They carry accessories ranging from ring pillows to cake knives as well.

We've been big fans of the options available at Michaels Arts and Crafts stores for a long time. Their wide selection of silk flowers, craft supplies and wedding accessories make them a unique and valuable alternative.

MJDesigns
(214) 929-8595

MJDesigns is a wonderful craft store with locations in the Dallas/Ft. Worth, TX, Buffalo, NY and the Washington, DC metro area. What makes these stores unique is their incredible selection of silk flowers. Shoppers in Dallas, for example, have told us they wouldn't shop anywhere else for floral supplies!

MJDesigns has a huge selection of fine quality silk flowers and supplies for the do-it-yourselfer. If you prefer to have your wedding flowers arranged for you but can't afford the high prices of retail florists, MJDesigns has the answer.

Each store carries a catalog of 10 different designs for brides' and bridesmaids' bouquets. When we looked through the catalog, we noticed all shapes and sizes including natural clutches, nosegays, cascades and crescents. Besides bouquets, there were ten possible corsage designs, and five boutonniere options. We also saw pew bows, hairpieces, flower girl baskets and veils—all at very affordable prices.

For example, bouquets range from a small nosegay for $15 up to a large cascade with Japhet orchids and stephanotis for only $60. Corsages range from $3.50 to $10.50, while boutonnieres are $2. After interviewing over 200 retail florists, we couldn't find any source for flowers (silk or fresh) that's more affordable than MJDesigns.

To order a bouquet from MJDesigns, you first pick a color from the display in each store. Then, you choose a style from their catalog. MJDesigns then sends your order to their main design studio where it takes about seven days to produce.

MJDesigns also provides other wedding accessories, including cake decorating supplies, toasting glasses, cake toppers and veil supplies. Overall, we highly recommend MJDesigns.

Other Do-It-Yourself Floral & Wedding Supplies

Do-it-yourself wedding supplies can be a significant source of savings. Here are our picks for the best craft stores in the country:

NATIONAL CHAINS
   Fabric Centers/Jo Ann Fabrics
   Fabric World
   Hancock Fabrics
   Michaels Arts and Crafts
   Petals catalog (800) 431-2464

NORTHEAST
   Hills

Craft Basket in Brookfield, CT
The Petals Outlet in Woodbury Commons
  in Central Valley, New York

MIDWEST
 Franks Nursery and Crafts
 Pat Catan Craft Stores (Ohio)

SOUTH
 White Rose Crafts and Nursery (also in Canada)

SOUTHWEST
 MJDesigns (Texas, Virginia, New York)
 Hobby Lobby (Oklahoma, Colorado, and Kansas)
 Crafts Etc. (Texas)
 Amber's (Texas)

WEST
 H & H Crafts (California)
 House of Fabric (Northwest)
 Sprouse Stores (Northwest)

Dictionary of Flowers

Here are a few flower names and descriptions we found ourselves running into frequently. Hopefully this will help you understand our "lingo."

LILIES
☙ *Calla*

Huge, long white flowers on thick stalks (as in Katherine Hepburn's ". . . the calla lilies are in bloom.") Smaller versions (called posy calla lilies) come in a variety of colors.

☙ *Rubrim*

Star flowers, come in colors from white to peach to deep maroon.

Rubrim Lily.

☙ *Lily of the Valley*

Small, white blooms that look like tiny bells. This flower is affordable in the north but quite expensive in other parts of the U.S. For a picture, see "Top Money-saving Secrets" earlier in the chapter.

ORCHIDS
☙ *Dendrobium*

Miniature orchids that come in sprays, may be used individually or as trailing pieces.

Dendrobium Orchid.

🌺 *Cymbidium*

Smaller than Japhet orchids with a curly edge only at the center.

🌺 *Japhet*

Large orchids with a curly edge all over, often have yellow throats.

🌺 *Phalaenopsis*

These are round-edged orchids that are white with reddish throats. They don't always wear well.

MISCELLANEOUS

🌺 *Stephanotis*

Small, white flowers with star-like petals and a deep throat (we've been told that these can discolor in extreme heat.)

🌺 *Anthuriums*

One of the few "true red" flowers, this has a heart-shaped bloom with a large stamen.

Chapter 6

Invitations

In this chapter, we'll tell you about a printing process that can save you 50% or more on your invitations. Then check out discount sources like mail-order catalogs and phone-order services. Next, we'll show you the five-step shopping process for finding invitations, and share several unique ideas such as edible invitations.

What Are You Buying?

 Buying invitations is a little like buying a meal at an à la carte restaurant. In other words, everything is priced separately: the appetizer, salad, entree, and dessert. With invitations, the entree is the basic invitation design itself (the paper style and the printing). Thankfully, the price does include the envelopes (two for very formal invitations and one for more informal options).

There also are other "accessories" (appetizers, salads, desserts) available but these are priced separately from the original invitation. Here are some options and a short description:

❧ *Reception cards* announce to the guest the location and time of the actual reception.

❧ *Response cards*(also known as R.S.V.P.'s) are just as they sound—a card that asks guests to tell you whether or not they can attend. An envelope (with your return address printed) is included with each response card. Most brides put postage on the response card envelopes to encourage your guests to respond.

❧ *Envelope linings* add a little flair and color to invitations.

❧ *Your return address* can be printed on the back flap of the envelopes.

❧ *Informals*, used mainly as thank-you notes, usually are blank cards with your names printed on the outside.

❧ *Exclusive (or photo) lettering* versus *regular lettering* refers to the style of lettering you choose for your invitation. Most invitation books offer you a choice between styles of script. Some, however also offer two separate lists to choose from called "exclusive (or photo)" and "regular." Exclusive lettering is more expensive than regular lettering but we recommend using exclusive lettering anyway. Why? Exclusive lettering gives you a wider choice of type-styles. Also, the size of exclusive lettering can be adjusted to fit the size of your invitation— a plus if you want a more intricate invitation design. The choice is up to you but the added expense is very small (about $4 or $5 per 100 invitations).

Average Total Costs The average couple pays about $200 for invitations and other stationery needs. However, fancier invitations can run two or three times that price. The average deposit is 50% down with the balance due when you pick up your order.

Where to Buy Invitations

Fortunately, brides today have a myriad of options when it comes to wedding invitations; not only are the styles endless, but the suppliers are equally plentiful. How does this process usually work? Well, most wedding invitations are printed by big, national printers. Some of these printers have a network of retail dealers (stationery shops, department stores, etc.). Others market invitations through the mail—they print up full-color catalogs and do business over an 800-number. You can also buy invitations through discount buying services.

Here are some common (and not-so common) places to find wedding invitations:

❧ *Retail sources.*

1 STATIONERY SHOPS. Look under "Invitations" or "Wedding Invitations" in the phone book and you'll find a smorgasbord of places, from party stores to gift boutiques. As dealers for the major invitations printers, they carry a selection of sample books containing examples of each invitation. Brides choose a design from these sample books and then place an order. The hands-on service is one of the chief advantages to this route—most can help you with etiquette/wording questions and, perhaps more importantly, deal with any problems that crop up with the printer. Of course, you pay for this service with full-retail prices and few discounts.

2 PLACES YOU WOULDN'T THINK OF. Some churches and synagogues offer invitations at discounted prices as a fund-raiser. We've even heard of several companies that

offer invitations as a perk for their employees. One bride who worked at Xerox told us she was able to order invitations through the company at a substantial discount.

Another great source is "out of home" stationers. These businesses operate from home-based offices and, thanks to low overhead, usually pass along savings from 10% to 20%. As with any merchant you deal with for your wedding, you'll want to make sure the company is reputable by calling the Better Business Bureau, checking references, etc.

Some department stores with bridal registries also sell invitations, as do off-set printers. Some local printers actually print their own invitations, while most send the orders along to the same national printers you'll see in stationery shops.

❦ Mail-order catalogs.

Of course, you can also order wedding invitations from the comfort of your home. Over 20 companies have sprung up in recent years to offer wedding invitations via mail (later in this chapter we'll review some of the best).

How do the catalogs work? First, you call the 1-800 number and wait two to four weeks for the catalog to arrive. The glossy four-color publication will have pictures of invitations, accessories and generic etiquette/wording advice. Most will also send along a sample or two of various invitation styles.

Ordering from the catalogs is rather easy. Prices (at least on the invitations) are hard to beat; we've found the same design in a catalog for 40% less than a retail store. Most take credit cards and are quick to fill the order—it takes as little as two to four days (plus another week shipping time). Expedited or overnight delivery may be available, but at a steep extra cost.

Later in this chapter we'll go into more details on mail-order invitations, including pitfalls to avoid.

❦ Discount buying services.

Later in the chapter, we review Invitation Hotline, an example of a discount buying service for invitations. What do they discount? You can get some of the same premium brand names you'd see in full-price stationary shops (examples of such brands are reviewed later in this chapter) at discounts from 15% to 25%!

Discount buying services are a hybrid between mail-order and retail dealers. They don't have any catalogs—you do the shopping and then call them for a price quote, once you've decided on the invitation (a page or style number will work). Once you place the order over the phone, the invitations are mailed back to you within a few weeks time. In a way, discount buying services offer the best of all worlds—the high-quality of premium brands at discount prices, combined with the convenience of mail-order.

Sources to Find Stationers

❧ *Friends.* Recently-married couples may be your best resource to find a good stationer.

❧ *Bridal shows.* Bridal shows are a great place to find little-known stationery companies. You may be able to look through some of their sample books at a show too.

❧ *Other bridal businesses.* Many other bridal businesses such as photographers, florists and bridal shops may be able to suggest a good local stationer.

❧ *Discount Bridal Service.* Quite a few DBS representatives also offer discounts on invitations as well as on bridal gowns. For a list of their representatives who also discount invitations call (800) 874-8794.

Top Money-saving Secrets

1 CHOOSE THERMOGRAPHED INVITATIONS instead of engraved. Right about now you may be wondering what is thermography. Let's take a quick look at the difference between the two printing processes. Note: we aren't talking about the style of script or the quality of the paper, this is just the actual printing process.

Engraving is the Rolls Royce of embellishments. It has been with us for quite a long time and actually was the only option available for invitations until about 15 years ago. Both engraving and thermography create raised printing. However, with engraving, a copper or steel plate is etched with the type and design. These etchings fill with ink and are forced against a die, lifting the ink out of the plate and creating a raised image on the paper. The paper is left with an impression from the back.

Thermography is often used to simulate engraving. A resinous powder is dusted over the ink while it is still wet. The pieces then are heated where the powder melts, fuses with the ink and swells to create a raised surface. While metal plates may be used, this process is much less expensive (up to 50% or even more!). This option also allows you to use a wide variety of ink colors. Thermography has become extremely popular, thanks to better production processes. The process is virtually indistinguishable from engraving except to those snobs out there feeling the backs of invitations. All the mail-order catalogs listed later in this chapter offer thermographed invitations.

2 ORDER FROM A PROFESSIONAL STATIONER who discounts. Discount Bridal Service (800) 874-8794 has

many representatives around the country who regularly discount invitations 10% to 20%.

3 CHECK THE LOCAL NEWSPAPER FOR SALES. Some professional stationers have periodic sales.

4 DON'T BUY ALL THE EXTRAS. As you've read above, there are quite a few different accessories and extras available to match your wedding invitation. Instead of ordering separate reception cards, consider printing "Reception Following" at the bottom of your actual invitation. This could save about 15% off your bill. Also, skip envelope linings and response cards if you don't see a need for them. To see how all these charges add up, let's look at the sample costs for an invitation with black ink from the popular Carlson Craft brand (for a dealer near you, call (800) 328-1782):

INVITATION PRICING EXAMPLE
Carlson Craft Invitation #WC 298-71
Price for 200 Invitations

BASIC INVITATION	$158.50
RETURN ADDRESS ON FLAP	40.30
RECEPTION CARD	77.50
RESPONSE (RSVP) CARD	95.50
LINED ENVELOPES	34.00
INFORMALS (THANK YOU NOTES)	77.50
TOTAL	**$483.30**

As you can see by this sample, the original invitation is much less costly by itself than after you add in all the options.

5 BUY AN EMBOSSER WITH YOUR RETURN ADDRESS instead of paying extra to get this printed on the back flap. The cost of an embosser is about equal to or less than the return address charge in many cases—the advantage here is you can use the embosser again.

6 TO SAVE ON POSTAGE, DON'T BUY AN OVERSIZED INVITATION. Oversized invitations require more postage. Also, an invitation with lots of enclosures (reception cards, response cards, maps, etc.) will be more expensive to mail. Remember that response cards require their own stamp, too.

7 FOR ENGRAVED INVITATIONS, CONSIDER ALTERNATIVES TO CRANE. The Cadillac brand of engraved invitations, Crane (see review in the next section) charges $300 to $400 for 100 engraved invitations. But what if you have to have engraved invitations but can't afford the Crane price? There are several affordable alternatives. For example, the Reaves Engraving mail-order catalog (910-369-2260) charges just

$181 for 100 engraved invitations on Crane paper. (It's even less for engraved invitations on their own in-house stock—$87 per 100). Another alternative: use a discount buying source like the Invitation Hotline (800) 800-4355 (see review later in this chapter). They'll sell you 100 engraved invitations by Encore (on 100% cotton paper) for just $259.

8 Response postcards save on money and postage. Instead of a response card (which needs a separate envelope and a 32¢ stamp), consider a response *postcard*. 50 postcards cost about $12.90 from mail-order catalogs like Invitations Etc. (800-709-7979, see review later in this chapter)—that's nearly a 50% savings over standard response cards-with-envelopes. And then the postcards only require a 20¢ stamp. That's a $12 savings for every 100 invitations you send out.

9 Design it yourself on a computer. Got a computer and a laser printer? Some brides today are producing their own invitations, with the help of desktop publishing programs and laser-compatible papers. Later in this chapter, we'll discuss do-it-yourself resources for the computer-savvy bride.

Helpful Hints

1 For large orders, engraved invitations may be a better bargain. While thermography is generally cheaper than engraving, there is an exception. After you get beyond 300 to 350 invitations, the reverse is often true. For example, we priced 400 thermographed invitations from a major printer at $575. The same number of engraved invitations from a buying source like the Invitation Hotline (see review later in this chapter) were $566. Not only is it cheaper, but also for that price you get invitations that are folded and stuffed into envelopes—no thermographer offers this service, which is no small task. Another tip: while mail-order catalogs have great prices on orders of 100 or 200 invitations, their price advantage drops as the quantity grows. You may find a better deal on large orders (over 300) from a local stationer.

2 Consider addressing options. Many stationary shops and even mail-order catalogs today offer envelope addressing services for busy brides and grooms. They'll take your guest list, feed it in the computer and then voila! Addressed envelopes ready to stamp and mail. While some services use a pen-based addressing machine (like Inscribe), more and more are turning to computerized output from laser and ink jet printers. Which is best? Consider the paper type before making a decision. If your envelopes are not made from paper that is laser-printer compatible (ask the stationer or catalog to find out), go with an ink jet printer service. Why? The laser printer toner might rub off at the post office, making the invitation undeliverable. Ink jet printing is preferable since it sticks to the envelope better.

Spotlight: Best Buys

Through our research for this book, we have identified a few "best brands" in wedding invitations—these are printers who sell their designs through retail dealers (and not directly to consumer via mail-order). Call the number listed after each review to find a local dealer who carries these brands:

The Ratings

★★★★ EXCELLENT — *our top pick!*
★★★ GOOD — *above average quality, prices and creativity.*
★★ FAIR — *could stand some improvement.*
★ POOR — *yuck! Could stand major improvement.*

William Arthur ★★★★ Our pick as the best bet for invitations is Maine-based William Arthur. Their fabulous collection of thermographed invitations offers a sophisticated and classic look for brides who want an alternative to the plain, traditional invitation. With a variety of unique type styles and card-type designs, Arthur's line runs $197 to $277 per 100 invitations ($302 to $462 for 200 invitations). Included in that price is return address printing, which is nice plus. The customer service is excellent, according to stationers we interviewed. "They're in a class by themselves," one told us, adding that their shipping (5 business days) is incredibly reliable. One and two day rush service is also available. For a dealer near you who carries William Arthur, call (207) 985-6581.

Carlson Craft ★★½ One of the largest invitation printers in the country, Carlson Craft has something for everyone. The thermography is very good quality and their 100% cotton (40 lb.) paper designs are a good buy at $150 per 100 invitations. For a dealer near you who carries Carlson Craft, call (800) 328-1782.

Chase Paper ★★½ From plain traditional to glitzy contemporary, Chase Paper has a very wide selection of unique papers. The quality of the thermography is top-notch, say our stationery sources. Prices run $60 to $140 per 100 invitations. Best of all, the lower-priced options are a definite step up in quality compared to other companies. Shipping takes about three weeks. For a dealer near you who carries Chase, call (508) 366-4441.

Checkerboard Invitations ★★★ Checkerboard's sample book features a wide assortment of designer invitations—you can even mix and match type styles (most printers don't let you do this). We saw designs with splattered ink, mylar prisms and marbled paper; they even have several recycled paper designs. Funky envelope linings complete the looks. Prices range from $59 to $169 per 100 invitations. For a dealer near you who carries Checkerboard, call (508) 835-2475.

Crane ★½ Pull out a dollar bill and you'll feel some Crane paper. Yes, this is the same company that provides Uncle Sam with stock for greenbacks. Their wedding invitations are equally legendary—"Crane engraved" invites were the preferred (some say only) method for announcing a high-society wedding in the past. Today, Crane offers both thermographed and engraved invitations at prices that will require bushel loads of those aforementioned greenbacks. For example, a basic engraved design will run $300 to $400 for 100 invitations. But those prices can vary dramatically from dealer to dealer (see Pitfalls to Avoid later in this chapter for more info). So, is Crane worth it? Well, the paper is nice, but the prices are so out-of-sight that it's hard to justify the huge expense for a plain, basic invitation. As a result, we can't give Crane a top-notch rating. For a dealer near you who carries Crane call (800) 472-7263.

Elite ★★ Elite offers invitations showcasing character, elegance and pizazz. Of course, this comes at a price. Pearlized, embossed and glittered designs can cost as much at $950 for 100 invitations. But if you have the bucks and desire a unique look, check out this brand, which is a division of industry behemoth Regency Invitations. New this year at Elite: the Infolio collection which features engraved and thermographed printing on stunning paper. The price for 100 engraved invitations in this collection runs $314. For a dealer near you who carries Elite call (800) 354-8321.

Embossed Graphics ★★★ If you're planning a large wedding, Embossed Graphics should be at the top of your invitations shopping list. That's because the company has incredible prices for large quantities of invitations. For example, 400 invitations from Embossed Graphics costs just $246! While the styles and extra options are limited, the heavy paper is high quality. Another incredible buy is their personal stationery album, which has a one-time $19.50 to $27 fee to print your return address on back flaps, regardless of the quality of invitations ordered. The only negative: Embossed Graphics is slow to ship some orders. For a dealer near you who carries Embossed Graphics, call (708) 369-0999.

Encore ★★★ In Encore's catalog, we have found some of the most wonderful papers, ranging from elegant taffeta moire to pearlized satins. If you want to match the flowers you'll be using in your wedding, Encore offers incredible embossed lilies, roses and more on textured papers and card stock. All the Encore invitations are thermographed and a wide variety of ink colors is available. The costs for these one-of-a-kind invitations range from $169 to $549 for 100 invitations. The average order however, falls in the range of $230 to $240. These designs may be rather pricey, but they're still popular since they give a contemporary look without compromising elegance. New this year at Encore is the Classic Collection, engraved invitations on 100% cotton papers. For a dealer near you who carries Encore, call (800) 526-0497.

Jenner ★★ In a hurry for engraved invitations? While most printers can take up to three weeks, Jenner engraves invitations on Crane paper with a five-day turnaround. Of course, you pay for this privilege—200 engraved invitations runs $438, about 25% more than the best price we found. In fact, Jenner's recent price increases have led us to lower their rating this year. Nonetheless, Jenner includes folding and stuffing of invitations into the envelopes (most printers don't offers this service). For a dealer near you who carries Jenner, call (502) 222-0191.

Pacific Thermographers ★★★½ Unimpressed with the flimsy, boring designs of the low-cost printers—but you can't afford the fancy designs of the super-expensive brands? Here's a solution: Pacific Thermographers offers excellent printing on incredibly heavy paper. And best of all, the prices are very down to earth—just $90 to $150 for 100 invitations. For example, their style #357 features either a single or triple panel design for just $90 per 100—an incredible buy for the super-heavy, 80 lb. stock. Fool your friends in thinking you spent hundreds of dollars on invitations! With both stylized and traditional paper designs, Pacific Thermographers is definitely a best buy. For a dealer near you who carries Pacific Thermographers, call (800) 423-5071.

Getting Started: How Far in Advance?

There are five steps in the shopping process for invitations: Overall, we recommend you order invitations at least three to four months before your wedding.

1 SHOPPING. Take a couple of weeks to visit two or three stationers in your area. If you are interested in mail-order, remember it takes two to four weeks to receive most catalogs.

2 ORDERING. This varies greatly by printer. Generally, it can take anywhere from 10 days to two months to order invitations. Most orders take two to four weeks, although some companies offer rush service.

3 MISTAKES. We suggest you leave a two week "buffer zone" in case your invitations come in with mistakes. One stationer told us that one out of every three orders comes in with errors from the printer.

4 ADDRESSING. Considering how busy you probably are with work and wedding planning, leaving four weeks here is prudent. If you choose to hire a local calligrapher, most take between one and three weeks to complete a job.

5 MAILING. Everyone knows how wonderfully efficient the U.S. Postal Service is. Give yourself plenty of time. Mail invitations to out-of-town guests at least six weeks before the wedding. For in-town guests, mail at least four weeks before the event. If your wedding is on a holiday weekend, consider mailing even earlier so your guests will have time to make plans.

Biggest Myths About Invitations

Myth #1 *"My aunt, who is a real stickler for etiquette, says that engraved invitations are the only option to consider. She says the quality of thermographed invitations is awful."*

Unfortunately, your aunt has been reading too many outdated etiquette books. In reality, thermography technology has improved so much in recent years that even Crane, the number-one seller of engraved invitations, now offers thermography. The only visible difference between thermography and engraving is the dent on the back of your invitation—and in your pocketbook.

Myth #2 *"I thought it would take 15 minutes to write up my invitations order at the stationer. Boy was I surprised when it took an hour and a half!"*

That's right! Many folks think writing an invitation is easy—until they actually try it. In reality, finding the right combination of words and type styles that make an aesthetically attractive invitation is challenging. That's why just writing up an invitation order can take an hour or more. Using a professional retail stationer or calling the customer service department at a mail-order catalog will make this process go easier.

Myth #3 *"I assumed when we ordered our invitations that extra envelopes would be included—is this true?"*

Nope, many printers send the exact compliment of envelopes as invitations ordered. If you want extra envelopes, they must be ordered in advance (there is a small additional cost). Why is this important? Well, if you're addressing your own invitations, it pays to have extra envelopes in case of mistakes. Even calligraphers will request you supply extra envelopes.

Step-by-step Shopping Strategies

 ❦ ***Step 1:*** Determine the number of invitations you need. This is not the same number as the guest count, because you send only one invitation per household. The exception: if a guest's child is over 18 and living at home, he or she receives their own invitation. This step, of course, actually involves the groom. You must compile a list of his, yours, theirs (parents' friends) and ours.

❦ ***Step 2:*** Confirm the place and time of the wedding and reception. Also, verify the spellings of the facilities and names of participants. (We heard one story of a bride who didn't know how to spell her fiance's middle name—the resulting invitation was misspelled! Doing your homework here is obviously helpful.)

❦ ***Step 3:*** Determine your overall wedding style. For example, an outdoor afternoon wedding followed by a barbecue reception will probably not have a formal, engraved invitation. On the other hand, a formal wedding with a sit-down dinner reception at the Waldorf-Astoria isn't the time for embossed hearts and flowers on parchment paper. The invitation is your guests' clue about what to expect. To decide how formal your wedding is, consider time of day, formality of dress, and reception style. At the same time, you and your fiance's personalities should also be reflected in the wedding invitation.

❦ ***Step 4:*** Decide on an invitation budget. Prices range from $25 to $900 per 100 invitations, so have some amount in mind.

❦ ***Step 5:*** Once you find a stationer (either retail or mail-order), look at their sample books or catalog. First, decide on the paper. Forget the wording, type styles, and ink colors. Instead, look at the paper design and quality. Any style of type, wording and colors can be put on any paper design, so key in on that aspect first. Paper grades and weights largely determine the price—inexpensive mail-order catalogs use lightweight 24 lb. paper, while more expensive brands use heavier (up to 80 lb.) stock. Papers made of 100% cotton are usually more expensive than other options, but give a more elegant look. (Most mail-order catalogs will provide a free sample of any invitation design so you can evaluate paper quality).

❦ *Step 6:* Next, consider the printing. Decide on the ink color, lettering style and printing method (engraving or thermography). Some invitation designs limit choices in these areas.

❦ *Step 7:* Given the paper design and printing that best fits your reception, choose an invitation in your price range. Don't forget to factor in the cost of extras including napkins, place cards and matchbooks if you want them.

❦ *Step 8:* Order at least 25 more invitations than your actual count in case you decide you need more later. Also, order extra envelopes in case of addressing goofs (calligraphers often ask for 10% extra for mistakes). After the order is written, proofread very carefully before the order is sent off. This is a critical step to catch any errors.

❦ *Step 9:* When the order comes in, proofread again and count the number of invitations to be sure you received the amount you ordered. Do this before you leave the store. Retail stationers have only a three- to five-day window allowed by printers to catch mistakes. Mail order catalogs have varying return policies, but most only allow 10 to 15 days.

Questions to Ask a Stationer

1 How many different lines do you carry? A wide assortment of styles and brands not only gives you more choices (and price ranges) but also a clue to how serious the retail stationer is about their business. Since stationers must purchase those sample books (at a cost of $35 to $250 a book), the number they carry indicates their commitment to wedding invitations.

2 Given my wedding and reception, what is your opinion of having response cards? Response cards, an extra expense, request that your guests reply to your invitation. However, in some regions of the country (parts of the South and Southwest) guests often don't send in their response cards because they prefer not to "disappoint" the bride by saying no. In other regions, particularly the Northeast, response cards are considered a must and are routinely returned by guests.

A retail stationer should be aware of what is most common in your area. Even if you do choose to send response cards, you may only receive as few as 30% back. We recommend response cards when you are inviting a large number of guests and/or are having a very expensive meal. If you are only planning a cake and punch reception or are having fewer than a hundred guests, response cards may not be needed. Remember that response cards also require their own stamp, raising your expenses accordingly.

3 CAN I SEE SOME SAMPLES OF ACTUAL INVITATIONS? This is one way to separate the part-time stationer from the full-time professional. Some part-time stationers may not keep samples while professionals should have samples from previous orders. The best mail-order sources also provide free samples of invitation designs upon request. Don't look at the style or color of the samples. Instead key in on the wording and the overall composition. Is the overall effect pleasing? Are the lines of type proportionate to the paper size? Is the type correctly aligned on the paper? If the invitation wording looks awkward, you may not want to trust your invitation to this business.

4 WHO IS RESPONSIBLE FOR ANY ERRORS THAT OCCUR? Some retail stationers may not offer to fix errors, whether you made them or they did. The true professional will take care of anything that goes wrong, regardless of who is responsible. If ordering from a catalog, be sure you get a written copy of the return policy and guarantee offered.

5 CAN I SEE A PROOF OF THE INVITATION? Some printers offer this at a very small cost ($20 or less). If you have a large order or complex invitation, this might be a prudent way to go.

Pitfalls to Avoid

Pitfall #1
UNDER-ORDERING OF INVITATIONS.
"When I first ordered invitations, I ordered exactly enough for the people on my list. Later, my mother came up with some long-lost relatives, and I had to go back and reorder another 25. I was shocked at the extra expense!"

If you guess wrong and need more invitations, the set-up charge to reprint will be tremendous. For example, let's look at a sample invitation order from a popular brand. The total for 100 invitations is $204.50. Let's say you're a smart bride and decide to order extra quantity, say 125 invitations. The total would be $246.20—a $41.70 difference. However, if you order only 100 and find out later you need 25 more, the total cost will be $363.50. Wow! Ordering 125 in the first place would have saved you $117.30! As you can see, ordering extras in your original order is much more cost effective. That's because the set-up charge for additional orders is the same as for the original order. There is no cost savings on invitations if you go back later to order more. Also keep in mind that if you "go back to press" later, the ink color and paper may not match the original order.

Pitfall #2
MAIL-ORDER SNAFUS.

"I ordered invitations from one of the catalogs advertised in a bridal magazine. Boy, am I sorry—the order came in with several mistakes and the whole design looked out of whack."

Sure, mail-order invitation catalogs offer great prices, but do you get what you pay for? We've heard the stories from brides who felt burned when their invitation arrived, looking nothing like they expected.

The reasons for this are many. In some cases, the composition (how the type is aligned) is off, due to a mistake in the printing process. Other times, the catalog made a goof with the spelling or wording. Later in this chapter, we'll review the companies we think are most reliable—including those who offer an unconditional guarantee, the best bet for getting what you want.

Of course, the mail-order companies sometimes have themselves to blame. At some catalogs, quality control is so bad they actually send out samples to prospective customers that include spelling errors and bad composition! In other cases, we've seen catalogs recommend invitation wording that is awkward at best. If you go the mail-order route, you may want to invest in or borrow a copy of *Crane's Wedding Blue Book* by Steven Feinberg ($12, available at your local bookstore, library or call 800-472-7263).

Pitfall #3
WHEN INVITATIONS ARE JUST A SIDELINE.

"My bridal shop offered to order invitations for me at a 10% discount. However, the salesperson who helped me didn't seem to know much more than I did about how to write up the order or word the invitation."

Competition in the invitation business is intense. Many bridal businesses (particularly bridal shops and photographers) now offer invitations as an enticement to order a gown or purchase photography. The discount is usually 10% to 20% off retail. The problem: many of these businesses are inexperienced. Their selection and knowledge of invitation printers is limited and service by low-paid clerks is lackluster. Many also lack the skills to word the invitations correctly.

Another twist on this pitfall are stores that advertise "up to

50% off" wedding invitations, as one bridal shop in Ohio recently promoted. As it turns out, you have to order five bridesmaids dresses (or 5 tux rentals) to get the discount, which only applies to the invitation itself—response cards, napkins and other accessories are full price. Hence, you might get a better deal on the *whole* invitation order from a mail-order catalog or retail stationer who discounts.

Pitfall #4
LAST MINUTE CHANGES.

"My church just called to say that we have to move up the time on our ceremony by one hour. The problem is I've already ordered invitations. Can I make a change?"

Not without incurring some big charges. First, understand that most invitations orders are faxed to the printer within 36 hours. Once received by the printer, it is very difficult to locate, change or stop the order. If changes can be made, there is always a charge. For example, one big printer we researched charges $10 "per inquiry" and another $10 per change.

Pitfall #5
CRANE SWITCHEROO

"I ordered Crane invitations from this store in the mall that was advertising a special deal. Yet, when the invitations came in, they didn't feel anything like what I expected. Did I get ripped-off?"

It's possible. Crane is one of the best known (and expensive) brands of wedding invitations. This notoriety has a down-side—some Crane dealers, desperate to compete with lower-cost alternatives, use tricks to discount the brand to brides. One common example is the "Crane envelope switcheroo:" sure, you get Crane engraved invitations, but the stationer substitutes cheaper, non-Crane envelopes without telling you. How can you stop this? Most (but not all) Crane envelopes have the distinctive Crane watermark—check for this when you pick up the order. Also, make sure you specify in writing that you're to get Crane envelopes.

Another Crane scam: we've documented several cases of stationery dealers who use Crane's "commercial" stock instead of the 40 lb. social paper more commonly used for wedding invitations. Why? The commercial stock is thinner and less expensive, enabling the dealer to give a "discount" on the order. Our advice: don't use it—this stock just doesn't look right for wedding invitations. Ask the dealer what type of stock they use for their Crane orders.

Pitfall #6
THE REVENGE OF THE ETIQUETTE POLICE.

"I just got in my invitation order and got a big surprise. With no warning, the printer had changed my order to fix an alleged 'etiquette error' in the wording! This is ridiculous."

Hard to believe, but it is true that some printers will change the wording on invitations to conform to "proper etiquette" as they see it. The only way you can avoid this problem is to tell the stationer or catalog that you want the wording (and any capitalization) to be exactly as you specify. This is usually accomplished by checking a box on the order form (which can be in very small type buried at the bottom) or noting it in some other way. You must also indicate if unusual spellings of names (like Henri instead of Henry) are correct. That way the printer won't substitute their etiquette rules or spelling corrections for your finely-crafted prose.

Pitfall #7
PET POSTAL PEEVES

"My stationer told me the invitations would cost just 32¢ to mail. However, after I added two maps and took the invitations to the post office, they said it would be 55¢. As a result, we have to shell out another $50 in postage. Is that fair?"

This is why we recommend taking your invitation (and all the enclosures) to the post office and getting it weighed *before* you buy all those cute "love" stamps. Start adding maps, response cards or other enclosures and you'll notice the postage bill soars.

Another interesting twist on this scam is a story we heard from Austin, Texas. A local company there was advertising an "addressing, stuffing and mailing" service for just $1 per invitation. Sounds great, huh? The problem was the service didn't tell brides they were mailing their invitations *bulk rate*. The post office treats bulk rate mail as a very low priority, to put it charitably. As a result, some of the brides' invitations arrived six weeks after the wedding—others didn't arrive at all. As it turns out, it's illegal to mail invitations (or any personal correspondence) bulk rate and the post office may have confiscated the invitations. The best advice: *always* mail invitations first class.

Pitfall #8
OUTRAGEOUSLY PRICED ACCESSORIES

"I was so excited with the savings on invitations from a mail-order catalog, I decided to order a slew of accessories too. Yet when I visited a local shop, I saw some of the same products at much lower prices. What's going on here?"

Ah, you've discovered the secret money-making machine behind the mail-order invitation catalogs. While the invitation itself is very affordable (perhaps as much as 50% less than retail), the prices on accessories can go through the roof.

Look through any of the mail-order invitation catalogs and you'll see plenty pictures of "suggested accessories," including matching napkins, programs, unity candles, cake toppers, toasting glasses, garters—even swizzle sticks printed with the bride and groom's name. Yet the prices can be amazingly high. We found much better deals on these items at party stores, gift shops, and other local stores. And then there's the whole question of whether you really need a matching "gold guest-book pen with heart-shaped, rose-etched lucite base" for $17. The best advice: comparison shop before you buy.

Do It By Mail

In a previous edition of this book, we weren't thrilled with the idea of mail-order wedding invitations. The quality of samples we saw from these catalogs just didn't impress us. In the past few years, however, mail-order invites have shown dramatic improvement. We've also received dozens of calls from brides who found these catalogs to be big money-savers.

So, we set off to find the best mail-order invitation catalogs. First, we poured over samples and catalogs from 20 mail-order companies. Then we looked at the feedback from brides we've received over the past year (our e-mail address is in the back of the book, by the way). Finally, we think we've come up with a list of the best resources for discount mail-order invitations.

A couple of thoughts before we get to the reviews: we noticed many of the catalogs carry some of the same designs. Yet comparing prices can be difficult—some catalogs charge more for fancy type styles, while others throw this in for free, for example. Also, the prices can be all over the board: some catalogs offer great deals on small quantities, while others give better discounts on large orders.

The designs themselves were generally quite traditional; some brides may find them too hokey. While most catalogs featured elegant invitations, others had bland, boring designs. The paper was often quite thin (24 lb. was a common stock weight). Even more offensive were the samples we got from the catalogs—some had printing that was off-center and the wording was incorrect, etiquette-wise. And this is an example of their best work?

On the other hand, the prices were hard to beat—sometimes 40% below retail for the exact same invitation. Mail-order is also a convenient option for many brides; you can shop in the comfort of your home and don't have to drag the groom to yet another wedding-related appointment.

So our advice is to shop carefully. Request a sample of the design you're thinking about ordering. Visit retail stationery shops to compare paper quality and prices. Make sure the mail-order company has a unconditional guarantee that allows you to return the invitations, no questions asked. Finally, we recommend paying with a credit card (in case a dispute develops, you may be able to get a refund from your bank).

The prices quote below are for invitations with black ink and regular lettering. Here is a round-up of 14 mail-order invitation catalogs:

Ann's Wedding Stationery
To Order Call: (800) 821-7011
Or Write To: PO Box 326, Carrollton, MO 64633
Credit Cards Accepted: MC, VISA, check or money order

"Sentimental" is how we'd describe the invitations designs in Ann's Wedding Stationery catalog. Among the most eye-catching designs was a framed card with marbled border in a variety of colors for $48 per 100. A plain panel invitation was priced at $25 per 100. Over 20 type styles and 16 ink colors are available. We were impressed with the selection of accessories, which outdid most other catalogs in variety. Another plus: Ann's order form is one of the best and most complete.

Dawn
To Order Call: (800) 528-6677
Or Write To: 681 Main St., Lumberton, NJ, 08048
Credit Cards Accepted: MC, VISA, Discover, checks

We liked the sample invitation Dawn sent—the folded card (#DMV687) featured embossed flowers in a Victorian motif ($60 per 100). In fact, many Dawn designs were highlighted by embossed accents like hearts, candles and doves. However, the "Cinderella"-type designs with castles and carriages may be too kitschy for some brides. Also, the pre-printed thank-you notes were the height of tackiness (one comes with the verse "We love your gift/How did you know/Just what to choose/To please us so!", followed by your names. What a nice personal touch.)

Elaine
To Order Call: (800) 323-2717
Or Write To: 6253 W. 74th St.,
PO Box 2001, Bedford Park, IL, 60499
Credit Cards Accepted: MC, VISA, AMEX, Discover

The heavy card stock on Elaine's sample invitation caught our attention. The "Filigree" ensemble features a single-panel design with "intricately embossed border, highlighting a frame for your name or monogram." Price: $105 for 100 invitations. While this is more pricey than other mail-order catalogs, the paper quality is better. If you're planning a wedding with a Victorian motif, consider the "Wedding Morning" collection, with famous English paintings reproduced on a folded card ($85 per 100). All in all, we found Elaine's to have more sophisticated and unusual designs than other catalogs.

Evangel Christian Wedding Invitations
To Order Call: (800) 342-4227 or (812) 623-2509
Or Write To: PO Box 202, Batesville, IN, 47006
Credit Cards Accepted: MC, VISA

If you're looking for a wedding invitations with a Christian theme, here's a great catalog. Evangel's designs feature biblical verses, religious wording and symbols. For example, a folded card with an embossed cross and deckled (ragged) edge costs $68 per 100. Evangel's catalog also has a wide variety of religious-themed accessories, from ring-bearer pillows to unity candles.

Heart Thoughts
To Order Call: (800) 648-5781
Or Write To: 6200 E. Central #100, Wichita, KS, 67208
Credit Cards Accepted: MC, VISA, Discover

We discovered this company when we researched the best baby announcements for our *Baby Bargains* book last year. Heart Thoughts wedding invitations are equally impressive— you won't find the same old cliched invitations here. Instead, we found a multitude of original, sophisticated designs, from translucent papers to ribbon accents. One stand-out was the "Fields of Flowers," a folded card embedded with wildflower petals. The actual invitation is printed on translucent paper and mounted inside the card with a ribbon accent. Price: $110 per 100 invitations. We liked the freebies Heart Thoughts throws in, like free envelope linings or free return address printing on some designs. They even offer a envelope addressing service (call for a quote).

Invitations Etc.
To Order Call: (800) 709-7979
Or Write To: PO Box 7700, Glendale, AZ, 85312
Credit Cards Accepted: MC, VISA, AMEX

The "white on white" embossed look is big this year at Invitations Etc., a rather basic catalog that features traditional designs. Typical of the offerings is "Blossom Bouquets," a folded card with embossed roses that frames the wording. Cost: $45 per 100. Invitations Etc.'s pricing seemed more convoluted than other catalogs—the minimum order is 50, with additional invitations priced per 25. On the plus side, the return address printing is free and all orders are shipped Fed-Ex economy (2-day service) at no extra charge.

Jamie Lee Fine Wedding Stationery
To Order Call: (800) 288-5800
Or Write To: PO Box 5343, Glendale, AZ, 85312
Credit Cards Accepted: MC, VISA, AMEX

Jamie Lee's "Super Savers" are good buys. These two folded-card designs (a raised panel or embossed corner rose) cost just $25 per 100 invitations. This no-frills option has a single envelope and no extras (like response cards, reception cards, etc). Other options were equally affordable, ranging up to $85 per 100. We liked Jamie Lee's order form, which clearly explained all service charges in plain English.

Now & Forever
To Order Call: (800) 451-8616
Or Write To: PO Box 820, Goshen, CA, 93227
Credit Cards Accepted: MC, VISA, Discover

Now & Forever's "Shades of Nature" series features embossed mountain scenes, pine trees and animals—perfect for that Pacific Northwest, pioneer-themed wedding. Of course, the catalog has many other styles, from classic single-panels to cutesy cartoon animals. For example, the "Romance by the Water's Edge" is a Z-fold invitation with a formally-dressed bride and groom frog. Yes, you read right—it's a formally-dressed frog couple about to make the leap into married life for just $54 per 100. Now & Forever offers a "lowest-price guarantee:" if you find the same design in another catalog for a lower price, they'll match it.

Precious Collection
To Order Call: (800) 537-5222
Or Write To: PO Box 3403, Merchandise Mart,
Chicago, IL 60654.
Credit Cards Accepted: MC, VISA

This catalog is owned by Regency, the big invitation printer who also sells their wares through a big network of retail dealers. In fact, Regency has not one but *four* wedding invitation mail-order catalogs—two of the best are "Wedding Treasures" (reviewed later in this section) and the "Precious Collection." Besides traditional designs you'd expect to see, this catalog is also sprinkled with a few contemporary invitations. For example, the over-sized square panel card with a brilliant pink poppy design (with black and fuchsia foil) was an eye-catcher. Cost: $65 per 100. Choose from a large selection of type styles (25 at last count) and 17 different ink colors. One nice perk to this catalog: the Precious Collection offers one of several freebies (such as envelope linings, printed return address or thank-you notes) with your order.

Reaves Engraving
To Order Call: (910)369-2260
Or Write To: PO Box 37, Riverton Rd., Wagram, NC, 28396
Credit Cards Accepted: None. Check, money order
or COD only.

A bride who called our hotline highly recommended this mail-order catalog and we have to agree—Reaves Engraving has an incredible selection of invitations at very good prices. While they offer thermographed designs, it's their engraved wedding invitations that caught our attention.

If you want an engraved invitation on Crane paper, Reaves lets you choose from seven different styles at just $185 to $276 per 100 invitations—that's just half the cost of retail! If you want to save even more money, check out their in-house paper stock, which costs just $75 to $87 per 100 invitations. Remember, these are prices for *engraved* invitations.

Of course, there are a couple of disadvantages to this catalog. First, Reaves has no 800-number; the order is on your dime. The company also takes a lengthy time to fill orders (four to seven weeks), although rush service (11 day turnaround) is available for a hefty up-charge. Another bummer: Reaves doesn't take credit cards, either.

On a positive front, Reaves sends out plentiful samples of each paper stock. The catalog also offers a computerized calligraphy service for 75¢ to 90¢ per invitation.

Rexcraft
To Order Call: (800) 635-4653
Or Write To: Rexburg, ID, 83441
Credit Cards Accepted: MC, VISA, Discover

Of all the catalogs we researched for this section, we have to say that Rexcraft is one of our top picks. Rexcraft's monster 232-page catalog has something for everyone. Well-organized and easy to use, the catalog has graphic icons that explain how an invitation folds and there's even a glossary to help demystify terms like "deckled edges" and "French fold."

We counted over 130 styles, from basic single-panel cards to elaborately embossed, foil-stamped designs. One stand-out was "Bridal Mist," a single-panel card with a delicate rose border, painted in an Impressionistic style. Price: $65 per 100 invitations. You can even buy matching rose envelope linings (an extra $12). All in all, most styles range from $28 to $120 per 100—very affordable.

Looking for a hard-to-find bridal accessory? You'll find over 90 pages dedicated to such items as paper napkin rings and "Just Married" signs. The selection of favors and related items was excellent.

Romantic Moments
To Order Call: (800) 635-1433
Or Write To: PO Box 299 Maple , Sugar City, ID, 83448
Credit Cards Accepted: MC, VISA, AMEX, Discover

This stylish catalog features many invitation designs you won't see in other catalogs. Typical of the offerings is "Chantilly," described as "old-fashioned charm with embossed floral detailing printed on white wedding vellum paper" for $63 per 100 invitations. Elaborate embossing also highlights the "Gold Impact" invitation, with its Victorian feel ($54 per 100). Choose from 25 different type styles and 14 ink colors. If you're looking for a more contemporary-styled invitation, this is one good catalog to check out.

Wedding Treasures
To Order Call: (800) 851-5974
Or Write To: PO Box 6678, Rockford, IL, 61125
Credit Cards Accepted: MC, VISA

As we mentioned earlier, invitation giant Regency has several mail-order catalogs, including the Wedding Treasurers line. This catalog seems to specialize in offering various color options for the same invitations design. For example, the embossed flowers on the single panel "Flower Garden" are available in three different color schemes (white-on-white, pastel on ecru paper, or pastel on white paper). The price ranges from $35 per 100 for the white-on-white to $50 for the colored options. Another nice look was the "Loving Touch," which featured embossed calla lilies with pearlized foil for $65 per 100.

Willow Tree Lane
To Order Call: (800) 219-1022
Or Write To: PO Box 263, Galena, IL, 61036
Credit Cards Accepted: MC, VISA

Excellent customer service was what one bride told us she liked most about Willow Tree Lane, an outstanding invitation catalog. And they put their money where their mouth is with a great low-price guarantee: Willow Tree Lane will give you *double* the price difference if you find a cheaper price elsewhere. Prices start as little as $20 per 100 for the simple, single-panel style invitations. We liked the splashy colors on the spring-flower square card invitation, which cost $70 per 100. Color accents also highlighted other designs, with purple, peach and pink hues the most popular. Willow Tree Lane also offers express delivery (overnight or second-day) for $15 to $25.

Unique Ideas

Looking for something truly different? If you can afford to splurge you might consider custom-designed invitations. No doubt there is someone in your town who can design something unusual, but if not, we have a few suggestions.

If money is truly no option whatsoever (and if so we'd like to meet you!), consider a company called *Creative Intelligence* in Los Angeles. Creative Intelligence custom designs invitations and can fulfill your wildest invitation fantasy (if you have one!).

Owned by Marc Friedland, Creative Intelligence has made quite a splash among the jet-set, including Ivana Trump, Dudley Moore and others. He offers hand designed invitations for all kinds of events at an average cost of $14 each (not per 100). His prices have even reached as high as $100 each. Designs have incorporated western themes, others have included plastic hula dancers and astro turf. Of course, Friedland custom designs these outrageous invitations for each event, so if you choose to hire him, your invitation will undoubtedly be quite unique (and expensive). The company's phone number is (213) 936-9009.

On a regional level, you can often find custom invitation makers that offer something different. Debbie Bodian of Denver-based *Paper Talk* (303) 759-1581 hand-paints mountain scenes on invitations for couples planning nuptials in the Rockies. In southern California, *Claudia Laub Studios* (213) 931-1710 produces beautiful invitations and placecards using engravings from antique gardening books.

Arlene Segal Design Group (call 305-651-8283 for a dealer near you) of North Miami Beach, Florida offers custom invitations that are hand-painted on elegant papers. A box of 10

Real Wedding Tip:
Do-it-yourself invitations

 If you have a computer, laser-printer and desktop publishing know-how, you can easily design your own invitation. But how do you find the appropriate paper?

We found several sources that help you create that truly custom invitation. For example, *Paper Direct* (800) 272-7377 (7205 Chubb Ave., Lyndhurst, NJ 07071) has an amazing collection of laser-compatible stationery, note-cards, placards, and more. For a rehearsal dinner, brides-maids luncheon or informal wedding invitation, Paper Direct's "Themes" collection has several fun options. The catalog even sells "Festive" papers with embedded silver and copper flakes.

Paper Journey (800) 827-2737 is a wonderful catalog of "unique papers and accessories." The "Exotic Printables" are laser-printer compatible, hand-made papers in four styles: ivory with grass & straw flecks, white with grey wool flecks, cream with green silk flecks and pink and indigo floral papers. Price: $15-16 for a 50 sheet box. The catalog also features guests books, photo albums, notecards and even custom invitations.

Looking for calligraphy supplies? *Paper & Ink Books* (301) 447-6487 sells calligraphy how-to books, supplies and unusual papers. You can learn how to make your own paper or select from a wide assortment of hand-made options.

costs $15 and includes coordinating hand-painted envelopes. Segal also offers a wonderful collection of blank stock with hand-painted borders and matching envelopes (perfect for laser printers). Speaking of hand-made invitations, *Dyan Law Design, Inc.* of New York City (call 914-638-1153 for a dealer near you) has a collection of hand-engraved, hand-painted invitations that are printed on hand-made specialty papers from around the world. This "Premiere" collection costs $14 each (for an invitation and envelope). Dyan also offers a more moderately-priced collection ("Classics") that features papers that are hand-gilded with gold leaf—these cost $5 and up per invitation.

Special thanks to Bridal Business Report (published by Marcy Blum's The Bridal Group, 212-644-6687) for providing some of the sources for this section.

Barbara Logan's Paperworks
(800) 458-9143 or (301) 774-2949

If you're tired of "traditional" (read: boring) wedding invitations, have we got a company for you. Barbara Logan's Paperworks in Rockville, Maryland has created some of the most unique wedding invitations we've ever seen.

What makes Paperwork's invitations special are handmade papers embedded with dried flowers or sparkling glitter. Matching parchment invitations with raised printing are inserted into the paper for a truly unique look. New this year are over-sized square invitations with handmade paper wraps.

The handmade papers are available in one of four styles: floral, glitter, parfait papers with threads and fibers, and earth-tone natural papers. A variety of color choices are available.

So, how much does this cost? Okay, it isn't cheap. The price ranges from $6 to $12 per invitation. That's right—100 invitations cost $600 to $1200. The cost difference depends on the invitation size, hand labor (some designs have tassels, ribbons and other accents) and amount of hand-made paper. Printed accessories like response cards and thank-you notes are available to complete the ensemble. Delivery takes four weeks.

While those prices seem high, Paperwork's designs may be within the budgets of brides planning a small wedding. If you're ordering 25 invitations from a mail-order catalog, you could spend $50 to $70—that's not too far from the $150 starting point for custom invitations.

Paperwork's Alina Zygmunt told us that their invitations "combine the best of both worlds—a unique innovative decorative cover with the more traditional invitation insert." And we couldn't agree more.

A discount buying source for invitations

If you love the quality of designer wedding invitations but not the designer price tag, consider the **Invitation Hotline** (800) 800-4355, (908) 536-9115, fax (908) 972-4875. The Manalapan, New Jersey-based company offers a 25% discount on such well-known brands as Carlson Craft, Elite/Infolio, Encore, and more. Over 90 albums are available to chose from and the company does take all major credit cards. Owner Marcy Slachman told us that all brides need to do is call her with the book name and style number. She'll help troubleshoot any etiquette or wording questions. Delivery takes about two weeks from the date the order is placed. Faster delivery is available via overnight services. The company accepts all major credit cards and personal checks.

The Invitation Hotline also carries favors, including a few more eclectic offerings. For example, we noticed their price list included a silver-plated dolphin bottle opener ($3.95) and a silver-plated ice cream scoop ($4.15). Other wedding accessories and calligraphy are available as well.

Spotlight: Wedding Favors

When we decided to write about wedding favors, we thought we should talk to an expert about their origin and popularity. We spoke to a major distributor and wedding favor manufacturer to answer these questions.

❦ **Where did favors originate?** Popular mainly on the East coast and in California, wedding favors have had a long, rich history. When we say rich, we really mean royal. In fact, in France in the 16th century, nobility and royalty gave valuable gifts (usually of porcelain) to their wedding guests as mementos of the occasion.

In the middle of the 16th century, almonds came to Italy from the Far East. These almonds were very expensive and became popular to give as favors to guests at royal weddings. To preserve these almonds, a sugar-coating was invented and Jordan almonds were born.

In the 17th century, three almonds, painted in bright colors and wrapped in bridal veiling, were given to guests. The significance of three almonds is this: from the union of two comes three—a baby. The veiling meant that the guests shared the couple's happiness.

❦ **What about favors in the U.S.?** In the U.S., favors are most popular with ethnic communities (particularly Italians). The manufacturer told us that nearly 25% of their orders come from Pennsylvania, New York and New Jersey. Brides and grooms in these states order more expensive favors with almonds inside a porcelain swan or champagne glass—these favors can cost as much as $3 to $10 each! In other parts of the country, potpourri is a more popular favor choice. While favors are also common in the Southeast (Georgia, Florida, North and South Carolina in particular), brides in the Midwest, Northwest and Southwest rarely give favors to guests.

The manufacturer we interviewed sells mostly traditional favors such as tulle wrapped around potpourri or almonds and foil-imprinted ribbons are also popular.

❧ *A source for wedding favors:* Favours Internationale (617) 383-1065 is a Massachusetts-based company that makes favors. Their show room in Cohasset features over 200 items. They can even design a favor from a verbal description. Call for a price quote or catalog sheets ($3, which is applied to any order).

If you're interested in edible favors, Elegant Cheesecakes of Half Moon Bay, CA (415) 728-2248 sells chocolate favors, placecards, and centerpieces. You can even tint the chocolate to complement your color scheme. A chocolate truffle place card and favor costs $5.25 each. With shipping available to the U.S. and Canada, the company's creations have been featured in the Neiman Marcus catalog.

REAL WEDDING TIP:
Do yourself a favor—and save money

 If there is one aspect of a wedding where you can put that do-it-yourself energy to work, consider making your own favors. And here's a great use for relatives and friends who want to "help" you with the wedding. Heather Remer of Pittsburgh told us she "didn't want to give my guests a crystal vase or dust collector that they will keep for a year because they feel guilty and then throw away. I wanted something simple and sweet—chocolates! Yet, when I looked at the prices some places were charging for a box of chocolates, I thought I would have to starve for a month (okay a little drastic) just to scrounge up the money. Then I got an idea—why not make them myself? A few weeks before the wedding, my four bridesmaids, mother, aunt and two cousins had a "chocolate party" to make my favors. The molds, chocolate and netting are all inexpensive—I figured my total savings to be $150." Another source: many of the mail-order invitation catalogs reviewed earlier in this chapter have extensive favor offerings—both finished designs and supplies to do-it-yourself.

PART II

Your
Reception

Chapter 7

Reception Sites

The reception is certainly the biggest expense area of any wedding. Think you can't save money here? Think again! We'll show you seven money-saving tips that could save you thousands—plus we'll give you the four most common pitfalls with reception sites and how to avoid them! Finally, we'll take a candid look at the real pros and cons of the five most common reception site types.

What You Are Buying?

 Basically, you are buying two things here:

❦ *Exclusive use of the facility.* Either you are charged a flat fee for a certain period of time or there is an hourly rate. Obviously, rates vary with the amount of ambiance. An historic restored mansion will cost much more than a local union hall. Most places require a booking deposit which can be several hundred dollars. A second deposit (to cover any damage or clean-up) may also be required at some sites.

❦ *Catering* (food, liquor, service and rentals). All reception sites either require you to use their in-house caterer or allow you to bring an off-site caterer. When a site has an in-house caterer, there is often no "room charge"—the facility makes its money from the catering. Unfortunately, some sites not only charge you for the catering but also tack on a facility rental fee. We cover wedding catering in-depth later in this book.

The Big Trade-off: Ambiance vs. Great Food

Many brides tell us that they must make a basic trade-off in their search for a reception site: the ambiance vs. quality of food. Often, you must decide which is more important—how the site looks versus how the food tastes. Many lovely receptions sites have just mediocre offerings for food. Other less attractive sites may have great reputations for sumptuous buffets or sit-down dinners. Of course, the perfect compromise is to find a beautiful site that allows you to bring in an outside caterer. As you will find in our later discussion, these sites are rare indeed.

Sources to Find a Reception Site

 Finding the right reception site for your wedding may be the most challenging task you face. That's mainly because of the big bucks involved here—the reception (and, specifically, the catering) is the most expensive part of getting married. Here are some top sources to find affordable sites.

❦ *Wedding coordinators at your ceremony site.* Yes, these folks probably have talked to hundreds of brides over the years. They might be able to give you the "word on the street" for several reception sites.

❦ *Caterers.* Most off-site (or independent) caterers are well aware of the best local wedding reception sites. That's because their livelihood depends on the existence of facilities that let outside caterers come in for receptions. Call around to a few local caterers to find leads.

❦ *Recently-married couples.* Ask your co-workers or friends if they know anyone who was recently married. These couples are often more than willing to share their research and experiences about reception sites.

❦ *Visitors/Tourism bureaus and local parks departments.* If you are looking for a civic site (such as an historic home), your local visitors/tourism bureau (or chamber of commerce) may have some suggestions. Many civic sites (like gardens and parks) are booked by local parks departments.

❦ *Bridal shows.* Yes, bridal shows can be a source for reception sites. Large expos with many vendors are your best bet. Reception sites often set up booths and hand out food samples and menus.

❦ *Our Web page.* In the back of this book, we'll give you information on how to access our home page on the World Wide Web. There, you'll find a list of local wedding guides with reception site info, as well as links to other web pages with local wedding information.

Top Money-saving Secrets

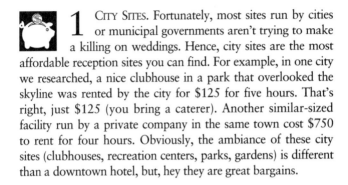

1 CITY SITES. Fortunately, most sites run by cities or municipal governments aren't trying to make a killing on weddings. Hence, city sites are the most affordable reception sites you can find. For example, in one city we researched, a nice clubhouse in a park that overlooked the skyline was rented by the city for $125 for five hours. That's right, just $125 (you bring a caterer). Another similar-sized facility run by a private company in the same town cost $750 to rent for four hours. Obviously, the ambiance of these city sites (clubhouses, recreation centers, parks, gardens) is different than a downtown hotel, but, hey they are great bargains.

2 CHOOSE A SITE WHERE YOU CAN BRING IN A CATERER. In every city we've researched, there are always a handful of sites where you can rent the facility and then bring in an "off-site" caterer. Often, this is where the big savings are found—see our chapter on catering for more details.

3 CONSIDER AN OFF-PEAK TIME. Everyone wants to get married on a Saturday night in June. Now, if you pick a time with less competition, you can often negotiate better rental rates. Many sites have stated discounts for Friday or Sunday weddings. In other cases, you may be able to negotiate a lower rental rate for less popular months of the year.

4 HAVE A RECEPTION LUNCH OR BRUNCH INSTEAD OF DINNER. The biggest expense of most receptions is catering, and the most expensive meal to serve is dinner. Wedding lunches or brunches often are much more affordable. Furthermore, a two o'clock wedding with cake, punch and light hors d'oeuvres will be even less expensive. Check the catering chapter for more tips to save money on this big budget item.

5 CONSIDER YOUR CEREMONY SITE. Many houses of worship have attached reception halls. In fact, almost one-quarter of all receptions occur at churches or temples. Perhaps this is because rental rates are particularly affordable. Either you are allowed to bring in a caterer or you are required to use the site's in-house catering.

6 YOUR HOUSE. Hey, at least the facility is free. Be aware that you may have to rent chairs, tables, etc. and this might add to the tab. If you plan to pitch a tent in the backyard, the expense can go even higher. Of course, the savings of bringing in a caterer (instead of holding the reception at a pricey hotel) may put you ahead overall. Between 10% and 20% of all receptions are held in private homes.

7 RESTAURANT RECEPTIONS. A Connecticut bride called in this tip: she found a restaurant with a nice banquet room that was perfect for her 50-guest reception. Instead of telling them it was a wedding reception, she said the party was a family reunion. As a result, she was able to get a great price for a complete sit-down luncheon. Two weeks before the reception, she told the restaurant it was actually a wedding— too late for the restaurant to raise the price! Many restaurants have banquet rooms, some that can hold large crowds. These may be a great alternative to pricey hotels or catering halls.

Getting Started: How Far in Advance?

 Don't delay the search for your reception site. As soon as you have confirmed your ceremony site, start the search for a reception facility. Time is of the essence. Most cities have a shortage of great reception sites; prime dates in the spring and summer often go quickly. In the South, December can book up to a year in advance for popular Christmas weddings. Since June is also popular in many areas of the country, booking a site nine months to a year in advance may be necessary.

Step-by-step Shopping Strategies

 ❦ *Step 1:* Figure out how many guests you want to invite. Then look for a site that fits that capacity. Many brides make the mistake of doing this the other way around—picking a site first and then having to adapt their guest list around its capacity.

❦ *Step 2:* Using the above sources, make appointments with three to five of the top prospects. Confirm the availability of your date before making any trip. Bring a friend along to help inspect the facilities.

❦ *Step 3:* When you visit a reception site, look carefully at the facility. Can the room really hold all your guests comfortably or does it looked cramped? Is the lighting on a dimmer system? How will the traffic of guests flow around buffet tables, the dance floor, etc.?

❦ *Step 4:* Try to meet the catering manager (if the catering is done in-house). Honestly discuss your budget and suggest the manager custom-tailor a menu for your reception. Read the catering chapter to make sure you cover all of those details. Get a detailed price breakdown—in writing—on everything (food, liquor, service, centerpieces, linens, china, etc.).

❦ *Step 5:* Ask to see the site set-up for a wedding. It's some-times hard to imagine an empty ballroom dressed to the nines for a wedding reception. Here's a good way to get a more realistic impression. Ask to visit just before the reception is to start. Check the traffic flow—for buffets, see if the lay-out of the food stations makes sense. Does the staff seem organized, or are they running around at the last minute like chickens with their heads cut off?

❦ *Step 6:* If the site has in-house catering, ask for a taste-test of the food. The quality of food varies greatly from site to site, so asking for this is a wise precaution. Most sites offer taste tests at no charge.

❦ *Step 7:* After visiting several sites, make your decision and put down as small a deposit as possible. Sign a contract that includes the date, the hours, the rental fee and any other charges and approximate guest count. Be very careful to get any verbal promises by the site ("oh, sure we can decorate that landing with flowers for no charge") in writing in the contract.

❦ *Step 8:* Any subsequent contact with the site from here on out will depend on whether the site is doing the catering or not. In any case, call the site back one month before your wedding to confirm the details of your reception.

Questions to Ask of a Reception Site

1 How many guests can the space accommo-date? Typically, the capacity is given in two numbers, one for a buffet/hors d'oeuvres (or stand-ing) reception and one for a sit-down (seated) dinner. Be care-ful about these figures—sites often fudge capacity numbers or give "approximate" guesses. Don't forget to account for any buffet tables or dance floors—these all take space.

2 How many hours does the rental fee cover? What are the overtime charges? Be sure to ask about whether set-up and clean-up time is included in the stated hours. Some sites don't count this time "on the clock" while others do.

3 Is there an in-house caterer or a list of approved caterers? Or can you bring in any caterer? Obviously, hotels have in-house caterers (that's how they make the big bucks). But many other sites are also picky about this—after they get burned by a sloppy caterer, a site may restrict brides to a list of "pre-approved" caterers. In case you can't find a caterer on their approved list who meets your specifications, ask if you can bring in another one.

4 ARE THERE ANY COOKING RESTRICTIONS? Are the kitchen facilities adequate? For a site where an outside caterer is brought in, check the kitchen facilities. Some sites restrict caterers from cooking on-site and just allow the warming of food that is prepared elsewhere. Make sure you confirm with your caterer to see if the kitchen facilities are adequate.

5 IS THERE A PIANO AVAILABLE? How about a dance floor? Obviously, bands don't cart around a baby grand with them to every reception, so ask the site coordinator. Don't assume anything is free. Ask the site about any extra charges to prevent surprises.

6 WHAT ELSE IS HAPPENING AT THE SITE THE DAY OF MY WEDDING? Hotels are often most guilty of this problem, but we've even seen smaller sites try to cram two or more weddings into a facility. Will you have to compete with a noisy convention of insurance agents that has a 10-piece band in the next room? Press the catering rep to give you exclusivity over the facility. Or at least, insist on a layout of the parties that minimizes overlapping noise.

7 ARE THERE ANY UNION RULES WE MUST FOLLOW? In some states (particularly the Northeast), union work rules may force certain restrictions on sites, including the serving of food and set-up of any audio equipment.

Pitfalls to Avoid

Pitfall #1
UNWRITTEN PROMISES.

"I booked my wedding and reception at an historic home. The wedding coordinator there told me all the wonderful things they would do for my reception at no charge. For example, they said they would decorate the gazebo for free if I brought them the fabric. Then, wouldn't you know? My contact person left and the owner of the site refused to fulfill the promises she made! I was furious! The only problem was I couldn't prove a thing since nothing was written down. Rats!"

Well, this is perhaps the most common complaint we hear about reception sites: unfulfilled promises. To get you to book the site, some unscrupulous site managers will make wild promises they never intend to keep. Another problem: the person you first meet with quits or is fired before your wedding. This happens more than you might think (catering and site managers hop from job to job like rabbits). A word to the wise: get every last promise and detail in writing in the contract. This protects you from dishonest people or from changes in personnel. If promises are made after the contract is signed, get them to write a note or type a letter putting the promises in black and white.

Pitfall #2
MENU GOOFS.

"My wedding and reception was at a popular hotel in our town. We spent hours going over the menu but what was served at the reception in no way resembled what we ordered. Worse yet, then we couldn't find anyone from the catering department to fix the problem! What happened?"

Sometimes the bloated bureaucracy at hotels and other reception sites can lead to snafus. Perhaps the catering manager "forgot" to inform the kitchen of your menu. Maybe the chef just had an extra 200 Chicken Cordon Bleus left over from a banquet the night before. In any case, you deserve a refund or the site should offer a fair reduction in the bill as compensation for their mistake.

As for fixing a problem the night of the wedding, good luck. While you might be able to have the maitre d' contact the catering director, there may be little that can be done at that moment. Another wise idea: if the catering director or representative won't be at the reception, get their home phone, pager or car phone numbers.

Pitfall #3
KICK-BACKS AND CATERING MANAGERS.

"I picked a band for my reception based on the recommendation of my site's catering coordinator. It was a disaster—the band was a flop! To add insult to injury, I later found out the catering coordinator received a 'commission' from the band!"

One scam we uncovered in this field are catering managers/coordinators who take kick-backs from bands (or other wedding merchants) they recommend. In California, one musician blew the whistle on a site that was charging a $200 fee to get on their "recommended list." We've also encountered this on the East Coast. Protect yourself by thoroughly checking out any of these "recommended" services.

A Look at the Five Most Common Reception Site Types

Hotels/Catering Halls

Catering halls and hotels may seem like an obvious choice as the site for a reception—both have spacious banquet rooms and full-service catering staffs to take care of every detail. On the East Coast, catering halls host as many as half of all wedding receptions. Meanwhile, in Texas, hotel ballrooms are the only choice for a bride trying to find a facility hold 300 or 400 guests (a typical wedding in the Lone Star State). While hotels may only account for 10% to 20% of receptions nationwide, they often host the biggest and most lavish receptions in many cities. Here are the pros and cons of having your wedding reception at a hotel or catering hall.

Advantages of Hotel /Catering Hall Receptions

1 ALL-INCLUSIVE PACKAGES. When you have a reception at these facilities, all the rentals (tables, chairs, serving pieces, bars, dance floor, etc) are generally included in the price.

2 LARGE WEDDINGS. For large weddings, hotel or catering halls may be the best choice. That's because their big ballrooms can accommodate large parties up to or over 1000 guests. Most other sites have peak capacities at about 200 to 300 guests.

3 CLIMATE CONTROL. In areas of the country with harsh weather, climate-controlled ballrooms are a plus.

4 DISCOUNTS ON ROOM RENTALS, HONEYMOON SUITES. Most hotels are willing to negotiate a discounted rate for a block of rooms. If you have many out-of-town relatives, this may be a big plus. Some hotel packages also throw in a honeymoon suite gratis—a nice touch. One caveat: make sure to double-check the hotel's special rate to see if you're getting a deal. More than one bride has told us they discovered the "special group rate" was no different than the regular room fees.

5 SPECIAL WEDDING RECEPTION PACKAGES. Many hotels and catering halls have special catering packages for wedding receptions. Unfortunately, these are sometimes more expensive than their à la carte choices! Why? The extra labor needed for a reception versus other functions might be one answer. Or maybe it's just pure greed (brides are sometimes seen as a money-machine for these guys). Be sure to crunch the num-

bers for different packages to see which is the best deal. On the other hand, some facilities aggressively pursue weddings by offering many freebees—you'd be surprised at the big difference in costs from one site to another.

6 DIETARY RESTRICTIONS. For those couples who need Kosher catering, hotels are often a best bet. Hotels must meet certain standards before they are certified Kosher. Call a local synagogue or rabbi to get a list.

7 SOME HOTELS AND CATERING HALLS CAN ALSO HOST A LOVELY CEREMONY. One West Coast hotel has an outdoor garden and gazebo for ceremonies. At a catering hall we visited in New Jersey, lush gardens offered several ceremony site options. The convenience of having everything at one location may be a big plus.

8 ADVICE ON ENTERTAINERS, FLORISTS, BAKERS, ETC. Catering managers at hotels and catering halls often have their pulse on the best wedding bands and entertainers. Use their experience, but be careful of unscrupulous managers who take kick-backs from "recommended" services. (See Pitfall #3 above for more info.)

Disadvantages of Hotel /Catering Hall Receptions

1 DRAB INTERIOR DECOR. Some sites look like they were decorated in Early Eisenhower.

2 THESE SITES CAN BE DARN EXPENSIVE. While hotels and catering halls offer all-inclusive packages, you definitely pay for this with high-priced food and liquor. Food quality varies greatly from site to site, so ask for a taste test. At best, these places have what could be charitably described as a "mixed" reputation for food, making many brides wonder where all their money is going.

3 FROZEN FOOD. Perhaps the biggest problem that plagues many hotels and catering halls is poor quality food. These sites often buy frozen food that can be quickly prepared. Ever seen those mini-quiches at a hotel wedding reception? Hotels can buy these and other popular buffet items in bulk from suppliers. Unfortunately, frozen hors d'oeuvres that are quickly warmed simply don't compare to freshly-prepared foods.

4 BUREAUCRACY OF CATERING DEPARTMENTS. From busboys to waiters to captains to catering assistants to managers, the multi-layer management of catering departments can be vexing. Ask if the catering manager (or the contact person whom you have dealt with) will be at your reception.

5 WEDDINGS CAN BE LOW ON THE PRIORITY LIST. Especially in December, hotels are distracted with corporate Christmas parties on large budgets. Competition with convention and reunion business can also be a headache.

6 REMEMBER THE CATERING REPRESENTATIVES ARE ON COMMISSION. The more money you spend, the more money they make. Hence, we find many hotels and catering halls pushing exotic (and expensive) foods such as shrimp to jack up the tab. Many hotels also "suggest" expensive wines and other liquor.

7 OVERPRICED LIQUOR. Here's one example: One moderately-priced hotel we researched had a $22 retail price on a specific bottle of wine. That same bottle wholesales at $4—and that wine was the most "affordable" option the hotel offered!

8 BE CAREFUL OF NICKEL-AND-DIME CHARGES. Never assume that anything is free. Extra charges could include valet parking, special table skirting, ice carvings, a dance floor, corking fees, cake cutting charge (see catering chapter), food station attendants, and any audio equipment (a microphone for toasts, for example). Also, silk table centerpieces and special linens or china may be extra. Compare the estimate on centerpieces with your florist's bid to get the best deal.

What Does a Hotel/Catering Hall Reception Cost?

Reception packages vary widely. Hotels and catering halls in downtown areas tend to be the most expensive (and also expect to pay extra for valet parking). In suburban areas, rates are somewhat less and these sites tend to be more aggressive in their competition for wedding business (since they can't rely on downtown convention traffic). In our research, we've found packages that start as low as $10 per person for a buffet at an Oklahoma hotel and go up to $125 per person for a complete sit-down dinner at a posh New York City catering hall. In general, most sites are in the $20 to $50 per person range for basic receptions (not counting liquor). In the biggest cities (New York, Los Angeles, Chicago, Philadelphia), you can expect to pay twice to three times more. Add in a big liquor tab and you can expect your total costs to soar.

Private and Country Clubs

Think you have to be a member of those fancy country clubs and private clubs to hold a wedding reception in their facilities? Not always. In fact, many clubs welcome non-members with open arms! That's because weddings often bring in badly-needed revenue. We define private and country clubs as any site that has membership requirements or restrictions. While you may have to be a member at some sites, others just require a "member-sponsor." Still others don't have any requirements at all.

Types of Clubs

1 BUSINESS CLUBS. Often downtown on top of skyscrapers, some business clubs have a restaurant open for lunch each day and host meetings and receptions. Various professional organizations (i.e., Engineers' Clubs, Doctors' Clubs) may own and operate these facilities. Such sites vary widely in appeal (we saw one Engineer's Club that looked like it was decorated by, well, engineers) but are generally more open to wedding receptions. Mostly likely, you must use the club's in-house catering.

2 COUNTRY CLUBS. These sites normally have a golf course and several acres of grounds. Here, the clubhouse is the focal point for receptions. Some of these sites can be quite stuffy, with the snob appeal often spread rather thick. Nonetheless, lush grounds can make more beautiful backdrops for photos. These sites may be the most restrictive, as most require a member (who can be a friend or just an acquaintance) to at least "sponsor" the reception. Many times, this sponsorship is just a token technicality where the member assumes responsibility in case you don't pay the bill and move to Peru. In most cases, you must use the country club's in-house catering.

3 CIVIC/SOCIAL CLUBS. Elks Clubs, Garden Clubs, Federation of Women's clubs, Junior Leagues, Junior Forums—each of these organizations may have facilities they rent for receptions. Often, you must bring in an outside caterer. Prices and quality are all over the board: Elks Clubs and Veterans of Foreign Wars (VFW) Posts, for example, are often quite affordable but offer rather Spartan decor. Other clubs are located in historic buildings that are beautiful but also carry a hefty price tag. Membership requirements are usually non-existent.

Advantages of Private Clubs

1 MORE PERSONAL SERVICE. Many of these sites don't have the bloated bureaucracy that hampers hotels. Less bureaucracy often improves service.

2 NICER SITES. Unlike the drab and sterile decor of many hotels, country and private clubs are often set on beautiful sites. In the South, many are surrounded by lush grounds with golf courses. In many metro downtowns, clubs may occupy the top floor of skyscrapers—offering spectacular views of the skyline.

3 SOME CLUBS PERMIT OUTSIDE CATERERS. While business and country clubs usually have in-house (read: expensive) catering, some clubs let you bring in a caterer of your choice— this can be a fantastic savings (see our catering chapter).

Disadvantages of Private Clubs

1 SOMETIMES YOU MUST BE A MEMBER. Frequently this depends on the local economy. Hence, if the club is in need of funds, they may let non-members in to boost a sagging financial situation. However, if the club is flushed with members (and hence, revenue), they will limit the use of the club to members only.

2 IF YOU AREN'T A MEMBER, SOME CLUBS REQUIRE YOU TO HAVE A MEMBER-SPONSOR. Here, a member of the club must "sponsor" your reception, agreeing to attend the event and pay for it if you skip town. If you have a friend who is a member, great. If you don't, some clubs may negotiate around this point—perhaps by requesting a larger deposit. We know one club that will find you a sponsor if you don't know one!

3 FOOD QUALITY CAN VARY WIDELY. Some clubs have gourmet chefs on staff who create wonderful dishes. Other clubs may not be as lucky and their food quality is, at best, as good as that of an average hotel. Ask for a taste test to confirm food quality.

4 EXPENSIVE RECEPTIONS. Some clubs can be just as, or even more, expensive than hotel weddings. Overpricing of liquor is a common problem. Just like hotels, club catering managers receive commissions based on the total amount you spend—giving them an incentive to inflate the tab. Many clubs also add on a high gratuity, similar to hotels.

What Does it Cost?

Well, it depends. Fancy country clubs may be just as expensive as the prices we quoted above for hotels and catering halls. Other clubs, that don't have in-house catering, just charge a rental fee for the facility.

Civic Sites

A "civic" site is any reception facility that is owned and administered by a city or municipal agency. Almost always, you must bring in your own caterer. Some civic sites have a recommended list of caterers that you may have to choose from. Be aware that some sites may have time and beverage restrictions (no liquor) and others require you to hire security officers. Civic sites are usually the best bargains. Why? Subsidized by taxpayers, these sites aren't out to make a quick buck like private facilities.

Types of Civic Sites

1 PARKS, GARDENS, AMPHITHEATERS. Often quite affordable, these sites are usually administered by city parks departments. Some sites even have clubhouses. If you decide to have an outdoor ceremony or reception, make sure you have a backup plan in case of inclement weather.

2 RECREATION CENTERS, CIVIC CENTERS, TOWN HALLS, CONFERENCE CENTERS. Quality varies greatly with these sites (some are spectacular while others are dumps), but they are often quite affordable.

3 SITES OWNED BY UNIVERSITIES OR COLLEGES. These sites include faculty clubs, chapels, etc. Some of these facilities can be expensive.

4 MUSEUMS. Rare but available in some cities, these sites may be quite expensive and even require you to be a "museum patron" (i.e. make a hefty donation).

Advantages of Civic Sites

1 LOW COST.
Most of these sites are very affordable.

2 BRING IN AN OUTSIDE CATERER. Off-site caterers can save oodles of money and offer creative, delicious menu options.

3 UNIQUE ONE-OF-A-KIND LOCATIONS.

Disadvantages of Civic Sites

1 VERY POPULAR SITES BOOK UP QUICKLY. Since civic sites are so affordable, they are also very popular. Many book months in advance.

2 EQUIPMENT RENTAL EXPENSE CAN BE HIGH. Some of these sites might require you to bring in rentals (tables, chairs, serving pieces, etc.). This could be a significant expense.

3 MAKE SURE THE CATERER IS VERY FAMILIAR WITH THE SITE. Some brides find hiring and dealing with an outside caterer challenging—increasing the complexity of the event by adding another person in the loop. On the plus side, the savings here can be tremendous. Kitchen facilities may also affect a caterer's flexibility.

Home Weddings

Yes, we can always tell when it's wedding season in Boulder, Colorado. Pick any road that winds its way up into the foothills and you'll see several signs directing guests to a remote location for the nuptials of "Spense and Lisa," "Cheyenne and Bob," and so on.

Home weddings are big here, as they are in other parts of the Rockies. While only accounting for 6% to 10% of all receptions in the U.S., Boulder seems to be the center of the universe for home nuptials and receptions—half of all weddings here are at home, according to our estimates. Perhaps it's the nice summer weather or the views of the Continental Divide that convinces brides and grooms to tie the knot at home. Or maybe we're just cheap—cost is definitely one factor that couples look at when planning a home wedding.

Advantages of Home Weddings

1 AFFORDABLE RECEPTIONS. Let's be honest: home weddings can be had cheap. Whether you have friends and family help with the food or order a meal from a restaurant or catering service, home weddings cost a fraction of receptions at traditional sites like hotels, catering halls and private clubs.

2 NO SCHEDULING CONFLICTS. If you want to have a wedding in June on a Saturday night, you may discover that so do

many other brides in your area. The competition for reception sites during popular months can lead you to consider a home wedding.

3 SMALL WEDDINGS. Unless you live in a mansion, the average home can only hold a minimal number of guests (usually under 100). This is a plus and a minus. While you may not be able to invite everyone you'd like to, you do have the perfect excuse for cutting down that guest list.

Disadvantages of Home Weddings

1 RENTALS, RENTALS, RENTALS. Planning a home wedding for 75 guests but you don't have tables and chairs for the crowd? You'll need to rent them, along with plates, silverware, glassware, serving pieces, bar set-ups, dance floors and more. Afraid it might rain on your parade? Renting a tent can set you back $500 to $1000 or more. As you can see, the money you save on catering with a home wedding may be partially eaten up by a big rental bill.

2 SURPRISE EXPENSES. Home weddings may entail several unexpected bills. You may need to move furniture out of your house and store it for the wedding weekend. At one home wedding we attended in Austin, Texas, the bride and groom hired a van service to shuttle guests to and from a nearby parking area—this cost an extra $250. You may also need extra insurance to cover liability at the event—call your homeowner's insurance provider to see what's covered.

Restaurants, Restored Mansions, Laundromats, Etc.

Yes, you can have a wedding reception just about anywhere. Smiley's Laundromat, in Denver, Colorado has hosted weddings and receptions where brides and grooms have exchanged rings between the spin and rinse cycles. The South (particularly Atlanta) has several stunning restored mansions available for receptions. Other possibilities include theaters, ranches, private estates, chartered boats and yachts, bed and breakfast inns, and so on. Anything goes!

What's the message here? Don't think you must have your reception in a hotel or club just because all your friends did that. Every city has many romantic and beautiful settings for receptions—it may just take a little creative searching.

In fact, that's perhaps the biggest challenge to using a "non-traditional" site—finding one! (Perhaps the second biggest challenge is convincing parents and relatives that the site is better than the traditional options!) To find a non-traditional site, look in bridal editions of local newspapers and other local wedding advertising publications. Ask local caterers for suggestions. Don't overlook even the national bridal magazines—each has "regional" advertising sections that are full of ads from local sites.

Often you must bring in your own caterer (the exceptions, of course, are restaurants). As a side note, a recent survey in *Bridal Guide* revealed that 11% of all wedding receptions are held in restaurants.

CAUTION: Many of these sites (private homes and estates, for example) can be quite expensive. Some have "all-inclusive" packages (catering, flowers, cakes, etc.) that provide dubious value.

Chapter 8

Catering

I f you read just one chapter in this book, make it this one. That's because we give you 14 little-known money-saving tips that could save you hundreds if not thousands on your wedding catering. Also, you'll learn the inside scoop on catering with 17 questions to ask any caterer and five pitfalls to avoid with wedding catering.

What Are You Buying?

 Wedding catering varies dramatically across the country. While we think of ourselves as a homogeneous society, we act more like several different nations when food is the topic. And these differences make weddings in one part of the country much different from other areas. Sometimes the differences are also social in nature. For example, in the Northeast, nearly all receptions are sit-down dinners—folks there like to have their own space to enjoy the meal. While, in the South and West, almost all weddings have buffets or hors d'oeuvre receptions—people there like to mingle, instead of being in one chair for the entire reception. No matter where you have your wedding, however, here are the four basic things you buy from a caterer:

❦ *The food.* Everything from hors d'oeuvres to dessert. Sometimes caterers will also offer to do the wedding cake (and the groom's cake, a Southern tradition). The typical method of calculating costs of wedding catering is based on a figure per guest. Cost can range from $4 to $6 per guest for a simple "cake, punch and mints" reception to over $100 per person for a full sit-down dinner with open bar at a posh hotel.

❦ *The beverages.* Whether your reception will just have punch and coffee or a full open bar with premium well brands, the cost of beverages can be a significant part of the catering budget. For one hors d'oeuvres reception at a posh hotel with a full open bar serving premium liquor, the total bar tab for 400 guests was $9200—almost half the $19,000 total cost of the evening! Of course, the charge for beverages

Open vs. Cash Bars

One big controversy in the world of wedding etiquette is whether bars should be open or cash. In the latter case, guests pay for their drinks. As you can imagine, etiquette gurus wildly flail their arms at the suggestion that guests pay for their drinks, reasoning that you are in a sense charging them to attend the reception. For couples on a fixed budget, however, the debate is moot—they simply don't have the funds to stock an open bar for several hours. Adding to the debate is the nation's recent trend toward sobriety—people are drinking less alcohol. Some couples compromise by having an open bar for an hour at the beginning of the reception and a cash bar for the rest of the evening. This also discourages guests from getting smashed toward the end of the evening when they might get behind the wheel. The liability issue is also forcing many couples (and reception sites) to rethink serving alcohol altogether.

depends on what you serve and how the reception site accounts for this.

🍃 *Labor.* Hey, don't forget those folks who actually serve the food. Of course, most sites won't let you forget to pay the staff—they impose a mandatory gratuity of 15% to 20%. This applies to the food and sometimes the liquor served at the reception. If you serve a buffet that costs $3000, you must pay as much as $600 extra for the servers, bus boys, etc. Frankly, we think a percentage gratuity is slightly deceptive—most sites don't pay their staff anywhere near the amount of money they collect for "service." They pocket the difference as pure profit. For example, in the above case, let's assume the reception was for 150 guests. Using an industry rule of thumb of one server for 25 guests at a buffet reception, we would need six servers. Hence, each server would theoretically receive $100 of the $600 service charge for the evening. If the reception lasts four hours, do you really think the site is paying the servers a wage that totals $25 per hour? In most cities, we wouldn't bet on it.

Perhaps a more equitable way of paying for service is a method adopted by some independent caterers. This involves paying a flat per hour fee per waiter at the event—usually $10 to $20 per hour per server. No matter what the total tab of your function, you pay only for the number of people actually serving your guests.

🍃 *Rentals.* Certain reception sites may lack tables, chairs, silverware, china, glassware, table linens, etc. All these items must be rented separately and brought to the site. Some caterers have an in-house supply of rentals while others arrange the needed rentals through an outside rental company. Charges for this service vary greatly—sometimes the caterer will charge you what the rental company charges them. Other caterers may tack on an extra fee of 5% to 10% of the rental bill to cover the administrative expense of dealing with the rental company. Some caterers (who charge this fee) also absorb any charges for broken or missing rental items. However, in some cases, you may be responsible for any breakage or damage.

❦ *Coordination of the reception.* In the past few years, many caterers have added a new service: coordination of the entire reception. This can range from simply referring names of good florists or entertainers to actually booking and negotiating with other services. Some caterers offer such coordination as a free customer service; others charge fees that are similar to that of a professional wedding consultant. The degree you will want your caterer to coordinate your reception will depend on how much you trust them.

❦ *Average catering costs.* Catering prices vary greatly from city to city. That's because a caterer's overhead is vastly different in, say, Minot, North Dakota than in San Francisco, California. The exact menu that costs $15 per person in Albuquerque could be as much as $75 in Chicago. For example, one bride told us she had to move her reception from Dallas, Texas to Washington, DC. In Dallas, she priced her reception at $24 per person. A very similar menu at a comparable hotel in Washington, DC cost $56 per person!

Most caterers require a deposit that is as much as 50% of the total bill to hold a date. The balance is customarily due a week or two weeks before the date—some caterers will let you pay the final balance the day of the wedding. Get all payment policies in writing before you sign the contract.

Types of Caterers

1 IN-HOUSE OR ON-PREMISE CATERERS. These are catering operations that exclusively provide the catering for a site. Examples are hotels and many country clubs. Unless they're really desperate, most of these sites won't allow outside or "off-premise" caterers.

2 OFF-PREMISE CATERERS. These caterers bring in food to an existing site. The caterer's services can be limited to just providing the food or include the coordination of the entire event. Here, caterers become more like party planners or wed

ding consultants—either providing or contracting out for services like decorators (table centerpieces, table skirting, for example) and entertainers.

No matter which type of caterer you choose, the following information will be crucial.

Sources to Find an Affordable Caterer

❦ *Ask friends and other recently married couples for suggestions.* Finding a good, affordable caterer is by far the biggest challenge faced by engaged couples. The best caterers work strictly by word of mouth and hence, don't do much high-profile advertising.

❦ *Reception sites that don't have in-house caterers.* Most will have a list of local caterers they recommend. This will be an invaluable time-saver. Ask them for their opinions as to which caterer offers the best service or most affordable prices. Also, we have found some photographers who have recommendations on catering (they usually sneak a taste during receptions!).

❦ *Don't look in the phone book.* Unlike some other categories, the best caterers do not have the biggest Yellow Pages ads.

Top Money-Saving Secrets

1 FIND A SITE WHERE YOU CAN BRING IN AN OUTSIDE CATERER. Outside caterers are not only more affordable but many times offer higher quality than caterers at hotels or other sites. The big savings come in lower overhead. Outside caterers may let you buy liquor at wholesale, provide rentals at cost and basically provide more food for the dollar. Best of all: outside caterers usually don't have lots of "nickel-and-dime" charges.

2 HOLD THE RECEPTION IN MID-AFTERNOON. A wedding reception at one or two in the afternoon will be much less expensive than evening affairs. Why? Because guests will probably have already had lunch, they won't be expecting a six-course, sit-down meal.

3 GO ETHNIC. Surprisingly, certain ethnic cuisines are affordable alternatives to traditional wedding fare. Chinese, Mexican, Italian and barbecue are crowd pleasers and happily 20% to 30% less than fancier, haute cuisine. Dress up an ethnic buffet with food stations (a taco bar or pasta station, for example) that lend some pizazz to the meal. Instead of an open bar, tie in affordable alcohol alternatives (a margarita machine for a Mexican buffet, bottles of Chianti for a Italian meal) to save even more money.

4 CONSIDER A WEDDING BRUNCH OR LUNCHEON. These meals will also be less-expensive than dinner. One new idea a Chicago bride suggested to us was a dessert reception. She planned a late evening ceremony (9 pm) and threw a reception for 200 guests that featured a lavish buffet of desserts. This included a fondue of fresh fruits, torts, cheesecakes, an ice cream bar, and favorite dessert recipes from relatives, along with the traditional wedding cake. An espresso bar with flavored coffees provided refreshments. Since there wasn't a full meal served, she saved $2000. (To avoid any confusion, it's appropriate to add on your invitation or reception card "Dessert Reception Following.")

5 AVOID SATURDAYS. Some on-premise caterers have reduced rate-packages for Fridays and Sundays with 10% (or more) discounts. Ask if they have any such deal.

6 NEGOTIATE. Yes, you can haggle with most caterers and reception facilities. Those written menus aren't cast in stone. If the caterer gives you a proposal for $28 per guest, ask what he or she can do for $25. If a competitor offers you a great freebie, ask if the facility will match the competition. Like all negotiations, you want to be reasonable and recognize that your leverage to get a good deal may depend on the date/time of year for your wedding.

7 AVOID "BUDGET-BUSTING" MENU ITEMS. Certain food items are extremely expensive and can bust your budget. Two common examples are shrimp and beef tenderloin. An universally-affordable item is chicken. Another tip: stay with fruits and vegetables that are in-season. Trying to get chocolate-dipped strawberries in December will cost you a pretty penny.

8 CHOOSE ITEMS THAT AREN'T "LABOR INTENSIVE." Certain hors d'oeuvres may be made of simple ingredients but require painstaking labor to assemble. For example, hors d'oeuvres like "Boursin cheese piped into Chinese pea pods" take a long time to prepare since the cheese has to be hand-piped into the pea pod. Caterers pass along that labor cost to you.

9 FOR BUFFET AND HORS D'OEUVRES RECEPTIONS, HAVE THE CATERER'S STAFF SERVE THE ITEMS instead of letting the guests serve themselves. This will control the amount of food served (and hence, cost). When guests serve themselves, the food always seems to go much quicker (wonder why)!

10 BUY YOUR OWN LIQUOR, IF POSSIBLE. While most hotels, catering halls and country clubs don't let you do this,

other sites may permit you to buy your own liquor. The savings
of buying liquor at or near wholesale prices will be tremendous
(perhaps a 50% to 70% savings). Ask the caterer if they will
refer you to a good wholesaler in your area. When you buy by
the case load, you can normally negotiate lower prices than
retail. Some liquor suppliers may even let you return unopened
bottles for full credit. One note of caution: the liquor must be
chilled down prior to the reception, so plan ahead.

11 PROVIDE YOUR OWN BAR SERVICE. In some cases, "free-
lance" bartenders are cheaper than the caterers' own
staff. If the caterer allows you to have your own bar service,
do a cost comparison between the two options. On the other
hand, some caterers may not allow free-lance bartenders
because of liability concerns.

12 DON'T MOVE THOSE HORS D'OEUVRES! Having hors
d'oeuvres passed on silver trays may look elegant but
watch out! One Florida wedding planner told us sites there
charge exorbitant prices for "passed hors d'oeuvres." The
more affordable alternative is to keep them stationary—scattered about the room at "stations" in chafing dishes. Of
course, these exorbitant prices aren't the rule everywhere. A
Wisconsin wedding planner says there is no premium price
for passed hors d'oeuvres in her area; as a result, she highly
recommends them to keep guests from over-indulging at a
buffet table. The bottom line: compare costs for these two
options carefully to get the best deal.

13 STEER CLEAR OF COURSE OVERKILL. For sit-down dinners, do you really need to serve both hors d'oeuvres
and an appetizer? Or soup and salad? Some brides eliminate a
dessert course and let the wedding cake suffice.

REAL WEDDING TIP:
Alcohol Alternatives

With the soaring cost of booze and worry
over drunken driving, many couples are
looking for alternatives to the standard-issue
open bar at receptions. In San Diego, one wedding featured an espresso bar with a selection of flavored coffees. Other couples are forsaking hard liquor for bars
that serve a selection of micro-brewed beers, sparking
waters, and other creative ideas. Go to any wedding in
San Antonio, Texas and you'll probably see a frozen
margarita machine humming away.

14 SLASH THE ALCOHOL BILL. If you still want to have that traditional open bar, there are a couple ways to save money. First, use only house brands instead of pricey "call" brands for hard liquor. If you're having a cocktail hour, serve affordable hors d'oeuvres to lower alcohol consumption (people drink less when they're munching cheese puffs). Finally, close the bar early (say an hour or so) before the reception ends. Have less expensive soft drinks or punch available for the rest of reception. Another idea: some hotels and catering halls offer flat-rate packages for beverages. Instead of being billed per drink ordered, you pay a flat fee per guest for beverages. This might be more an affordable alternative.

Spotlight: Best Buys

Affordable Wines and Champagnes

Liquor prices vary greatly. For hotels, there is often a killer markup. The house brands are often the most affordable bet (but do a taste test, first.) If the choice of wines and champagnes is up to you, here are some recommendations that are not only tasty but also affordable:

Wines

❦ *Glen-Ellen Chardonnay.* 750 milliliter bottle. Retail price: $4.99. A nice California Chardonnay that's very affordable.

❦ *Moreau Blanc.* 1.5 liter bottle. Retail price: $5.99. This French white wine is packaged in affordable, big bottles.

❦ *Sebastiani White Zinfandel.* 1.5 liter bottle. Retail price: $7.99. Popular California blush wine that also is also a best buy.

❦ *Kendall-Jackson Vintners Reserve Chardonnay.* 750 milliliter bottle. Retail price: $10.99. Very popular California wine.

Champagnes

❦ *Codorniu Blanc de Blanc.* Retail price: $8.99. Excellent champagne from Spain.

❦ *Chardon Brut or Blanc De Noir.* Retail price: $14.49. Very dry California champagne in both white and blush.

❦ *Castellblanch Brut Extra.* Retail price: $5.98. Good, affordable champagne from Spain.

Remember, the taste of wines is not always related to the price. We've tasted some very expensive wines that weren't winners.

Getting Started: How Far in Advance?

 Book your caterer as soon as you confirm your reception site. Many book up far in advance (as long as a year) for popular summer wedding weekends. Also, December is an extremely busy time for caterers because of Christmas parties.

Biggest Myths about Catering

 Myth #1 *"If I invite fewer guests, I assume my catering bill will go down dramatically."*

Well, yes and no. Obviously, fewer mouths to feed will have an impact on your total bill. However, if you invite fewer guests, the price per person may go up. Why? That's because a large part of the per-person price caterers quote you is "fixed." Fixed costs include office expenses, the caterer's time, etc. No matter how many guests you invite, caterers still have to pay these administrative expenses. Hence, you're paying for more than just the food. In a sense, most caterers have an unwritten base price or minimum that engaged couples must pay—no matter how many guests they want to invite.

Myth #2 *"Buffets are always less expensive than sit-down dinners."*

This is one those great debates that has no one answer. The bottom line: the cost of a reception is often *what* you serve rather than *how* (buffet vs. sit-down) you serve it. Hence a basic sit-down chicken dinner will be cheaper than a fancy buffet with shrimp, sliced beef tenderloin and other pricey dishes. Conversely, a five-course steak dinner may cost several times a simple buffet with hors d'oeuvres like fruit, cheese and mini-sandwiches.

We've noticed that caterers tend to steer couples toward the type of reception they do most often. Hence, a caterer who frequently does buffet receptions will tell you a sit-down dinner is too expensive. In the Northeast (where sit-downs dinners are most common), caterers will advise just the opposite.

Of course, you can combine both types of receptions if you prefer. A "seated buffet" is set up like a sit-down dinner, with tables and chairs for every guest. The salad or first course is served at the table by waiters, while the main dish(es) is served buffet style.

Myth #3 *"Given the expensive prices caterers charge, you get the feeling these guys make big, fat profits off weddings."*

Gosh, it may be hard to believe, but most don't. Profits only range from 8% to 15% of the total bill. In the past few years, food and insurance costs have soared for most caterers. Don't shed too many tears for them, though. Since the average business only earns a 5% profit on sales, caterers' profits aren't all that bad. Different caterers make more money in different areas. For off-premise caterers, the biggest revenue area is the food. For on-site or in-house caterers (like hotels), the biggest money-maker is the liquor.

Myth #4   *"We're having a buffet reception. Isn't using plastic plates and glasses more affordable?"*

Nope. In many cases, the cost of renting glass is actually almost as affordable as using plastic! Besides looking nicer, glass also doesn't have the negative environmental impact caused by throwing away plastics. Ask your caterer to do a cost comparison between plastic and glass.

Deals at Wholesale Clubs and Gourmet Supermarkets

Liquor prices too much for you to swallow? Full-service catering charges too high to stomach? Consider two alternatives that offer great deals: wholesale clubs and gourmet supermarkets.

Popping up in most major cities, wholesale clubs like Sam's and Price Club (also known as Price/Cosco) offer cut-rate prices on everything from electronics to groceries. Best of all, some of the clubs have fully stocked liquor departments where you can buy in case quantity at fantastic discounts. We visited a Price Club and found prices 15% to 30% below regular liquor stores. Name brands of wine, beer and spirits were available in big quantities. If you're hiring a caterer who will let you purchase your own liquor, be sure to get a quote from a local wholesale club.

While many wholesale clubs have been adding liquor and groceries, many supermarkets have remade themselves into "gourmet markets" with full-service catering departments. The quality has also improved. We've spoken to brides who have found affordable catering options for small at-home receptions at a local gourmet supermarket—and they found the quality to be excellent. Many markets also have pastry chefs on staff that can whip up a respectable wedding cake. With full-service floral departments as well, some markets offer an affordable one-stop shopping service. Prices for catering, cakes and flowers tend to be about 10% to 20% below retail.

Step-by-step Shopping Strategies

 ❦ *Step 1:* Using the sources above, set up appointments with at least three recommended caterers. When you call for an appointment, notice how promptly the caterer returns your call. Within the business day is good—if it takes them more than a day, that's not good. Prompt attention is your first clue to the caterer's commitment to service. Before your meeting, discuss with your fiance your likes and dislikes for catering.

❦ *Step 2:* Ask to see photographs of their previous work. Look for a colorful and creative presentation of food. Is it artfully arranged with flowers and garnishes or just piled up on mirrored trays?

❦ *Step 3:* Ask for sample menus. These may list some popular hors d'oeuvre choices or sit-down options. Hopefully, their prices will be listed to give you a better idea of costs. While most caterers customize menus for each reception, they should be willing to give you basic cost parameters for certain items.

❦ *Step 4:* Be honest about your budget. If you're not sure, give them a range of costs per guest that you feel comfortable with. What one caterer will offer you for $25 per person may be vastly different from what another may propose. Also, be specific about your menu likes and dislikes as well as any dietary restrictions.

❦ *Step 5:* Ask for a proposal that details possible menu options. Also, the proposal should clearly identify costs for liquor, rentals, and labor. Call the caterer back and ask them to clarify any part of the proposal that isn't clear. One bad sign: caterers who promise to send you a proposal and then fail to do so.

❦ *Step 6:* Confirm any "minimums." Some caterers require you to purchase a minimum amount of food (in dollars or meals). Hence, you may have to pay for 125 meals even if only 100 people show up to your wedding. While some of this is negotiable (depending on the date and time of your wedding), never book a caterer who has a minimum you don't think you'll be able to meet. Also ask the caterer about the opposite case: when more guests show up than expected. Most caterers make 5% to 10% more food than is ordered, but confirm this to be sure.

❦ *Step 7:* Given the different proposals from each caterer, pick the one you most like and ask to visit one of their weddings during the set-up. Look for how organized they are and how the staff is dressed. Just observe.

❦ *Step 8:* Ask for a taste test of proposed menu items. Most likely you are planning to spend several thousands of dollars on catering, so this is the least caterers can do. You may be able to combine the taste test with the visit to one of their weddings. Another suggestion: take pictures of the food at the tasting, in case the chef or catering manager changes before your wedding. That way you'll be able to show the new staffers what you expect.

❦ *Step 9:* Once you select a caterer, get everything in writing—down to the very last detail. Food, labor, liquor, and rentals (if necessary) should be clearly stated in a written contract. Make sure you understand any price escalation clauses (where the caterer has the right to up the price within a certain time period) and get any price guarantees in writing. Also get a drawing of the physical layout of the room with placement of the tables, dance floor, buffet tables, etc.

❦ *Step 10:* Before you sign anything, take the contract home to read it. Pour over any fine print like refund policies and cancellation fees. Remember that just because something is in the contract doesn't mean it's set in stone and can't be changed—ask the caterer to alter or change any wording that makes you uncomfortable. Make sure any modifications or cancellations are made in writing.

Questions to Ask a Caterer

1 CAN WE HAVE A TASTE TEST OF THE FOODS ON OUR MENU? We positively loath caterers who expect you to pay thousands of dollars for food on faith. Equally reprehensible are caterers that say "why do you need to taste such basic items? Hors d'oeuvres are hors d'oeuvres." We suggest you find another caterer if you get this line.

2 CAN WE SEE ONE OF YOUR WEDDINGS DURING SET-UP? A truly organized and professional catering company should have nothing to hide.

3 DO YOU PROVIDE A WRITTEN ESTIMATE AND CONTRACT? Verbal agreements are a prescription for disaster. Make sure every last promise and detail is in black and white.

4 ARE YOU LICENSED? Almost all municipalities (or counties) require caterers to be licensed. Local standards will stress clean and adequate facilities for food preparation and storage. Liability insurance on liquor and food may also be part of the requirements. Ask the caterer about insurance. Operating a catering business out of a home or residence is often illegal.

5 Do you specialize in certain cuisines or types of menus? Although they may claim to handle all types of weddings, caterers usually specialize in certain types of receptions (smaller versus larger, finger hors d'oeuvres versus full sit-down dinners). Some caterers may have chefs who specialize in certain cuisines (Continental, Greek, Southwestern, Indian, etc.)

6 Where is the food prepared? Will you need additional kitchen facilities at my site? Make sure these details are confirmed by the caterer to prevent any last minute surprises.

7 When is the menu "set in stone?" How close to the wedding can we get and still make changes in the menu? Trust us, there will be changes. Different family members, friends and relatives will add in their two cents on the perfect wedding menu.

8 How is your wait staff dressed? The key here is professional attire. Don't assume the wait staff will be wearing tuxedos (the exception is hotels who always have uniformed servers).

9 For cocktail or buffet receptions, how often will the food be replenished? Will the servings per guest be limited? Who makes the decision on when to stop serving?

10 Given the style of my reception, how many waiters do we need? For seated receptions, one waiter per 16 to 20 guests is adequate. For buffet or cocktail receptions, one waiter per 25 guests is standard.

11 How is the charge for labor figured? Is the clean-up (dish-washing, etc) extra?

12 How much does a dessert table cost? Is the wedding cake price included in the package? Dessert or Viennese tables are popular in the Midwest and in parts of the Northeast. Be sure the costs of a dessert table are clearly identified.

13 What are your cancellation/postponement policies? Since catering is the biggest expense area, confirming this aspect would be prudent.

14 Do you have a liquor license? How is the cost of the beverages calculated? What brands of liquor will be served? Most caterers offer both "premium" (or "call") and generic or "house" brands. If you plan to serve alcohol, you'll want the caterer to carefully explain what brands you are buying and how the cost is calculated. Per drink charges are often the most expensive, although per bottle charges can be just as costly.

15 ARE YOU FAMILIAR WITH MY RECEPTION SITE? If not, will you visit it with me? For off-premise caterers, don't assume they know your facility. Confirming details such as the kitchen facilities and the clean-up rules are very important if you want to get your security/damage/cleaning deposit back from the reception site. The site will hold you responsible for any damage or rule violations by your caterer.

16 DO YOU RECEIVE ANY COMMISSIONS FROM SERVICES YOU RECOMMEND? Caterers may recommend bakers, florists or musicians but watch out! Some take "commissions" (we call them kick-backs) from the businesses they recommend. Don't just take their word—thoroughly check out any services before contracting.

17 WILL YOU GUARANTEE THESE PRICE ESTIMATES? Many caterers raise their prices at the beginning of the year. Since we urge you to plan in advance for this chapter, your reception may be several months away. Our advice: negotiate a price guarantee in writing (or at least a cap on future increases). Most caterers will be willing to do this to get your business. One couple we interviewed in Colorado found out this the hard way—the site they booked raised their prices 15% just weeks before their event. Their wedding budget was thrown into complete disarray.

Helpful Hints

1 MAKE SURE THE CATERING REPRESENTATIVE WHO PLANNED YOUR WEDDING WILL BE THERE THE NIGHT OF THE WEDDING. Hotel catering staffs are frequently guilty of not showing up to make sure everything is right. If you contract with a smaller, off-premise caterer, make sure the owner is there. Obviously, the owner may not be able to be at your wedding reception every minute, but there should be a clear chain of command in case a problem arises.

2 HAVE THE CATERER PREPARE YOU A GOING-AWAY PACKAGE. Believe it or not, you probably won't get to taste any of the food at your reception. You'll be too busy shaking hands, giving hugs, posing for pictures, etc. Considering the amount of money you're spending, ask the caterer to prepare a going-away package with a sample of the evening's menu (don't forget to include the cake!). You and your fiance will probably be starved when you leave the reception!

3 CAREFULLY BUDGET LIQUOR AMOUNTS. Wedding planner Pattie Cox of Grafton, Wisconsin (Events by Pattie, 414-375-8503) provided us with this rule of thumb to budget how many drinks guests will consume at an open bar: 2.5 drinks the first hour, 1.5 drinks the second hour and one drink per hour thereafter. Hence, for a four hour reception, you should budget five drinks per guest. Wow! Do people really drink that much at wedding receptions? No, Pattie told us. Remember that you are charged for the number of drinks *ordered*, not consumed. "So, when Uncle Joe can't remember what he did with his nearly full drink, he figures it's 'free' and he just gets another one," Pattie said. Another scam that inflates liquor tabs: waitstaffs that clear half-full glasses before guests can finish them. As you'll read later in the Pitfalls to Avoid section, this is but one way some sites can boost the beverage charges.

4 TIPS ON TIPPING. We always get many questions on tipping from brides and grooms. Who do you tip? How much? First, understand that most wedding reception sites have a mandatory gratuity added into the final tab. (The same goes for most limousine companies). As a result, you don't *have* to tip anyone. However, if you believe an individual staffer has gone "above and beyond the call of duty," it may be nice if you slipped them an extra $20 or more. A server who tracks down a missing special dietary meal for a relative, a limousine driver who makes a special return trip to your house to retrieve an errant bridesmaid, a catering manager who works miracles with a cake that's collapsed—these are examples of extraordinary service that you may want to reward with an extra tip. You may also give a tip to the band or disc jockey if they turn in a stellar performance.

Pitfalls to Avoid

Pitfall #1
FROZEN FOOD.
    "We went to a friend's reception last weekend at a hotel. I know the bride spent a lot of money on the buffet, but the food was just so-so."

In our opinion, too many sites like hotels rely too much on frozen food. Bought in bulk, frozen versions of mini-egg rolls and mini-quiche are mainstays on some reception site menus. Obviously, its cheaper (and hence more profitable) to buy these items frozen and quickly warm them in chafing dishes than to painstakingly make the same items from scratch. The problem? Besides obviously tasting "frozen," caterers who use frozen food often aren't any less expensive than those caterers who hand-make food from scratch ingredients. If the food at your reception is one of your high priorities, shop carefully for a caterer who doesn't use shortcuts.

Pitfall #2
THE INFAMOUS CAKE-CUTTING FEE.

"Boy am I steamed! The reception site I chose for my wedding said they would charge me $1 per person to cut my wedding cake. After spending thousands of dollars on food and liquor, I think they're trying to wring every last nickel from me!"

WE COULDN'T AGREE MORE! Boy, this is our #1 pet-peeve with caterers and reception sites. Some of these guys have the audacity to charge you a ridiculously high fee to cut your wedding cake. Ranging anywhere from 50 cents to $3 per guest, this "fee" supposedly covers the labor involved to cut the cake, as well as the plates, forks, etc. The real reason some reception sites charge this fee is to penalize you for bringing in a cake from an outside baker (instead of having the site bake you one). Even more amazing are some sites that don't even bake wedding cakes themselves but still charge cake-cutting fees! Talk about abusive—these fees are pure greed! We say if you are spending hundreds or thousands of dollars on food and liquor, the caterer or reception site should NOT tack on $100 to $400 more just for the privilege of cutting and serving the wedding cake! First of all, you are already paying a mandatory service gratuity to have a staff present at the reception. Hence, the cake cutting fee is often double-charging. Secondly, do you really think they pay the cake-cutter $100 to $400 for fifteen minutes of work? We suggest you try to negotiate away this charge—don't forget that everything is always negotiable.

(Note: some caterers or sites try to sneak in the cost of serving coffee into the cake-cutting fee. We suggest you tell the caterer to forget the cake-cutting fee and just price the coffee out separately. If the site still insists on a cake-cutting fee, try to negotiate a flat fee, say $50 or $75, instead of a per guest charge.)

Another inflated price we've discovered: the cost of punch. One hotel in the West charges brides and grooms a whopping $35 per gallon of punch! Since a half gallon of Minute Maid Fruit Punch goes for $2 to $3 at grocery stores, you can see how outrageous this stuff can get.

Pitfall #3
CORKING FEES AND THE LIQUOR THAT RUNNETH OVER.

"My friend had her reception at a country club that seemed to push liquor on the guests. Every five minutes, they

went around to the guests and pitched more drinks. I also understand they charged the couple for every bottle that was opened! Isn't this a bit excessive?"

Not only excessive but also quite expensive. When couples are charged based on the number of $20 bottles of wine or champagne that are opened, one mad staffer with a corkscrew can inflict heavy financial damage. Such charges (called corking fees) are perhaps one of the biggest cost pitfalls of any wedding reception. That's because couples must pay for any opened bottles whether or not they were poured! Think you can just recork the bottles and bring them home? Think again—most sites prevent the removal of liquor from the premises.

In a different twist on the same problem, some sites push drinks on guests when the bar is "open" (i.e., the engaged couple pays for each drink). Why would sites or caterers do this? BIG PROFITS! Liquor is the biggest profit area for sites like hotels and catering halls, and hence the temptation to push booze or open unneeded bottles is too great for the greedy. The solution to the corking fee pitfall is to give the caterer or reception site a limit on the number of bottles they can open. Tell them to confer with you before they go beyond that limit.

Another version of this scam surfaced in California. We spoke with a former employee of a catering company who admitted they brought empty bottles to receptions. Since the liquor charges were based on the number of empty bottles at the end of the evening, the caterer was able to make a killing. We recommend you count the bottles at the beginning of the evening and again at the end. If there are 100 full bottles at the start, there better not be 125 bottles (80 empty and 45 full) at the end.

Sites can also inflate the liquor tab by picking up half-full glasses, forcing guests who have just returned from the dance floor to go back to the bar to get something to drink. One wedding planner we spoke to suggested couples should explicitly tell catering managers to make sure the waitstaff is not overzealous in clearing half-full glasses. If you see specific examples of this behavior, you should be able to negotiate a 10% to 20% reduction in the beverage bill.

Pitfall #4
GRATUITOUS GRATUITIES

"When we saw the final bill for our reception, the facility charged us a 'gratuity fee' on everything including the room charge! Is this fair?"

Many facilities look at the gratuity as "extra profit," not something that is paid to the staff. One bride in California called in the above story, where the facility was charging an 18% gratuity on the *room rental fee*, of all things (this worked out to an extra $300). In our opinion, the gratuity should only be charged on the food and liquor. (We should note in some states it is illegal to charge a mandatory gratuity on the liquor tab—as an alternative to the gratuity, facilities often charge "bartender or bar set-up fees.") Placing a gratuity on other charges (like room rental, valet parking, coat check) is price gouging.

Another similar rip-off is the "double-charging" of labor. In Denver, Colorado, for example, many caterers charge both a gratuity and a "labor fee." While the staff generally gets the gratuity, the owners usually pocket the labor charge, which, by the way, is illegal in the state of Colorado. As a result of this double-charging, couples are being socked with an effective 25% gratuity rate on receptions—an outrage in our opinion.

What about sales tax? In some states, food and liquor is taxable. A few states even slap sales tax on labor charges like the gratuity and other services. Since the sales tax rate can be 5% to 10% in some cities, this can add to the bill in a hurry. Be forewarned: some brides have told us that their sites have slapped sales tax on items like room rental that were clearly not taxable. Why? Maybe it's just sloppy bookkeeping. Or they may be pocketing the tax. If you have any questions on what's taxable and what's not, check with you local city or county government (listed in the white pages of your phone book).

Pitfall #5
PRICE RISE SURPRISE

"I booked my reception site a year in advance and we agreed on a certain price per guest. One month before my wedding, the catering manager informed me of a 20% price increase and pointed to fine print in their contract. Is this fair?"

Our office has received several complaints from brides and grooms who believe they were stung unfairly by "surprise" price increases. Ironically, these couples may be tripped up by their own advance planning—they booked their wedding site so far in advance that the facility won't guarantee a price for food and liquor.

Instead, these couples received a written proposal and contract that included a "price escalation" clause. This enables the site or caterer to raise the price with little or no notice. Obviously, that can be a painful lesson for brides and grooms who get socked with unexpected extra costs.

Certainly, the best course of action is to get a firm price guarantee. If that's not possible, try to negotiate a "reasonable" price increase cap in the contract—paying a small 5%

The Wisconsin Pig Scandal

Here's a true story about a catering rip-off that zapped a Wisconsin couple, as reported by their videographer. "I was videotaping a wedding last year that had a Hawaiian theme to it. The bride contracted with a hotel to have the reception and wanted a menu with a roast pig, to be cooked on site. The hotel said yes, promising the roast pig.

"The bride had a list of "must haves" for her video, which included a shot of the pig coming out of the oven. When I approached the kitchen to video it, the cook and the manager came out to read me the Riot Act about coming in the kitchen. They quoted me chapter and verse from the Wisconsin Food Preparation Act, which states in so many words that if you're not doing the cooking, you're not allowed in the kitchen."

"I tried to figure out how I was going to get a shot of the pig when a busboy told me the real reason I wasn't allowed in the kitchen: the hotel was unable to roast the pig on site; they had to send it out to be cooked!"

"Well, I was going to get that pig on video because the bride was the type of person that if she didn't get EXACTLY what she wanted, she wouldn't pay on the rest of the video bill. Armed with the information from the busboy, I went back to the cook and manager and I read them the Riot Act. I told them I had found about the deception and unless I got a video of the pig coming out of the oven, I was going to inform the bride about the pig scandal (why should I take the fall for them when I'm only getting $1500 and she's spending $9500 on the hotel—it was the hotel that broke their end of the bargain)."

"Surprise . . . the manager let me into the kitchen (it was amazing how quickly they forgot the Wisconsin Food Preparation Act). I told them I wanted a shot of a pig coming out of an oven, so I set my camera up in a way that the oven looked larger than it really was. When the pig arrived (which was, of course, late) they put part of the pig into the oven (it was a clean oven, so they dirtied it just for me—weren't they nice!). I got the shot of the pig and they got to keep their $9500. The moral of the story is: make sure you get what you pay for at the reception, because some sites will say anything to get your business if you spend enough money."

increase isn't fun, but it's much better than being surprised with a 20% whopper.

Also look out for clauses that let the caterer substitute food items. Insist in the contract they get your written approval first before any changes to the menu are made. You want to be reasonable, of course. While a sudden frost in Florida might change your plans for Mimosas, you don't want your caterer or reception facility to start making wholesale substitutions to the menu without your approval.

Chapter 9

Photography

E ver hire a professional photographer before? Probably not—that's why this chapter will be invaluable. This country has over 27,000 wedding and portrait photographers, making it a daunting task to find the perfect one for you. From key questions to important pitfalls to avoid, this chapter will give you a clear and concise guide to finding a great photographer at an affordable price.

What Are You Buying?

 When you hire a professional wedding photographer, there are three main areas where your money goes:

1 CANDIDS: These are the pictures taken at the wedding and reception which are assembled into an album for the bride and groom. Photographers often assemble candid packages for the parents (referred to as parents' albums) and gifts for attendants (usually 2 or 4 pictures in a gift folio). Note that parents' albums (usually 20 to 60 pictures) and gift folios are extra and are not included in our "average" photography tab.

2 ALBUMS: Most photographers offer a wide selection of albums to hold the candids. The best are Art Leather, Leather Craftsman and Capri. Unfortunately, they are also the most expensive and are sold only by professional photographers. Art Leather albums (which include the less-expensive Aristohyde and super-expensive leather brands) are guaranteed for a life-time. With Capri or Leather Craftsman albums, the pictures are mounted to the pages, which are permanently bound in the album. Some photographers skimp by using cheap, vinyl albums with plastic-covered pages. We'll explain later why these cheaper albums can damage your pictures.

3 PORTRAITS: Pictures taken prior to the wedding day fall into this category. A bridal portrait is a formal portrait of the bride in her wedding gown. Particularly popular in the

Southern U.S., bridal portraits are taken in an indoor studio or "on location" typically four to six weeks before the wedding. An "engagement portrait" is a more informal picture of you and your fiance. This portrait is often used to announce your engagement in the local paper. Two expenses are involved with portraits: the sitting fee and the portrait itself. "Sitting fees" are a charge for the photographer's time and range from $50 to several hundreds of dollars. The most popular print size is 16x20 and this can cost $100 to $500 depending on the photographer and city.

Photography customs and traditions vary greatly across the U.S. For example, in Sacramento, California, many couples have a formal portrait taken after the reception at one of the area's many parks. In the South, a formal portrait of the bride taken a month before the wedding is often framed and displayed at the reception. Several Colorado photographers bring studio-quality lighting systems to the wedding in order to do portraits of the bride and groom before the ceremony.

AVERAGE TOTAL COSTS: In most U.S. cities, the average tab for professional wedding photography—you might want to sit down—is $1000 to $2000. So what does that buy you? That figure just covers your album of candid coverage at your wedding and reception. Keep in mind that certain "celebrity" photographers in larger metropolitan areas charge several times more than the average. Meanwhile, competent photographers in smaller cities can be hired for $700 or less.

No matter where you are, however, the process of selecting pictures is relatively the same. We should note that photographers don't usually talk in plain English, so here are three typical terms you will come across and their simple translations:

❦ *Exposures:* Basically this is defined by every time the camera goes "click." At least 150 to 200 exposures are taken at the typical wedding and four-hour reception. Be careful of packages that limit the number of exposures below that level.

❦ *Proofs:* Exposures are developed into proofs. The proofs are often 5x5 pictures from which you choose the final prints that will appear in your album. Unretouched, the proofs chronicle all the pictures that the photographer took at your wedding. Photographers often have packages that guarantee the selection from a certain number of proofs. This can range from 80 proofs for small packages to over 200 for the largest.

❦ *Prints:* The proofs are enlarged into final prints. For photographers who use medium format cameras (we'll explain this later), popular enlargement sizes are 5x7, 8x8, 8x10 and 10x10. The final prints are assembled into the album.

Okay, so now you know the basics of what you are buying. But how do you find a competent, yet affordable, professional wedding photographer in the first place?

Sources for Finding a Photographer

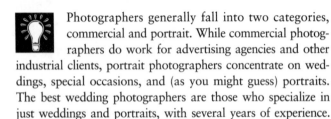 Photographers generally fall into two categories, commercial and portrait. While commercial photographers do work for advertising agencies and other industrial clients, portrait photographers concentrate on weddings, special occasions, and (as you might guess) portraits. The best wedding photographers are those who specialize in just weddings and portraits, with several years of experience. They should do at least 10 to 15 weddings per year. Here are three sources to find the very best wedding photographers:

❦ *Recently-married couples.* Yep, word-of-mouth referral from friends are your best bet for finding the best photographers. Ask them how happy they were with the photographer and final prints. Was there anything they would change?

❦ *Wedding coordinators at ceremony and reception sites.* What an incredible resource! These people have seen hundreds of wedding photographers come through their door. Ask them who they thought were the best. Of course, their impressions are limited to the photographer's behavior at their particular site. Site coordinators rarely see the final photo album. Nevertheless, their opinions are valuable.

❦ *Bridal shows.* These shows (sponsored by local bridal shops and reception sites) often have several exhibits by local photographers. Be aware that these shows may feature young or new photographers who are looking to build their business. Unfortunately, these shows also tend to showcase large photography studios whose quality can vary greatly from associate to associate (we'll discuss these studios later). Keep your eye on the local paper for shows in your area.

Where not to look. Unfortunately, the phone book is not a good source for wedding photographers. Many of the best wedding photographers do not invest heavily in this type of advertising. In fact, many don't advertise at all, working exclusively by word-of-mouth referral. Some photographers will also put a book of their work in local bridal shops. However, whose work is displayed has more to do with politics than merit. Another place to avoid looking are any wedding advertising publications—most good photographers shun these like the plague.

Understanding Wedding Photographers: Some Basics

As you shop for a good wedding photographer, there are three key areas that you must always keep in mind:

1 EQUIPMENT. Obviously, the quality of equipment the photographer uses is directly related to how good your wedding pictures will look. No matter how talented and personable the photographer is, the resulting pictures will be a disappointment if he or she uses an inferior camera.

"I visited a wedding photography studio yesterday that said they use 35 millimeter cameras. They claimed the pictures look just as good as others shot with more expensive cameras. Is this true?"

Not exactly. To understand why, let's look at the two types of cameras mainly used for wedding photography: 35 millimeter and medium format cameras.

❦ *35 millimeter cameras:* Most of us are familiar with these widely-available cameras. There is quite a debate in the professional photography community when it comes to which (and what type of camera) is best. Some professional wedding photographers shun 35mm cameras because of their small negative size. Since some wedding photos are blown up to 8x10 or larger, this negative can produce pictures that are "grainy." Other photographers also say 35mm pictures look "flat" and the colors are not as vibrant.

Photographers who are fans of 35mm point out that the quick action of the shutter on 35mm cameras lets them take more "candid-style" pictures. They also say the equipment and film has improved dramatically in recent years, closing the quality gap with more expensive cameras. What about the problem of grainy blow-up pictures? They claim that most couples don't request pictures blown up bigger than 8x10, the upper limit on 35mm pictures for acceptable quality.

❦ *Medium-format cameras:* The main distinction between medium format cameras and 35mm is their negative size: a medium format's square negative is usually 2¼" wide and 2¼" long. This provides much clearer photos when prints are enlarged. Medium-format cameras produce pictures that have richer depth, warmer colors and sharper contrasts than 35mm cameras. (To be technical, the "warmth" of a photograph is determined by the amount of flash light. However, medium-format cameras deliver pictures with more "color saturation" than 35mm. Color saturation relates to the richness of color in the print). The "Hasselblad" is apparently the Lexus of medium format cameras. The Hasselblad (which was the one NASA used on the moon for astronaut snapshots) is incredibly popular among the best wedding photographers, apparently for the beautiful pictures it takes. Another popular medium-format camera is the Bronica.

We should note in passing that there are also several larger-format cameras that produce even bigger negatives (and hence, greater color saturation) than standard medium-format. Cameras, such as the Mamiya RB67, are considered the "ultimate" camera in this category. That camera takes a negative that is 6cm by 7cm.

"Well, now I'm confused. Should I hire a photographer who uses a 35mm or medium format camera?"

The key is to look at the pictures. As we'll discuss later in this chapter, there are several ways to evaluate photographs and some key questions to ask the photographer.

Also, consider the style of wedding photography you want. If you'd like a heavy emphasis on candid or spontaneous pictures, a photographer with a 35mm might be a best bet. Traditionalists who like a more posed look or who want to blow up pictures for portraits should insist on a photographer who shoots on medium-format. Since most formal bridal portraits are blown up to 16x20 (or larger), these should always be shot with a medium-format camera.

Why do some wedding photographer's use 35mm cameras? One reason is money. 35mm cameras suitable for wedding photography cost several hundred dollars. Medium format cameras cost several thousand dollars—each. For example, a completely-outfitted Hasselblad can cost up to $7500. Obviously, amateur photographers opt for the cheaper 35mm when they are starting out. What's most disgusting, however, are large studios who use low-quality 35mm cameras in order to cut corners. While the studio makes a few extra bucks of profit, engaged couples are left with inferior-looking photographs.

Just as important as the camera is the lighting equipment. Lighting equipment and techniques often separate the amateurs from the pros. Amateurs will use only a flash mounted on the camera—the resulting pictures are flat and of poor quality. Professional wedding photographers will use a powerful flash placed about 45 degrees to the side of the subject. The resulting light provides shadows and depth. Some photographers will add one or more flashes aimed at the background. Photographer Mark Spencer of Mountain View, California told us he even puts light behind posed groups and dancing couples to give his pictures additional depth.

Who holds all these extra flashes? Usually it's an assistant. Pros have one at their side the entire day. Not only does the assistant hold the additional flashes, but he or she also makes sure the photographer doesn't miss any detail. In Dallas, Texas, we found one expert photographer who brings *two* assistants to each and every wedding.

2 SKILL: Equally as important as having a high-quality camera is knowing how to use it. Photographing a wedding takes a tremendous amount of skill. This is not something that can be taught in a classroom. Only by actually going out there and clicking the camera can anyone learn how to be a good wedding photographer.

Skill involves not only knowing where to stand to get the best shot of the couple as they are showered with birdseed, but also how to coax a reticent flower girl into that perfect pose. The best wedding photographers learn how to work around adverse lighting conditions and, perhaps, adverse relatives.

The only way to tell a wedding photographer's skill is by looking at many albums of their work. After seeing hundreds of wedding albums, we are convinced that you can tell the skilled pros from the unskilled amateurs. One key: posing. Does the photographer creatively pose his or her subjects or are they lined up against a blank wall (like police mug-shots).

One last caution about skill: don't believe studios that tell you that "every one of their associates is trained in the same style." This has to be the biggest lie told by wedding photographers. True, studios may have a professed quality standard that they strive for but what matters most is the talent and skill of the individual photographer who will actually photograph your wedding. Despite the smooth sales pitch, quality can vary widely from associate to associate.

3 PERSONALITY: Beside professional equipment and the skill to use it, great wedding photographers also must have great people skills. This isn't nature photography where the photographer patiently sits out in a field for six hours waiting for that perfect photo of the yellow-finned butterfly. Wedding photography involves real people.

Obviously, this doesn't come as a surprise to you, but apparently this is news to some wedding photographers. Communication is key. Besides a sixth sense for good pictures, photographers must be persistent in getting the shots the engaged couple requests. Controlling large crowds of unruly bridesmaids and groomsmen for a group shot can be trying on even the best of nerves. Wedding photographers walk a fine line between being gentle conductors and absolute dictators. In the latter case, some fall victim to "director's disease:" barking orders at the bride and groom and turning the wedding and reception into a military exercise.

Remember that you will spend more time with your wedding photographer than any other service you will hire. For example, you won't see your florist or baker during or after the wedding. Not only do you meet with the photographer prior to the wedding, he or she will follow you around the entire wedding day. Then, you may spend several more hours with them viewing proofs and ordering prints. Make sure you like this person. We mean you need to really like this person. If anything makes you the slightest bit uncomfortable, consider hiring someone else.

Top Money-saving Secrets

1 GET MARRIED ANY TIME OTHER THAN SATURDAY EVENING. Many photographers offer discounted packages for weddings held during Saturday afternoon or any other time of the week. Savings typically range from 10% to 20%. For example, a 15% discount off a $1000 package would bring the price down to $850. Total savings = $150. (As a side note: some photographers charge extra to work on Sundays for family reasons.)

2 HIRE A PHOTOGRAPHER WHO WORKS OUT OF HIS OR HER HOME. When you walk into a photography studio in a fancy office complex and see all that plush carpeting and furniture, who do you think pays for all that? That's right, you do. No one has ever explained to us how designer wallpaper translates into great wedding photography. Our advice: seek out a photographer who works out of his or her home. Quite simply, the lower overhead of a home studio/office is often passed along in more affordable prices. Believe it or not, after visiting with 200 wedding photographers, we found some of the best wedding photography comes from home-based photographers rather than those who have plush offices. Savings here can range from 20% to 40% off our photography average. Total savings = $300 to $600.

3 SKIP THE EXTRA FRILLS. Forget about the extras that photographers will suggest you buy. Gift folios (pitched as the "perfect gift" for wedding party members) are fluff. Bridal and

engagement portraits are expensive extras. Instead, if you really want a portrait, take a candid from the reception and have it enlarged to a 16x20. You'll save the sitting fee (anywhere from $50 to $300) and the print is often less expensive too. Forget about ordering a frame from the photographer; this service is grossly overpriced. Instead, go to your favorite framing store. Sample savings: $30 each for two gift folios, $100 for a sitting fee, $300 for a 16x20 portrait. Total savings = $460.

4 HIRE A PROFESSIONAL FOR THE CEREMONY ONLY. Then let your guests capture the reception candids with their own cameras or single-use cameras (see tip below for more information). Many engaged couples don't realize photographers offer a ceremony-only (two hours or less) package for "small weddings." Of course, there is no law that says couples must have a small wedding to use this package. To see how the savings can stack up, here's one example: a photographer we met in Texas offered a one-hour, ceremony-only package for $300—significantly less than his $930 full-coverage plan. That's a savings of almost 70%! Obviously, prices will vary depending on the city you are in, but you can expect a savings of anywhere from 40% to 70%. Using our $1500 average cost of wedding photography, these packages would be in the $450 to $900 range. Total savings = $600 to $1100. (Note: beware of studios that might assign less-experienced photographers to shoot the ceremony-only packages.)

5 GET YOUR GUESTS INVOLVED. Kodak has a great deal on single-use (also known as disposable) cameras: The Wedding Party Pack has five cameras with built-in flash (call 1-800-242-2424 for a dealer near you). The retail is about $50-$55 but we've seen it for as little as $43 at K-Mart and other discounters. Since each camera has 15 exposures and it costs about $4 to develop each roll, your total cost is $65 for 75 pictures (only 86¢ per picture). Fuji has a great deal too— the Wedding Cam with built-in flash is $12 for 24 exposures. We found a Fuji 4-pack (96 exposures) at Bridal Discount Boutique in Houston, TX (713) 589-8901 for just $48. With the developing cost about $6 per roll, your total cost is $73 for 96 pictures (just 76¢ per picture). Will these cameras replace professional photographers? Of course not. Instead, we suggest hiring a professional photographer to cover the ceremony and let the guests snap away at the reception (they'll probably get pictures your photographer wouldn't take anyway). In your album, you can mix the candids taken at the reception with the professional pictures. Worried about the quality? Pictures from single-use cameras have dramatically improved in quality the last few years. If you still have

doubts, buy yourself a camera and do a little experimenting. With professional photographers charging as much as $10 to $20 for a single print, single-use cameras offer an affordable way to hold down the photography bill.

6 BUY THE ALBUM SOMEWHERE ELSE. Chances are you will get a photo album as a gift. If your budget is tight, forget the fancy leather album. If the photographer includes the cost of the album in the package, ask him or her what the discount would be for an album-less package. The retail price of an album from photography studios ranges from $150 to $350. Hence, total savings = $150 to $350. Where can find a great album for your wedding pictures without spending those kind of bucks? Check out the Real Wedding Tip below for a mail-order source.

7 CONSOLIDATE YOUR ORDERS TO TAKE ADVANTAGE OF QUANTITY DISCOUNTS. Okay, you've decided which pictures you want but, hold it, now your parents want a few extra prints. And Aunt Bea wants an 8x10 of you and your fiance exchanging vows. By consolidating several small orders

---

REAL WEDDING TIP:
Mail-order albums

Our favorite catalog for photograph albums is Exposures (800) 222-4947, 1 Memory Lane, PO Box 3615, Oshkosh, WI, 54903. Their 48-page color catalog features albums, frames and accessories you won't find anywhere else. For example, the "Grande Floridian" album is softly padded with a checked damask fabric and closes with a white ribbon. The album comes with one set of 10 photo pages (which hold up to 80 pictures). Cost: $79. Most Exposure albums use album pages made from "archival quality mylar" which does not contain chemicals that damage pictures. Other albums are "scrapbook-style," where you use old-fashioned photo corners to mount pictures to the acid-free pages, separated by protective tissue. The Millefiori is a linen-bound, scrapbook-style album with 50 pages for $55. Other scrapbook albums from Exposures cost $40 to $60, not cheap but much less expensive than albums from professional photography studios. You can also add in invitations, newspaper clippings and other mementos from your wedding. Exposures' frames and other accessories are equally intriguing—great gifts for bridesmaids, friends and other relatives.

into one large one, you may be able to take advantage of quantity discounts offered by your photographer. Also, you'll be able to avoid "service charges" some photographers slap on orders after the bride and groom's album is delivered. One photographer charges an extra 20% "service fee" on such reorders. In addition, we found several photographers who offer discounts if you turn in your order within a certain number of days after the wedding. Read the fine print.

Getting Started: How Far in Advance?

 Obviously, photographers can only be at one place at one time. Hence this "limited capacity" to do weddings makes the competition among brides for good photographers intense. Once you book the ceremony site (and therefore confirm your date), consider shopping for a photographer. While some photographers can be had on short notice (a few weeks to a couple of months), booking nine to 12 months in advance of your date is prudent. That way you won't have to settle on a third or fourth choice. During the "wedding season" in your town, prime dates will go quickly.

Biggest Myths About Wedding Photography

 Myth #1 *"A photographer I visited told me he has won several awards for his portraits. If he has won all these awards, that makes him a pretty good wedding photographer, right?"*

Not necessarily. To understand why, let's look at how photographers "win" these contests. According to a recent article in a professional photography magazine, some photographers hire models to pose for these portraits and then take hundreds of exposures to get just the right pose. Then, an army of "professional retouching and airbrushing artists" are used to enhance the image into an award-winner. "The final work presented before the judging panel [bares] little resemblance to the original print or negative," the article stated, adding that many "award-winning" photographers "create exceptional prints specifically for competitions, while exerting little effort toward producing the same caliber of images for customers."

Myth #2 *"I always see those photography specials advertised by big department stores. You know, the ones for $19.95 that include several dozen prints. Shouldn't wedding photographers be similar in price?"*

Sorry to say, but that isn't true. Stores that set up these portrait specials hire an amateur to shoot 35mm pictures in a high-volume operation. Unfortunately, professional wedding photography ain't cheap. The time involved in shooting a wedding is one big factor. Weddings take hours of time, shooting on location with expensive professional equipment.

Myth #3 *"I heard that the best bridal portraits are those that are mounted on canvas."*

Not necessarily. Studios like to pitch canvas-mounted portraits as "top-of-the-line," but there is a catch. In fact, a bride in Alexandria, Virginia alerted us to this rip-off. She spoke with a professor of photography who does not recommend canvas-mounted portraits for a couple of reasons. First, in order to be mounted on the canvas, the print must be peeled. As a result, the portrait may crack and reveal the canvas beneath. Second, canvas-mounted portraits must be oiled periodically to preserve the print. And guess who pockets these hefty "re-oiling" fees? You guessed it, the photographer. All in all, the extra expense of canvas may not be worth the hassle.

Step-by-step Shopping Strategies

 ❦ *Step 1:* Once you have booked your ceremony site, contact three to five wedding photographers you have identified by using the sources we listed above. Make an appointment with each studio and be sure to request to meet the actual photographer who will be available on your wedding day.

❦ *Step 2:* On your visit, view as many pictures as you can from the photographer's past work. Be sure that you are looking at the photographer's own work, not a compilation of the studio's "greatest hits." If possible, ask to see a proof book from a recent wedding.

❦ *Step 3:* While looking at the work, decide if the pictures strike an emotional chord with you. Is the posing natural or do the subjects look uncomfortable? Are the pictures in-focus and well-framed? Check for any over or underexposed prints—a common problem among amateur photographers. Look to see icing details in wedding cakes and delicate lace in bridal gowns—if these subjects look "washed out" then the pictures are overexposed.

❦ *Step 4:* Ask to see photos taken under low-light conditions, especially if you are planning to have a candle-lit ceremony. This is good measure of the photographer's skill, since low-light photography is a technical challenge for even the most experienced.

❦ *Step 5:*   Ask the photographer the questions we list later in this chapter. Make sure you get a good reading on the photographer's style and personality.

❦ *Step 6:*   After visiting with several photographers, pick the one you think offers the best quality for the most affordable price. Be sure to compare prices on an "apples to apples" basis, accounting for differences in package sizes and prices. Don't let any photographer pressure you into a quick decision.

❦ *Step 7:*   Once you make your decision, get a written contract from the photographer. Before signing it, take it home to read it thoroughly. A good contract should specify:

❦   The name of the actual photographer who will be at your wedding.

❦   When the photographer will arrive and how long he or she will stay.

❦   A minimum number of proofs the photographer will provide you to choose from.

❦   The exact number of prints and the type of album.

❦   The exact dates the proofs will be ready and the final album will be delivered.

❦   Provisions in case the photographer gets sick or can't make the wedding.

❦   A specific payment schedule that indicates when deposits and final payments are due.

❦   Any additional charges for travel time, overtime costs, or other fees.

❦ *Step 8:*   A few weeks before the wedding, set up another meeting with the photographer to go over details. Discuss your expectations of the photography and clearly state the types of pictures you want. Identify on a written list any special friends or relatives that you want photographed. The more explicit your instructions to the photographer, the better the odds your wedding photography will meet your high expectations. Frankly, you're paying a ton of money to this person so they better do as you say. Bring a copy of this list with you to the reception. After taking all the time to make this list, you want to be prepared in case the photographer forgets his or her copy.

🐾 *Step 9:* In Chapter 15 "Last Minute Consumer Tips," we recommend you pick a trusted friend or relative to be a "surrogate bad cop." This person insures all the vendors are doing their job correctly, while letting you enjoy your wedding day. Introduce the photographer to your "bad cop" early on the wedding day so the photographer knows who to turn to for help when trying to take all your requested photos.

Questions to Ask a Photographer

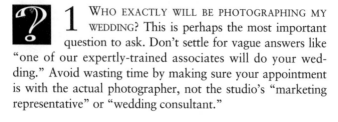

1 WHO EXACTLY WILL BE PHOTOGRAPHING MY WEDDING? This is perhaps the most important question to ask. Don't settle for vague answers like "one of our expertly-trained associates will do your wedding." Avoid wasting time by making sure your appointment is with the actual photographer, not the studio's "marketing representative" or "wedding consultant."

2 CAN I SEE A COMPLETE ALBUM FROM ONE WEDDING YOU PHOTOGRAPHED? By viewing a complete album from one wedding, you can see how the photographer tells a story from beginning to end. Try to look at several albums.

3 CAN I ALSO SEE A PROOF BOOK FROM A RECENT WEDDING? This is the best way to see what you are buying. Proof books are an unedited and uncensored look at what you might receive after your wedding. Good wedding photographers probably have at least one proof book that is waiting to be picked up—ask to see it.

4 DESCRIBE TO ME YOUR PHILOSOPHY AND APPROACH TO WEDDING PHOTOGRAPHY. Ooo, this is a good question. Sit back and listen to what they say. How active a role do they take in the direction of the day's events? Obviously, some photographers may have a canned speech for this question, but you can shake them up by asking good follow-up questions.

5 WHAT IS YOUR SHOOTING SCHEDULE DURING A WEDDING? When do you arrive and what is your general order of shots? How long do the traditional pictures after the ceremony take? This is a real controversial area of wedding photography. See the "The Great Before or After Controversy" discussion after this section.

6 WHAT IS THE BALANCE BETWEEN POSED AND CANDID SHOTS? Some photographers prefer to stage most pictures by formally posing the subjects. Ask the photographer's opinion about whether pictures should be posed or candid. A recent trend in wedding photography is "photo-journalism."

Here the photographer documents the wedding as it happens without any formal posing.

7 HOW MANY EXPOSURES WILL YOU TAKE AT MY WEDDING? IS THERE A LIMIT ON THE NUMBER OF EXPOSURES OR YOUR TIME? Be careful of photographers who limit the number of exposures or time. Too many times we have seen weddings shift into "fast forward" because the photographer's clock was running out. Limiting the number of exposures is also a problem since it restricts the possible choices for your album. About 150 to 200 exposures should be taken to provide enough choices for an album with 60 to 80 prints (our recommendation to adequately cover the day's events).

8 DO YOU BRING ANY BACKUP EQUIPMENT? What will you do if you are sick and unable to shoot the wedding? Cameras (even expensive ones) are just machines. Sometimes they break down. Good photographers should have backup cameras and lighting systems ready in case of a mechanical problem. Having an associate on call in case of emergencies is also prudent.

9 CAN I SEE THE ACTUAL ALBUM THAT COMES WITH MY PACKAGE? A favorite trick of wedding photographers is to show you their past work lovingly bound into leather albums. Then they "forget" to mention to you their packages come with cheaper vinyl albums with plastic-covered pages. And, oh yes, after the wedding, the photographer slips in that "the leather albums are available at an extra fee." Besides the deceptive nature of this practice, some vinyl albums with plastic pages are also problematic since the chemicals in the plastic can damage the prints over time. (Some plastic is okay if it is of "archival-quality;" that is, free of damaging chemicals). Insist on seeing the actual album that is mentioned in the package before you sign the contract.

10 DESCRIBE TO ME THE MOST DIFFICULT WEDDING YOU EVER PHOTOGRAPHED. How did you handle it? Ooo, this is another good question! It can be fascinating to see what the photographer defines as "difficult."

11 HOW LONG WILL YOU KEEP THE NEGATIVES? Here's a good money-saving tip: don't purchase a large number of prints right after your wedding. Instead, buy the minimum now and wait a year or two to finish out the album. Most photographers store negatives for a few years after your wedding and will be happy to do reprints later when you have more money. The photographer who shot our wedding called us five years later and offered to sell us the negatives for $1 each (an offer we accepted)—you may want to ask how long the photographer will store the negatives, whether you'll have an option to buy them and so on.

Helpful Hints

1 PHOTOGRAPHERS' PRICING METHODS MAY BE AS EASY TO UNDERSTAND AS THE FEDERAL INCOME TAX CODE. We are not quite sure why this is. One possible explanation is that photographers want to give you maximum flexibility in choosing prints, albums and portraits. The only problem is that every photographer approaches pricing with a different philosophy that ends up confusing you, the consumer.

Another, more Machiavellian explanation is that photographers want to make comparison shopping more difficult. The lack of a pricing standard makes it very difficult to compare "apples to apples." Instead you have one photographer who offers a complete package with an album of 50 8x10's for $800 and another has an a la carte system. The only way for you to make sense of this is to try to equalize the prices, in the same way the grocery stores often display the price per ounce of certain products. We do this by asking ourselves "So how much does a four-hour package with 50 5x5's and 20 8x10's in an Art Leather album cost?" This package provides adequate coverage for most weddings.

2 SOME OF THE BEST WEDDING PHOTOGRAPHERS ARE WOMEN. Sadly, wedding photography was once (and some say still is) a profession dominated by men. In many cities, men are the majority of professional photographers. The only women at studios are secretaries or the wives of photographers who come along as assistants. Fortunately, today more and more women are actually behind the camera. This is an especially great development for brides and grooms.

Why? That's because weddings are filled with emotions. In our opinion, professional photographers who are best at capturing those emotions are often women. Many times we see male photographers who seem preoccupied with the technical aspects of photography. Obviously, you need a professional photographer who has a firm grasp on the technical end. However, no one benefits when the photographer worries more about F-stops than getting an intimate moment between the bride and her parents.

Unfortunately, sexism in photography is rampant. For example, we have seen evidence that some male photographers (who control photography guilds) have attempted to block women photographers from the wedding market. Some argue that the women are too inexperienced to shoot an event as complex as a wedding. As a result, many women photographers have to work twice as hard to enjoy the same level of reputation as their male counterparts.

Frankly, good wedding photography is not dependent on the sex of the photographer. Just remember not to let outdated sexist attitudes influence the important decision of choosing a wedding photographer.

The Great Before or After Controversy

Ever attended a wedding where it seemed like the bride and groom took forever to make it to the reception? Where are they? Was their limo hijacked by an UFO? More than likely the bride and groom were hijacked by a wedding photographer who took an amount of time equivalent to the Creation of heaven and earth to do the "after-ceremony pictures."

So what exactly are the "after-ceremony pictures?" Basically, these are pictures of the bride and groom with the officiant at the altar, with the bridesmaids, with the groomsmen, with the whole bridal party, with their various relatives, etc. Also, since some churches restrict photography during the actual ceremony, several events from the ceremony (exchanging rings, lighting of the unity candle, the kiss, etc.) may be restaged for posterity. All told, we are talking quite a few pictures here.

Photographers often lie about how long this process takes. Sometimes photographers sound like a cartoonish version of "Name that Tune." (Yes, Bob, I can take those after-ceremony pictures in 20 minutes. Well, Bob, I can do those same pictures in 15 minutes.) In reality, we have known several couples who took one to two *hours* to make it to their reception thanks to the after-ceremony session.

Of course, some bright person recently came up with a solution to this problem. Hey, why not do all those pictures before the ceremony? The only problem: this would require the bride and groom to see each other before the ceremony on the wedding day. OH NO! The screams of wedding etiquette gurus could be heard miles away! "How can you break such a sacred superstition?" they screeched.

Well, let's take a closer look at the prohibition of seeing each other before the ceremony. As far as we can tell, this started back in the year 1008 A.D. when all marriages were arranged and brides and grooms didn't see each other until the wedding day. Keeping the bride and groom separate was intended to prevent Thor the Viking (the groom) from running away in case Freya the Bride was not the beautiful Viking goddess he was promised. Or vice versa.

Today, brides and grooms not only know each other before the wedding, they also probably share the same tube of toothpaste. It seems a little silly that you wouldn't see your fiance the day of the wedding when you were just sharing the same pint of Ben & Jerry's 24 hours earlier.

Furthermore, brides today are taught to believe that the groom stands at the end of the aisle and looks down toward his beautiful bride, all the while thinking "Wow! Isn't she beautiful? Aren't I lucky?" In reality, most grooms are thinking "Thank God she's here. Now we can get this over with."

We're not trying to take away from this special moment but there are several advantages to doing the "after-ceremony" pictures before the wedding (i.e., seeing each other before the ceremony):

🍂 *Everything is perfect:* Hair and makeup are fresh prior to the ceremony and hence those important pictures will capture you at your best. After the ceremony, all the hugging and crying can alter that perfect make-over, etc.

🍂 *You can leave immediately after the ceremony for the reception:* You can have more time seeing relatives and enjoying the party you spent so much effort (and money) planning.

HERE'S OUR RECOMMENDATION: Get to the ceremony site two hours before the wedding. After everyone is dressed, clear out the church with just the groom at the head of the aisle. Then, with appropriate music playing, the bride emerges and walks down the aisle. After this initial meeting, all the formal group pictures are taken before the guests arrive.

Or here's another variation: in a private room at the ceremony site, have the bride and groom meet prior to the ceremony. Here, you and your fiance can exchange gifts, marvel at each other's dapper appearance, gaze at the gown, etc. What's especially nice about this approach is that you actually get 15 minutes alone, just you and your fiance. For the rest of the day you'll be surrounded by friends, relatives, and that ever-present photographer. On a day that's supposed to celebrate your relationship, it's ironic that most brides and grooms have their first private moment in the car *leaving* the reception—after the whole shebang is over.

Pitfalls to Avoid

Pitfall #1
BAIT AND SWITCH AT LARGE PHOTOGRAPHY STUDIOS AND "CELEBRITY" PHOTOGRAPHERS

"My friend who recently got married contracted with a well-known, large studio to do her wedding. Everyone was shocked when the photographer arrived—the studio had sent out a person who had never shot a wedding before! The pictures were a disaster! How can I prevent this from happening to me?"

A practice we call "bait and switch" is definitely the #1 problem we hear about photography studios. Unfortunately, some large studios "bait" engaged couples with a great reputation only to "switch" them by delivering less-than-great wedding photography. How does this happen? Basically, some studios "farm out" their weddings to poorly-trained associates or (even worse) "stringers." Stringers are free-lance photographers who are often amateurs working on the weekend for a few extra bucks. The work of these photographers can be far inferior to professional wedding photographers.

"A famous photographer in our town has taken many pictures of celebrities. Since the studio also does weddings, I assume my fiance and I will get the same high quality photography."

Don't bet on it. Here's how it works in this case: every city in the U.S. probably has at least one "celebrity photographer" who attracts engaged couples to their studio based on their famous name. So who does the wedding photography? Instead of the famous photographer, weddings are often assigned to a no-name associate or a stringer. Hence, couples are "baited" into the studio by the famous photographer and then "switched" to a less-famous associate. While an associate may do good work, this is obviously deceptive since couples are duped into paying a hefty premium for "celebrity photography," then often get much less.

SOLUTION: You can prevent these problems by doing one simple thing: make sure the name of the actual photographer who will shoot your wedding is specified in the contract. Most importantly, before you sign the contract, meet with the actual photographer who will do your wedding and view several albums of his or her work. Don't let the studio show you a few slick sample albums and feed you the line "all our associates are trained in the same great style." Remember your wedding pictures are dependent on who is behind that camera, not any fancy name that's embossed in gold on the studio's stationery.

Pitfall #2
HIDDEN CHARGES.

"I really liked my wedding photographer. Yet, when the final bill came in, we were charged an extra $200 for 'travel time' at 30¢ a mile! When we protested this fee, the photographer pointed to the fine print in his price list. And if we didn't pay the extra fee, he said he wouldn't give us our pictures!"

Beware of fine print or hidden charges for travel time, over-time, special handling and other services. Sometimes, these fees are mentioned only in fine print on the price list, not your contract. One photographer charged an out-of-town bride we met a $500 penalty fee when she returned her proof book three days late, thanks to the post office.

This is why we recommend taking the photographer's contract home first and reading it thoroughly before signing. As we mentioned earlier in the catering chapter, you can request a change in the wording of any clause that makes you uncomfortable. Be wary of deadlines or other provisions that may be unreasonable and ask for an adjustment to fit your needs.

Pitfall #3
SMALL PACKAGES AND HEAVY SALES PRESSURE.

"I contracted with a photographer for one of his small wedding packages that had 20 8x10's in an album. After the wedding, the studio tried to pressure me into buying more prints than the original package—-at those high reprint prices! My only problem—I never realized how many more pictures I would want for my album! Help!"

Ah, this is a popular deceptive practice by wedding photographers. Here, the studio attracts wedding business with low package prices like "just $495 for complete coverage and an album with 20 8x10s." Sounds like a great deal? No, it isn't. That's because most weddings generate dozens of great pictures—photographers often snap 40 to 50 pictures before the ceremony even begins!

The result is that most albums need at least 60 to 80 prints to adequately tell the story of an "average" wedding. Of course, photographers are well aware of this and realize couples will want order many more pictures than those packages with just 20 prints. The result is that the $500 package ends up costing $1000, $1500, or even $2000 by the time the total order is placed. We have talked to photographers who admit this deceptive practice is commonplace. Some studios even make matters worse by adding some heavy sales pressure after the wedding to increase the size of the order.

The most blatant example of this practice was one studio we visited that offered a package for $995 which included just 40 5x7's. The price list then went on to say that "brides and grooms may purchase additional 5x7's or 8x10's to create a more complete story." Those "additional prints" cost $12 for a 5x7 and $20 for an 8x10.

You can prevent this practice by selecting a package that offers the amount of coverage that will realistically tell the story of your wedding. For small weddings (under 100 guests with a short reception), this might just be 40 to 60 prints. Most will require 60 to 80 and some large weddings (with big bridal parties and long receptions) may require 100-plus prints. Be realistic and don't get hooked by low-price packages that only give you a miniscule amount of actual pictures.

Pitfall #4
UNREASONABLE TIME LIMITS.

"I recently attended a wedding where it seemed like the reception moved at the speed of light. Apparently, the photographer was in quite a hurry."

We can't tell you how many weddings we've seen where the reception looked like a sped-up film because the photographer's clock was ticking. After researching this book we now know why: photographers often sell packages with unreasonable time limits.

For example, we interviewed one photographer whose main package had only two and half hours coverage. Since most photographers start their coverage one hour before the ceremony and since the ceremony itself can take up to one hour (including those pesky after-ceremony pictures), this would leave just 30 minutes to cover all the reception activities! No wonder why the bride and groom seemed in a frantic rush to cut the cake, throw the bouquet, toss the garter, and so on! Instead of enjoying the reception, the couple was racing to get everything on film before the photographer's clock expired.

You can prevent this from happening to you by selecting a package with reasonable time limits, or better yet, no time limits at all. In the latter case, the photographer stays at the reception until both of you leave. However, some photographers argue their time is precious and want to impose some time limit. In that case, select a package with at least four hours coverage for an "average wedding." You'll need more coverage (perhaps five or six hours) if you have a long ceremony (Catholic mass) or a large wedding party (all those pictures take more time).

Of course, it shouldn't come as a surprise to you that those same photographers who have those unreasonable time limits also offer overtime at a pricey charge per hour!

We should note that a close kin to this pitfall are photographers who limit the number of exposures they take at a wedding. Ask the photographer about any such limits before you sign a contract.

Pitfall #5
GREATEST HITS ALBUMS.

"I visited a photographer who only showed me an album with pictures from several weddings in it. Shouldn't this person have shown me more work?"

Yes. This problem is what we call the "Greatest Hits Album." Even lousy photographers can occasionally take good pictures. In order to convince you of their "excellence," these photographers compile all those "greatest hits" into one album. Obviously, you are only getting a tiny glimpse of their work.

When you visit a potential photographer, try to see as much work as possible. The best photographers should have sample albums that chronicle one wedding from beginning to end. This allows you to see how the photographer will tell the story of your wedding. Another helpful album to look at is a proof book. Typically, good photographers may have a proof book in the studio that is about to be delivered to a customer. Proof books give the most accurate picture you can get about the photographer's skill since that's exactly what you will use to select your prints later. Unedited and uncensored, you really see what the photographer can (and can't) do well.

Pitfall #6
FRIENDS AND RELATIVES.

"A friend of mine decided to let her uncle, who is a shutterbug, photograph her wedding. What a disaster! His flash didn't work for half the pictures and the other half weren't that exciting anyway."

As you realize, having friends and relatives do various part of your wedding can save you a tremendous amount of money. While you might have a talented aunt who can help alter your gown and a helpful friend who bakes great cakes, you may want to draw the line at the photographs.

Photography is typically high on everyone's priority list and its no wonder—the pictures are all you have left after the wedding. Investing the money in professional photography is a wise choice. Trying to save money here is tempting but we say resist the urge—at least when it comes to your ceremony, the most important pictures of the day. Well-meaning friends and relatives who are amateur photographers often bite off more than they can chew when they shoot a wedding. Adverse lighting conditions and other technical challenges can vex even the most talented amateurs.

If you are on a tight budget and can't afford a professional photographer, consider some of the money-saving tips mentioned earlier. Specifically, hire a professional for the ceremony only and have friends and relatives cover the reception with their own cameras or single-use cameras you provide.

Also be aware that many photographers' contracts specify that they must be the only photographer at the ceremony or reception. They claim that friends and relatives who snap pictures of the bride and groom compete with their work and equipment (their flashes may set off the photographer's flash prematurely). Ask your photographer about any such prohibitions.

Pitfall #7

"YOU GET THE FILM" PACKAGES.

"I met a photographer at a bridal show who told me that he can save me money by giving me all the film after the wedding. Then I go and get the pictures developed. Is this a good deal? What's the catch?"

The catch is that you have to develop the film, which is much more complicated that it sounds. Unlike 35mm film (which you drop off at Kmart and then a few days later—POOF! You have pictures!), medium format negatives must be developed by professional labs. These labs produce negatives that must be "cropped and masked" to produce final prints. We won't go into more detail on cropping and masking, but we can say that we did this for some publicity pictures and it was quite challenging.

The other main problem is dealing with the lab. As a consumer, you may not know the "photo-speak" that photographers use to communicate with the lab. For example, many labs offer less-expensive machine prints and also custom prints, which include touch-ups and artwork. We found communicating with the lab that did our publicity pictures difficult. Furthermore, you have little leverage over the lab in case the developed pictures have quality problems.

Most professional photographers do not sell their negatives (at least not initially after the wedding). Also, what incentive does the photographer have to correct any problems if the last you see of him (or her) is when he gives you the film at the reception? Unless you have an intimate knowledge of professional photography development, you may want to steer clear of these "get the film" packages.

Trends

❦ *Hi-tech touch-ups and proofs:* Computer technology has even invaded the staid field of photography. Some studios use computers to do electronic "touch-ups" on negatives. Others have done away with "proofs" and instead show you computerized previews of portraits within minutes (instead of days.) Art Leather has a new computer software system called Montage that lets you see a preview of your wedding album on a storyboard (call 718-699-6300 for a photographer near you who has this system). The advantage? Once you've decided on the album layout, Montage sends the order to Art Leather automatically, cutting processing time in half.

Another intriguing trend coming soon: video cameras that will take high-quality stills. These could be conceivably printed out on souped-up color laser printers. It's quite possible that in the coming years, photography and video will merge into one—a video/photographer will use one device to take photo stills and live action video. Stay tuned.

❦ *More candids, fewer posed shots:* Perhaps the biggest trend in wedding photography is a move away from posed shots and a larger emphasis on candids. Obviously, the best wedding albums feature a mix of both candids and posed pictures. However, traditional photographers who pose every shot seem to be falling out of favor.

❦ *Black and white photography:* Yes, it's back. Some couples are rediscovering the contrast and beauty of black and white photography. We've seen several truly striking albums that mix black and white and color photography—à la *The Wizard of Oz*.

Special Touches to Make Your Wedding Photography Unique:

1 ADD A MEMORY PAGE TO YOUR ALBUM. This is a page at the front of the album with a copy of your invitation. We've seen couples add a few of the dried flowers from the bride's bouquet and some lace from the bridal gown to this page.

2 PERSONALIZE YOUR WEDDING PHOTOGRAPHY. Instead of an engagement portrait in a studio with a boring blue background, have the picture taken at a special location. Perhaps the place you first met or had your first date. If this isn't practical, a romantic picture in a favorite park at sunset is nice. Obviously, photographers will charge a little more to go on location (perhaps $50 to $100) but it is a nice way to personalize the photography.

3 CHRONICLE YOUR ENGAGEMENT WITH PICTURES. With your own camera, document the wedding process (trying on gowns, tasting cakes, visiting various reception sites) from the proposal to the big day. Undoubtedly, you will receive a photography album as a gift, so here's a use for it. Add your honeymoon pictures in the back to complete the album.

Chapter 10

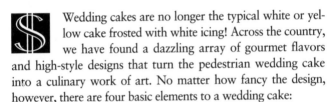

Wedding Cakes

With the four surprising sources discussed in this chapter, we show you how to find an affordable wedding cake that looks as good as it tastes. We'll tell you the biggest myth about wedding cakes and five questions to ask any baker. In short, you will learn how to have your cake and eat it too!

What Are You Buying?

Wedding cakes are no longer the typical white or yellow cake frosted with white icing! Across the country, we have found a dazzling array of gourmet flavors and high-style designs that turn the pedestrian wedding cake into a culinary work of art. No matter how fancy the design, however, there are four basic elements to a wedding cake:

❧ *The cake, itself.* Traditionally, wedding cakes are vanilla-flavored confections. However, today anything goes. Some of the unusual flavors of wedding cake we've found include Mississippi Mud, Pina Colada Rum, white chocolate mousse, and mocha chip.

❧ *The filling.* In addition to cake flavor possibilities, many bakers also offer a variety of fillings. Fillings used to be fruit jams or butter cream icing, but have expanded today to include liqueurs, fresh fruit, custards and mousses. The traditional wedding cake has two layers of cake with one layer of filling in each tier. Lately, we've seen more European torte-style cakes: confections with four or five layers of cake and filling. This torte-style cake tends to be much richer and more moist than an American-style cake.

❧ *The frosting and decorations.* As for the outside of wedding cakes, two key elements are involved. The actual composition of the icing can vary in a wide variety of ways. Some opt for the traditional butter cream icing (to which liqueurs are often added) while rolled fondant or marzipan is also popular (for a Victorian look). Whipped cream icings and meringue icings are other pos-

Wedding cakes don't have to be boring—check out this cheesecake wedding cake draped in imported French chocolate. Created by Elegant Cheesecakes of Half Moon Bay, CA (415) 728-2248.

sibilities available from some bakeries. No longer are you limited to the typical white icing; many brides want their cakes tinted to match the bridal party colors or merely prefer the antique look of an off-white icing.

The second element, decoration, has also changed dramatically. Wedding cakes used to be decorated with icing swags and maybe a few frosting flowers. Today's wedding cakes feature delicate detailing that even copies the lace motif of the bride's dress. Basket weaves are also extremely popular and provide an attractive, contemporary look.

Rather than relying on the standard plastic bride and groom to decorate their cake tops, many brides are using fresh flowers as decoration. Also silk flowers or hard sugar (gum paste) designs are available. The cost of these decorations may be included in the price of the cake or may be extra.

❦ *Delivery and set-up.* Another element you are buying is the delivery and set-up of your cake. This means the actual engineering of the cake with its several layers, possible separations (or stacking if you prefer the tiers to sit one on top of the other) and decoration if you want flowers and greenery. Rental items like the columns and plates for separating tiers are another cost. Some bakers have actually made a special stand for their cakes which they rent to couples for the day.

AVERAGE TOTAL COSTS. Cake prices range from $1 to $4 per serving (this is the typical way cake is priced), but may range up to as much as $8 per serving in places like Manhattan. There is a controversy over how big a serving is; we'll address this question later in the chapter. Deposits range from $50 up to 50% of the total bill. The balance is due usually a week or so before the wedding.

Sources to Find an Affordable Baker

We'd first like to describe the three types of wedding cake bakeries out in the market:

1 CAKE FACTORIES. Better know as commercial bakeries these folks bake and deliver over 10 cakes per Saturday. These businesses may be less personalized than the other two types of bakers. Grocery stores fall into this category, too.

2 RECEPTION SITES AND/OR CATERERS. Quality is sometimes great, sometimes not.

3 OUT-OF-HOME/SMALL BAKERS. These are the hardest to find, but often the best and most creative of these possibilities.

Here are our sources for finding great bakeries:

❧ *Florists.* Because they often work with bakers to help coordinate the floral decorations, florists may have the most contact with bakeries.

❧ *Photographers.* Since they attend many receptions, photographers see the best and worst creations of local bakeries. They also often hear praise or complaints about the cake while they are working.

❧ *Reception sites.* Besides helping set up the cake, as well as serving it, catering managers notice whether guests like the cake or not.

❧ *Bridal shows.* Bakeries often offer samples of their cakes at bridal shows, so here's a great opportunity to taste some without any pressure to buy.

Top Money-saving Secrets

1 ORDER LESS CAKE THAN THE NUMBER OF PEOPLE. If you have a sweets table or groom's cake, consider fewer servings. Also if you will be eating a heavy sit-down meal or have a crowd that doesn't eat a lot of sweets, consider cutting back.

2 CHOOSE AN INDEPENDENT OR OUT-OF-HOME BAKER. This could mean as much as $1 to $2 difference in cost per serving. Out-of-home or small bakeries often have lower overhead which they pass on to brides. Caution: Local health laws may prohibit bakers from operating out of their home. Each city is different, so you may want to check with your local health department.

3 SKIP THE ANNIVERSARY CAKE TOP (SEE PITFALLS).

4   IF YOU WANT THE LOOK OF A LARGE CAKE WITHOUT THE COST, CONSIDER USING FROSTED STYROFOAM "DUMMY" CAKES to make your cake look larger. This may cost as little as $25 extra. A variation on this tip: have your whole cake made out of Styrofoam. After posing with it for pictures, have the reception site wheel it into the kitchen where several sheet cakes are waiting. The site slices up the sheet cakes and guests never know the difference. Why do this? Sheet cakes cost a mere fraction of wedding cakes (50¢ or less per serving) and taste the same.

Getting Started: How Far in Advance?

Because bakeries can make more than one cake on a Saturday, brides may only need two to four months to plan. With some of the large commercial bakeries, you may even need less time (as little as a week's notice). Popular bakeries and popular dates may require more advance planning (between three and six months) and you may want to do this part early anyway to get it out of the way. You will need to know how formal the wedding will be and have a general idea of the number of guests you will have. You can finalize this number later, when the guest count becomes more concrete.

Biggest Myth of Wedding Cakes

Myth #1 *"At every wedding I've ever been to, the wedding cake was tasteless and dry. It's impossible to find a good-tasting cake."*

Wrong. This fallacy is based on all those tasteless white cakes with Crisco-based icings that we remember from the 1970's. Nowadays, with the variety of flavors and choices among bakeries, brides have the ability to serve a beautiful and delicious cake!

Step-by-step Shopping Strategies

❦ ***Step 1:*** Before visiting a baker, you will need to have a general idea of the number of guests invited. Final exact numbers won't be required until a week or two before the wedding date; this will allow you to get a basic price for a cake. Also, knowing your wedding colors will help guide the baker.

❦ ***Step 2:*** Given the resources above, identify two to three bakers who have skill levels and style ideas to fit your needs.

Make an appointment with them and ask if you can have a taste test. Time the appointment to make it easier for the baker to give you a sample (like Friday while they are baking cakes for Saturday weddings).

❦ *Step 3:* At the baker's shop, be sure to look at real photos of their cake designs. Some bakeries use standard cake-design books and tell brides they can make anything from these books. We have found cases, however, where bakeries have promised this and been unable to deliver. It is preferable to see actual photos of what they can do!

❦ *Step 4:* Given the size of your reception, ask the baker for a proposal or estimate of the cost of a cake based on one or two of their styles. Also ask for suggestions on how much cake to buy. The amount of cake to order will depend on several factors: if you will be having a groom's cake or sweets table; how much other food you will be serving (sit-down dinner vs hors d'oeuvres); the time of day; and the size of the slices (paper thin or birthday cake size).

❦ *Step 5:* Make sure you taste a sample of their cake. There is no substitute for having actually tasted it before buying. If a baker doesn't offer taste tests, you should be very cautious. You may have to buy a small six-inch cake from the baker in order to get a taste, but we prefer bakeries who offer free samples—these are usually the best.

❦ *Step 6:* Choose the baker and ask for a signed proposal detailing the design, flavors of both cake and filling, any rentals (like columns or stands), delivery and set-up fees, and deposit information. Don't forget to have the date, place and delivery time clearly written on the proposal. If you are planning far in advance, you may have to adjust the number of servings you will need—find out the last possible moment when you can change numbers.

❦ *Step 7:* Confirm any last-minute details and pay the balance on the cake a week or two before the wedding.

Questions to Ask a Baker

1 DO YOU HAVE ANY PHOTOS OF PREVIOUS DESIGNS? The idea is to see the bakery's actual work, not to look through generic picture books with designs they may never have baked.

2 CAN WE HAVE A TASTE TEST? You may have to wait for a day when they are making cakes, but the best bakeries will offer you a free taste test.

3 ARE THERE ANY EXTRA CHARGES? Some bakeries prefer to break down the charges for almost everything. These items may include: fillings, complex decorations, silk or fresh flowers, delivery, set-up, cake plates and columns, and more. Find out exactly what these items will cost and get a written proposal.

4 WHO WILL DECORATE THE CAKE WITH FRESH OR SILK FLOW- ERS? If you prefer this type of decoration on your cake, you will need to find out how the flowers will be provided and who will decorate the cake. Some bakers can purchase the flowers and decorate it themselves. Others will get the flowers from your florist. Still other bakers are willing to allow the florist to decorate the cake.

5 HOW FAR IN ADVANCE IS THE CAKE PREPARED? This may be a delicate question to ask, but you will want to know how fresh the cake is that you are buying. Some high-volume bakeries will make up cakes ahead of time and freeze them until a day or so before your event. We don't recommend these bakeries since we believe fresh cakes are usually more tasty.

Pitfalls to Avoid

Pitfall #1
ANNIVERSARY CAKE TOPS

"The baker I visited told me that 'of course you will want to save the top tier of the cake for your first anniversary.' This sounds like a silly tradition!"

Yes, we agree. Saving the top of the wedding cake to eat on your first anniversary is a common tradition in many areas of the country. This entails having mom or someone else remember to take the top home, wrap it very carefully, and put it in your freezer. Even supposing you have room in your freezer, the taste of the cake after 12 months may leave much to be desired. In fact, if you serve the cake at your wedding instead, you may be able to save 10% to 20% off your bak- ery bill—a much better deal than a stale year-old cake! If you want to follow this tradition, we recommend calling up your baker in a year and buying a small, freshly-made cake to cele- brate with on your first anniversary.

Pitfall #2
MYSTERIOUS WHITE ICING.

"We attended a wedding last weekend that had a beautiful wedding cake. But, when we tasted the cake, there was this terrible, greasy aftertaste. Yuck! What causes this problem?"

So what makes a cake's icing white? Well, a key ingredient in icing is butter—which creates a problem for bakers. Most butter made in the U.S. is yellow, which gives icing an off-white or ivory color. To get white icing, bakers must use expensive white butter (imported from Europe). Unfortunately, some bakers use a less expensive short-cut to get white "butter-cream" icing—they add white shortening like Crisco. Yuck! That's why some cake icing has a greasy aftertaste. If you want white icing, you might ask your baker how they make their icing white. For example, some bakeries offer a meringue icing (made from egg whites), while others do fondant, a paste of sugar, water and corn syrup that's rolled over the cake. Both of these options don't sacrifice taste for a white look.

Pitfall #3
WELL-MEANING FRIENDS AND RELATIVES.

"My aunt has offered to bake my wedding cake. She's good at baking birthday cakes but isn't a wedding cake much more complicated?"

That's right. Offers like this are made with the best possible intentions but, if accepted, can be disastrous. Baking a wedding cake is far more complex than baking a birthday cake from a Betty Crocker mix. The engineering skills required to stack a cake and keep it from falling or leaning are incredible. Unless you have a friend or relative who is a professional baker or pastry chef, politely refuse their offer. Consider telling them you've already contracted with a baker to make your cake if you don't want to offend them.

REAL WEDDING TIP:
Disappearing Deposits

 Julie Jauregui Holloway e-mailed us this interesting story about a disappearing deposit that is a good lesson for all brides. "Our baker charged us a $75 deposit for the lucite tiers in our wedding cake—he told us we had one month to return them or we'd lose the deposit. Well, after the wedding, we had our maid of honor drop them off since we'd be on our honeymoon. Unfortunately, she forgot about the deposit and didn't ask for any money back. The bakery also wouldn't give her a receipt. Well, you can guess what happened next—we got back, asked the bakery for the money and they claimed they gave it to maid of honor. It took three visits to the bakery before the manager agreed to refund our money."

Pitfall #4

EARLY DELIVERY AND COLLAPSING CAKES.

"My baker delivered my cake nearly five hours before my reception. In the interim, someone or something knocked the cake over and destroyed it! How could I have prevented this?"

This is a problem that often occurs with large bakeries that have many deliveries. The cake is dropped off (and set-up) hours before the reception and left unattended. As you can guess, Murphy's Law says that an unattended wedding cake is a collapsed wedding cake. No one at the reception site may admit to knocking it over but you can imagine how "things happen" during a wedding reception set-up. Prevent this problem by insisting the baker deliver the cake within two hours prior to the reception. You may want to coordinate with the catering staff to limit any scheduling snafus.

Trends

❦ *New flavors.* Look out, plain vanilla. New flavors are also coming into vogue, ranging from well-known favorites like carrot or pound cake to exotics like Amaretto mousse cake and orange ginger poppyseed. Fillings are also becoming a popular addition for many cakes and include fresh fruits, custards and liqueurs.

❦ *Chocolate wedding cakes.* In the South, chocolate groom's cakes are very popular and are served on the wedding day with the bride's cake. In areas where groom's cakes are unknown, some brides opt for a white-frosted chocolate cake as the centerpiece of their wedding reception. Some brides add chocolate cakes or truffles to their sweets table in other areas of the country to satisfy the tastes of those chocoholics out there.

❦ *New decorations.* Instead of traditional columns, we've seen more stacked cake designs, with ornate decorations such as hand-molded sugar flowers. Just as bridal gowns are becoming simpler and more elegant, so too have cakes. Victorian-style cakes with smooth marzipan icing and delicate royal icing detailing are popular as well. As you can see, cakes are now a personal statement, instead of uniform white creations that look the same from wedding to wedding.

Unique Ideas

1 ETHNIC TRADITIONS. Many couples incorporate ethnic traditions into their wedding cake. For example, the French wedding cake is actually a cone-shaped confection

made up of cream-filled pastry puffs stuck together with caramelized sugar. Guests serve themselves by merely grabbing a cream puff from the cone! Another ethnic cake is the Kransekai (as the Norwegians call it) or Mandelringstarta (as the Swedes refer to it). Popular among the Scandinavians in Minnesota, this confection is made of almond cake arranged in graduated rings. You may be aware of other ethnic cakes that will adapt well to your wedding.

2 DIFFERENT FLAVORS IN DIFFERENT TIERS. Can't decide between Italian Creme, mocha chip and carrot cake? Why not try all three in different tiers of your cake?

3 CHEESECAKE. Ah, here's an unique idea we are particularly fond of: cheesecake wedding cakes. Available in many different flavors, cheesecakes can be frosted with cream cheese icing or left plain and decorated with fresh fruit or flowers. Yum!

Spotlight: Home Bakers

One home baker we know describes her business as the "hobby that got out of hand." Lucky for brides-to-be that this hobby did evolve into a business! Home bakers are often the most talented bakers in a city because their cakes are individually hand-crafted—unlike commercial bakeries that churn out copy-cat cakes. We've found home bakers are more willing to try something unusual—like a new flavor or design. Low price is, of course, another big advantage: home bakers may be less expensive than commercial bakeries because of lower overhead.

A disadvantage of home bakers, however, is their popularity. Because they can only make and deliver a few cakes on a Saturday, some bakers may be booked up far in advance. If you are considering a home baker, contact him or her three to six months before the wedding to set up a visit. You may even have to plan further in advance. With one baker, we had to make an appointment 10 months prior to the wedding date!

Another problem may occur with the health department regulations in your area. Many cities and counties have legal restrictions on food preparation companies operated out of a residence. Therefore, some home bakers operate illegally—ask if you have any doubts.

If you are looking for a home baker, a good source is area caterers. Also ask reception sites and other wedding businesses like photographers and florists. Friends are a good way to to find a talented in-home baker, too, so ask any recently married couples you know.

Chapter 11

Wedding Videos

Lights! Camera! Money! Wedding videos are an expensive newcomer to the wedding market. In this chapter, we cut through the technical mumbo-jumbo to give you a practical guide to finding an affordable yet talented videographer.

What Are You Buying?

 Basically, there are two things you are buying when you hire a videographer: the cameraperson's time, and the video itself.

❧ *The cameraperson's time.* Many videographers will charge you for their time first and foremost. Most offer packages with a time limit of three, four, five or more hours. Overtime is charged on an hourly basis. Some other videographers will charge a flat fee for the whole wedding and reception.

Besides hiring a cameraperson for a certain amount of time, you are also buying his or her talent and personality. As with photographers, it is very important to find a videographer who is not only skilled at camera work but who also is compatible with your personality. You will be working with him or her as much as with the photographer. And, of course, the videographer's investment in equipment is important—we'll discuss this later.

❧ *The final product.* The most important item you're buying is the videotape. There are several types of tapes (or styles of videographers) available:

RAW FOOTAGE. This is a tape that simply starts at the beginning of your ceremony and runs, uninterrupted, to the end of your reception. There is no editing or post-production graphics. Raw footage videos should be the least expensive option.

EDITED "IN CAMERA." This type of video also does not have post-editing or added graphics. However, the videographer edits your video "in-camera." This means the cameraperson shuts off the camera during any uninteresting moments or rewinds and tapes over any unnecessary footage. If done by a professional, this option can work very well. It will usually be moderately priced in comparison with other types of tapes.

POST-EDITED. This type of tape is usually the most expensive because the videographer spends the most time on it. Videographers "post-edit" a tape after the wedding and reception. During this production, the videographer will take raw footage, cut out the boring parts (if there are any!), smooth the transitions, and add in titles and music. Some videographers add still photos (baby pictures, honeymoon photos) to give the tape a truly personal feel. If you have multi-camera coverage, post-editing blends the footage from several cameras to make for a more interesting tape. We've even seen tapes with special effects similar to those seen on television newscasts. Many videographers charge an additional hourly fee for post-editing, while others may have packages which include editing and special effects.

HIGHLIGHTS. In addition to tapes that cover the entire wedding and reception, some videographers offer brief highlight tapes that condense the day's events into a short montage that's 10 or 20 minutes long. Set to music and crisply edited, these tapes are perfect when you don't want to torture your friends with the full-length version of your wedding tape.

Most wedding video packages include one copy of the video tape. Extra copies often cost more; however some videographers have packages that include copies for parents.

AVERAGE TOTAL COSTS: The average wedding video costs about $850, although prices are all over the board depending on what you get. In small towns, a one-camera, unedited video could cost under $500. On the other end of the scale, you may pay over $5000 for multi-camera coverage with fancy editing and graphics in the country's largest cities.

Sources to Find a Videographer

 Wedding videos are a relative newcomer to the bridal market. Only in the 1980's did the videotaping of weddings really take off. Finding a good videographer can still be a challenge. Here are some of the best sources:

❧ *Recently-married couples.* These folks can give some of the best advice about videographers. Look at friends' videos to decide what styles, editing and extras you might want.

❦ *Professional associations.* The Wedding and Event Videographers Association International (WEVA) offers a toll-free line (800) 501-WEVA or (941) 923-5334 for brides to call to get a referral to local videographers. WEVA has nearly 4000 members internationally. While the organization does not certify videographers, they do require members to adhere to certain professional standards. Another source: national videographer franchises like Video Data Services (800) 836-9461 or (716) 424-5320. With over 200 franchises, Video Data Services has been in business since 1978.

❦ *Television stations.* Many camerapersons at TV stations moonlight on weekends shooting weddings. They may have access to high-tech editing and special effects computers. In Ft. Worth, Texas, for example, one of the most popular videographers for weddings is the chief videographer for the NBC affiliate. One tip we heard from a reader: when you call a TV station, bypass the receptionist and ask to speak directly to a cameraperson. Why do this? Some stations don't like their camerapeople moonlighting at weddings and instruct receptionists to tell callers that this service isn't available.

❦ *Wedding photographers.* This may be one of the best sources. Photographers will be able to recommend good videographers they've seen at other weddings. Occasionally, photographers and videographers have conflicts at weddings. You can avoid this by choosing two people who have worked together before. Don't, however, feel obliged to use a photographer's suggestion without checking out the videographer carefully to see if he or she fits your needs.

❦ *Ceremony site coordinators.* These folks often have firsthand knowledge about videographers since they are responsible for reciting the rules to them and determining where they can stand. Site coordinators can recommend people familiar with the site who are also easy to work with. And they may also hear back from brides about how good (or bad) the finished video is.

Understanding Videographers: Some Basics

When shopping for a professional wedding videographer, there are several elements to remember as you look at their work and talk about their options.

1 LIGHTING. As with photography, lighting is key to a good video. Often, existing room light is not bright enough to get a good picture. In fact, one of the biggest fears couples used

to have about videographers was their use of bright lights to compensate for dark rooms. In the past, videographers would need to flood a room with light in order to get good video.

Well, we have good news for those of you out there who are hesitating about wedding videos. Advancements in technology have led to new professional video cameras that are sensitive enough for use with only available room light. If they do require any extra light, videographers can use smaller, low-wattage lights that are less distracting and still get good video.

2 SOUND. Especially during your once-in-a-lifetime wedding ceremony, it is vital to get perfect sound on your video. Thanks to high technology, great video sound is possible in a number of ways.

There are basically three ways to capture sound at the ceremony. The least effective is through a "boom" microphone. This is attached to the video camera and often picks up every sound in the room, including your vows. If you don't want to hear your seven year old cousin Joey squirming around in his seat and fidgeting, the boom microphone is not for you.

The next option is the "hard-wired" microphone. This type of microphone has a wire which connects it to the camera. The other end, typically a small clip-on mic, is attached to the groom's lapel, the official, the podium or the kneeling bench. This may not be ideal for some people, especially if there is a lot of movement during the ceremony. The sound quality is usually average to good.

The final (and most common) option is a "wireless" microphone. This microphone sends sound to the camera via a radio transmitter (about the size of a small Walkman) attached to the groom's waist. Wireless microphones that are not "high band" may pick up interference from police radios or other radio equipment. High band microphones, on the other hand, can weed out most interference and produce a clean, clear "I do" on your tape.

Remember that audio is as important as video. When looking at sample tapes, listen for rough transitions or conversations that are cut off. Sloppy audio can keep you from following the sequence of events on the tape.

3 EQUIPMENT. *"All this video camera stuff is so bewildering—I hear there are 8mm cameras, VHS, Super-VHS . . . I'm so confused! I can't even program my VCR! Help!"*

Well, you're on your own with the VCR. But we can help you to understand the different cameras used for wedding videography.

We've extensively interviewed videographers across the country, so here's the scoop. There are three broad categories of cameras: consumer, professional and industrial. Also, there are three tape formats most used by videographers: VHS, Super VHS and Hi8 (a high definition 8mm format). In the next section, we'll explain more about videotape itself.

As for consumer-type cameras, you are probably familiar with their tape quality. Frankly, they aren't the best, clearest pictures we've ever seen.

In contrast, professional-grade cameras (called "prosumer" in the trade) provide much clearer pictures and brighter colors. These professional cameras (one such brand is the Panasonic ProLine) use advanced computer technology to produce better video.

The best professional cameras use "three-chip" technology—a separate computer chip to process red, blue and green colors. Unfortunately, these cameras are also quite expensive ($5000 to $15,000 in price!). As a result, fewer than half of all videographers use them. The balance use "one-chip" cameras.

Is it bad for videographers to use single-chip cameras? No, many combine single-chip cameras with Super-VHS or Hi8 tape to provide very crisp video. Are you confused yet? Well, in the next section, we'll try to explain why Super-VHS and Hi8 formats have become so popular.

What about industrial cameras? This category includes broadcast-quality cameras used by TV stations. These ultra-high priced cameras need bright light to produce good video and, hence, are rarely used by videographers who shoot weddings. Perhaps they're just overkill.

So, what does this all mean? Well, don't get bogged down in this technical mumbo-jumbo. What makes this even more challenging is the fact that video technology (cameras and formats) changes so quickly. The key is to look at the final product—the camera skills of the videographer are just as crucial as the type of equipment he or she uses.

4 THE VIDEOTAPE *"My maid of honor and bridesmaids are planning to give us a VCR as a wedding present from themselves and their spouses. They wanted to know whether we want a VHS tape player or a Super VHS player. What difference does it make and will the videographer be able to provide the right kind of tape?"*

Basically, the difference between VHS and Super-VHS machines is that the Super-VHS format provides more lines of resolution. Translated into English, this means the picture is even sharper for Super VHS tapes than for regular VHS tapes. If you're offered a Super-VHS VCR as a gift, by all means take it. Yet, it is probably an unnecessary expense for most couples—regular VCR's will play most wedding tapes with acceptable clarity. In the next few years, look for digital tape (and digital VCR's) to make a splash on the video market (currently all the formats mentioned above use analog tape).

Many videographers are capable of producing either type of videotape. If you have to have Super VHS, check with the videographer before you make an appointment—some companies still shoot with regular VHS cameras.

What if the videographer shoots with a Super-VHS or Hi8 camera and all you have is a regular VHS player? Well, both formats can be transferred to plain VHS.

5 CAMERA ANGLE *"Some sample videos I've viewed show the bride and groom only from the back or from strange angles in the church. Is there any way I can avoid such problems?"*

Some of the responsibility for these strange angles and shots belongs to the church or synagogue you choose. Many don't allow the videographer to move once the bride begins her walk down the aisle. They may also assign the cameraperson to a particular part of the sanctuary (like the back balcony!). This is why it is important to check with the policies of your ceremony site. Also, you can ask the clergy if your videographer can get a better view (they might respond more to a bride and groom's request than that of the cameraperson).

Also, it is just as important to have your videographer visit the ceremony site (even attending the rehearsal) to see where he or she will be setting up. This advanced preparation may help avoid those camera angle problems. Be aware that some videographers will scout out the ceremony site for free—others charge a fee.

Many videographers today offer multi-camera shoots with two or even three cameras at the ceremony. Do you need three camerapeople? Not always. Some of these cameras may be remote-controlled from the back of the church. The different views are edited together on the final tape to provide a much more interesting video than single-camera coverage.

Top Money-saving Secrets

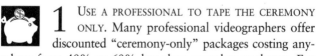 1 USE A PROFESSIONAL TO TAPE THE CEREMONY ONLY. Many professional videographers offer discounted "ceremony-only" packages costing anywhere from 40% to 60% less than complete packages. For the reception, consider asking friends and relatives to bring their cameras to shoot footage. Note: beware that some studios use their least-experienced videographer to shoot the "ceremony-only" packages. Confirm who will be your videographer and view their work before booking.

2 HAVE A FRIEND TAPE YOUR WEDDING. *ONLY AS A LAST RESORT!* If you choose to go this route, make sure your friend or relative has a tripod (to avoid those wobbly shots) and plenty of extra batteries. We don't really recommend this strategy since the quality of consumer-type cameras is less than professional-grade equipment. Also, your guests may enjoy your wedding more if they aren't stuck behind a camera.

3 NEGOTIATE LOWER RATES for less-popular wedding days/months.

4 ASK THE VIDEOGRAPHER IF THEY WILL DO A SCALED-BACK PACKAGE FOR LESS MONEY. Fewer bells and whistles (post-editing, special effects) mean less time for the videographer. Ask them if they can work out a "special package" that meets your budget.

5 REQUEST A VOLUME-DISCOUNT FOR TAPE COPIES. If you need several copies, the video company should be able to offer you a volume discount off their normal prices.

6 USE MULTI-CAMERA COVERAGE ONLY AT THE CEREMONY. While it's a nice luxury to have two or three cameras to cover the wedding ceremony, it may be overkill at the reception.

Getting Started: How Far in Advance?

 As with photographers, good professional videographers can book months ahead of the date. Popular summer months are often spoken for by January or February in many major metropolitan areas. In New York City, videographers are commonly booked up to two years in advance! We recommend you hire your videographer six to nine months in advance (as soon as or even before you book a photographer).

Biggest Myths About Wedding Videography?

 Myth #1 "*We had a friend videotape our wedding. The tape was just OK—there were several parts that are out of focus and shaky. Our friend said we could just get that fixed.*"

Don't count on it. You just can't "fix" a bad video that's blurry or missing audio parts. The best you can do is cut out the bad parts and try to piece it together. We've heard quite a few horror stories from engaged couples who had a well-meaning friend or relative tape their wedding, only to end up with a disaster.

Myth #2 "*I watched my friend's wedding video and found myself straining to hear the couple say their vows. We're writ-*

ing our own vows and we really want to be able to hear what we say to one another on our video. Is it true that it's impossible to get clear sound on a video?"

Sound quality depends heavily on the type of microphone. We recommend the use of a high-band wireless microphone attached to the groom's lapel. This type of microphone will overcome the disadvantages discussed earlier that come with boom microphones and hard-wired microphones. If you can't find anyone with a wireless high-band microphone, listen carefully to the sound quality on sample tapes and decide which offers the best sound.

Some videographers today use multiple microphones to capture audio at the ceremony. The best even mix the audio "live" at the site, adjusting the volume level during the ceremony to make sure the best possible tape is made.

Myth #3 *"I saw one sample tape that had interviews of the guests on it. I thought the interviews were kind of embarrassing and the guests seemed uncomfortable. Do I have to have interviews on my tape?"*

The answer is an obvious "no." We've seen several tapes where a good friend had too much to drink and related a sick joke. In another case, a guest suddenly had a microphone shoved into her face and made a few comments that don't need to be saved for posterity.

Well this doesn't have to happen in your video. First, if you don't want any interviews, be specific with the videographer—especially if he or she has these segments on sample tapes. But if you do want interviews, choose a package that will allow you to edit out any embarrassing comments made by your guests. And don't forget to specify what kind of interviews you want. One couple we talked to asked their videographer to only interview relatives. Another couple only wanted guests who really wanted to speak on the tape. These precautions should help you avoid the "video from hell."

Step-by-step Shopping Strategies

 ❦ *Step 1:* Using the sources discussed above, make appointments with two to three video companies. Ask to see a demonstration tape or a tape of a recent wedding. If you contact a studio with several associates, make sure you will be meeting with the person who will videotape your wedding. As with photographers, each videographer's style is different, so meeting the actual cameraperson is key.

❦ *Step 2:* See the sample or demo tape of each company. View more than just "highlight" tapes—ask to see a complete wedding. Even better, ask if they can show you any wedding videos shot at your ceremony/reception site. Don't let the videographer fast-forward through any parts of the tape you want to see or hear.

❦ *Step 3:* Check for sound quality, harsh lighting or uncomfortable-looking guests. Make sure you can hear the vows. This is the most important aspect of the video—the part you want to capture. If the lighting is extremely bright, guests may squint or turn away. You want everyone to feel comfortable so watch this aspect carefully.

❦ *Step 4:* If this is an edited tape, ask yourself if the editing is smooth and professional. Does the tape have a home-movie feel or a raw-footage quality? Or is it seamlessly edited with a smooth flow? Is the video enjoyable or boring? Decide if the special effects (if any) add or detract from the video.

❦ *Step 5:* Make sure the personality of the cameraperson is pleasant. If you don't feel comfortable with this person, shop for another videographer.

❦ *Step 6:* Get references from previous customers. Ask these recent brides if they were satisfied with their tapes. Did they meet their expectations? If they had to do it over again, would they choose that same company? Checking references here is especially important since many video companies are young and some lack professional track records.

❦ *Step 7:* Once you have decided on a videographer, get a signed contract. Specify the date, time, place, editing and other special points. Make sure they note any preferences too: will there be any interviews, for example.

❦ *Step 8:* Meet with your videographer again closer to the wedding date to discuss any special people you'd like on your tape. It may even be a good idea to draw up a list of names. Also go over the sequence of events and talk about any changes or additions.

Questions to Ask a Videographer

1 WILL YOU ATTEND THE REHEARSAL? Are you familiar with my ceremony/reception site? These are critical questions since the videographer must determine the best angle, lighting options and sound needs for your wedding and reception. Many ceremony sites

have specific rules about where the videographer can set up. Some sites may also present sound or lighting challenges—the more familiar he or she is with the site the better.

2 EXACTLY WHAT WILL THE FINAL PRODUCT LOOK LIKE? Find out how long the tape will be, what type of editing or graphics will be done or any additional touches that may be added. Often we've seen demo tapes with music synced to the action, fancy cursive graphics and even dissolves or other effects. Then we've been informed that all those options are extra on top of the package price. Watch out for these tactics.

3 WHO EXACTLY WILL BE SHOOTING MY VIDEO? Again, remember that some companies, especially in busy summer months, may send out unskilled amateurs to some of their weddings. Meet the actual videographer and see their work before booking. Unfortunately, some studios only assign their best camerapeople to the highest-priced packages.

4 ARE THERE ANY PHOTOGRAPHERS IN TOWN THAT YOU HAVE HAD DIFFICULTY WORKING WITH? The fit between photographer and videographer is critical—if they don't work together as a team, the scene may get ugly. Obviously, it may be difficult to get a truthful answer here since many videographers don't want to offend you or bad-mouth local photographers.

5 EXPLAIN YOUR GENERAL WEDDING SHOOTING SCHEDULE. This way you can find out what they do before the ceremony, whether they do interviews or not and how they expect the evening to run.

6 WILL I GET THE MASTER TAPE AND HOW MANY COPIES COME WITH THE PACKAGE? The master tape is the original tape. Some videographers keep this and give you copies just as photographers keep your negatives. If you want the master, shop for a videographer with a different policy. As for tape copies, they are usually extra. Plan ahead for this additional expense. The cost per copy could range from $20 to $80.

7 DO YOU HAVE BACK-UP EQUIPMENT? Do you edit your own work? Do you offer a guarantee? Back-up equipment is a critical issue—the best videographers have back-up equipment with them at the ceremony/reception sites, not in a car or office across town. Even if it takes just a few minutes to run out to a car, you can miss important moments.

8 WILL YOU TAKE A LITTLE TIME TO EDUCATE ME ABOUT VIDEO PRODUCTION? This is a trick question suggested to us by Bill Kronemyer, a New Jersey videographer. Bill told us you're

not looking for a technical lecture but insights into the videographer's philosophy. The videographer should acknowledge that each wedding is different—and be honest about the shortcomings of his or her work. "Beware of the person who doesn't or can't explain things to you. Or one who thinks he's the greatest on earth. Deep down, he is probably insecure. Picking a down-to-earth 'realist' is often a better bet than a 'braggart.'"

Helpful Hints

1 CHOOSE A PACKAGE WITH ENOUGH TIME TO COVER THE EVENT. A four to six hour package should provide enough time to capture a typical wedding (allow more time for sit-down dinners or receiving lines). If you think your reception will go over, ask about overtime availability and charges. Some packages end when the cake is cut while others run to the reception's end. Ask when overtime kicks in—if the cake is cut an hour late? What if the bride gets to the church 45 minutes late? Confirming the exact conditions that lead to overtime charges is important.

2 MANY UNCONTROLLABLE FACTORS CAN AFFECT THE QUALITY OF YOUR VIDEO. For example, church P.A. systems can interfere with low-band wireless microphones. Another problem may be caused by your officiant or site coordinator. At one wedding we attended, the priest requested the videographer stand in a certain spot. The videographer thought she would have a good view of the couple's faces. However, the priest then decided to hold the entire ceremony with the couple facing the congregation. This left the videographer taping their backs for the entire wedding!

We feel its best to try to keep a sense of humor about these uncontrollable events. Having the videographer attend the rehearsal should also cut down on the surprises.

Pitfalls to Avoid

Pitfall #1
"DIRECTOR'S DISEASE"
  "I was a bridesmaid in a friend's wedding recently and I was very shocked at the behavior of the videographer. He kept ordering everyone around, telling us what to do. Is there a way to avoid this problem at my own wedding?"

Occasionally, we've run into an inexperienced wedding videographer who suffers from that strange malady known as "director's disease." These camerapeople tend to expect weddings and receptions to conform to some sort of script for an all-star movie production. Instead of simply capturing the day as it happens, they try to direct the actors (bride and groom) in a performance (the wedding).

In many ways, however, a wedding is a videographer's nightmare—unscripted and unrehearsed, things often happen spontaneously. Experienced videographers will have discovered this fact and (hopefully) will adapt to each fun, yet frantic event on your wedding day. If you check references carefully and ask former brides about this aspect, you can avoid a videographer infected with "director's disease."

Pitfall #2
MISSING KEY EVENTS

"One of my friends complained that her wedding video was missing one of the events of the evening she thought was most important: her brother giving the toast. I don't want anything to be missed at my wedding. How can I prevent this?"

The bouquet toss, garter throw, toast and cake cutting among other things, are of paramount importance to most brides and grooms. Your videographer should at least be around for these events at your wedding. Amateurs and unseasoned professionals have been known to miss them—be sure to check with references.

When you hire a professional, you should also meet with him or her prior to the wedding to discuss those things you want in your video. Be specific and have him write your preferences down. Also bring him a list of important people you want in your video. Have a copy of this list with you at the wedding.

Pitfall #3
AMATEURS WITH LOUSY CAMERAS

No need to beat a dead horse! Just avoid amateurs with lousy camera skills, trying to pass themselves off as full-price professionals.

Pitfall #4
BIG SCREEN TVS.

"My wedding video doesn't look very good on my parent's big-screen TV. It looked fine on our 19" TV—what's the problem?"

The problem with big screen TV is that it uses a projection process to get the picture onto the screen. Unfortunately, this process causes a video's resolution to suffer. In other words, most videos (including movies) may look fuzzy on a big-screen TV. Don't blame the videographer for this problem!

Pitfall #5
DECEPTIVE DEMO TAPES.

"We saw this video company at a bridal show. They were playing a demo tape that looked great. When we asked them where it was shot, however, they sheepishly told us it wasn't really their work. What gives?"

Some franchised video companies will give their new franchisees generic demo tapes to help drum up business (since the fledgling company may not have examples of their own work yet). Confirm the tape your seeing is actually their work. While every new videographer has to start somewhere, we'd recommend he or she not learn the ropes on your wedding.

Pitfall #6
NICKEL AND DIME CHARGES

"One video company in my area advertises a super-low price for wedding coverage. When I met with them, however, there were several 'additional charges' that inflated the package price."

We've heard this complaint from several of our readers. In Wisconsin, for example, we discovered a video company that charges extra for each microphone ($50 a pop). And, wouldn't you guess it, the videographer recommends *lots* of microphones. Other additional charges could include exorbitant fees for editing, music, graphics, special effects and tape copies. The best tip to avoid this is to get "apples to apples" bids from several companies. Don't be fooled by super-low prices that seem too good to be true.

Trends

❧ *Digital editing.* Instead of editing on analog tape, cutting-edge videographers now edit tapes digitally on souped-up computer workstations. This speeds the process and gives a cleaner look.

❧ *Splashier graphics.* These new and constantly improving techniques make tapes less like home movies and more like Hollywood productions. Some unique additions we've noticed include dissolves and fades and even a technique called posterization (which freezes the picture and "colorizes" it). Adding still photos of your childhood at the tape's beginning and snapshots of your honeymoon at the end provides a complete video "album" feel to your tape. Of course, all these goodies tend to push up the price of packages.

❦ *Multi-camera shoots.* More and more videographers are using multi-camera shoots to capture the ceremony. Thanks to remote controlled cameras, however, this doesn't mean you have to have multiple camerapeople, which will inflate the final tab. Another trend: inter-format editing. Here the videographer combines Super VHS footage from a balcony angle with a remote camera that's shooting Hi8. Thanks to new editing techniques, all the footage can be seamlessly edited and transferred to regular VHS.

❦ *Combination photo/video studios.* Some photography studios have the attitude "if you can't beat 'em, join 'em" when it comes to video—many are adding "video divisions." Whether this involves sub-contracting out to another video company or actually having a "staff videographer," photographers have seized on the video trend as a lucrative side-line. Of course, just because the studio offers excellent photography doesn't mean they know beans about video. Be skeptical. Shop for each service as if they were separate companies.

Chapter 12

Entertainment

From harpists to dance bands, choosing music for your wedding and reception can be challenging. In this chapter, you'll learn ingenious ways to find your city's best musicians. We'll also take an in depth look at the controversy between bands and disc jockeys as reception entertainment.

What Are You Buying?

 ❦ *Ceremony Music.* From royal weddings to simple civil ceremonies, music has been an integral part of wedding ceremonies for hundreds of years. However, the role music plays varies from religion to religion. The main issue is the difference between liturgical and secular music. Basically, liturgical music features sacred words from the bible while secular music does not. Policies about what is and what is not appropriate will vary from site to site.

Nevertheless, most churches have a staff organist or music coordinator who will help you with selections. Organists charge a fee based on the amount of time needed to rehearse, learn new pieces, etc. Other musicians (such as soloists, pianists, harpists) may also be employed for the ceremony. Ceremony music can generally be broken down into three categories:

1 THE PRELUDE. Typically 20 to 40 minutes prior to the ceremony, prelude music sets the mood. Even if you don't have specific pieces in mind for the prelude, you can tell the organist/musicians your preferences for happy, upbeat music or perhaps more somber, quiet pieces. Sometimes an eclectic mix of different tempos and musical styles is a nice compromise.

2 PROCESSIONAL/RECESSIONAL. Processional music heralds the arrival of the bridesmaids and, later, the bride to the wedding ceremony. At the end of the ceremony, recessional music is basically the music everyone walks out to. Typically, the slower processional has a more regal and majestic feel than the quicker-paced recessional music. Sometimes, different musical selections are played for the entrances of the

bridesmaids and the bride. Or the same piece can be played at a different tempo as the bride enters the ceremony site.

3 MUSIC DURING THE CEREMONY. Soloists or the congregation's choir are often used during this part of the ceremony.

AVERAGE TOTAL COSTS: So, how much does this all cost? Most ceremony musicians charge $50 to $150 per musician per hour. Some may have two to three hour minimums. When you hire ceremony musicians, the only thing you may need to supply is sheet music for unfamiliar pieces. If you're having a string quartet, don't forget to provide chairs without arms so they can bow!

❦ *Reception Music.* Ah, now the party starts! Whether you plan to have only soft background music for listening or a raucous rock and roll bash, there are several aspects to what you're buying. For listening music (a harpist or string quartet), you may simply want to employ the same musicians who played at your ceremony. If dancing is preferred, you have two basic choices:

1 BANDS. When you hire a live band to play at your reception, you are contracting for a particular set of musicians to play a specified period of time. Most bands require periodic breaks throughout the evening and union rules may mandate break times. Bands provide everything (from instruments to the amplification system), but your reception site may need to provide a piano. Sometimes bands throw in a free hour of light cocktail music while guests dine. A specific repertoire of music is often implied in the contract—the best reception bands play a wide variety of music to please everyone's preferences.

So how much does a band cost? The price for four hours on a Saturday night can range from $500 to $5000. The key variables are the number of musicians and the popularity of the band. The majority of four-piece bands in major metropolitan cities charge $1000 to $2000 for a four-hour reception. Deposits for a band can range from nothing (which is rare) to one-third down.

2 DISC JOCKEYS. When you contract with a DJ, you basically get one DJ (plus, perhaps, an assistant), an entire sound system and a wide variety of music on compact discs, albums or tapes. Some DJs will add specialized lighting (colored spots that pulse to the music, for example) for an extra charge. Also extra may be rare or unusual song requests (such as ethnic music).

DJs are much less expensive than bands since, quite simply, DJs require less manpower. The average price for a professional

DJ for four hours on a Saturday night can range from $200 to $1000. Most DJs in metropolitan areas charge $300 to $500 for a typical reception. Less experienced DJs may charge only $100 to $200, while in-demand club or radio DJs command higher fees than average. Deposits roughly average $100.

AVERAGE TOTAL COSTS: Overall, couples spend about $1000 on the average for music at the ceremony and reception.

Sources to Find a Good Entertainer

 Every major metropolitan area probably has a plethora of good wedding entertainers. The only problem is finding them. Ceremony musicians, reception bands and DJs typically keep a very low profile, choosing to work by word-of-mouth referral. Many of the most successful bands don't advertise their services. So how can you find these people?

❦ *Ceremony/reception site coordinators.* For ceremony music, the wedding coordinator at your ceremony site may be able to suggest a few names of harpists, soloists, trumpeters, etc. Music directors are also another source since they have worked in close contact with local musicians. For reception music, the catering manager at your site will undoubtedly have heard a wide variety of bands and DJs. Ask who really kept the crowd hopping. See the pitfalls section later in this chapter for a disadvantage to using this source.

❦ *Independent caterers.* If you are having your reception at a site where you are bringing in a caterer, you may ask that caterer for entertainment suggestions. Caterers often are reliable sources.

❦ *Wedding announcements in the local paper.* Here's a sneaky way of finding good entertainers. Some local newspapers print wedding announcements that often list the names of the musicians that played at the ceremony or reception. Call the ceremony or reception site to find out how to contact the musicians.

❦ *Music schools at local universities/colleges.* Many students who are talented musicians pick up extra bucks by performing at weddings and receptions. A nice plus: most are more affordable than "professional" musicians. Be sure to get a contract from them, however. Also make sure the student will be dressed appropriately.

❦ *Municipal symphony organizations.* Most symphony musicians moonlight by playing at weddings and receptions.

Call your local symphony for any leads. Looking for a DJ? Call the American Disc Jockey Association (215) 675-9567 for a local referral.

❦ *The union directory of local musicians.* Most cities have musicians' guilds or unions that publish a directory of members. If you know a musician who is a member, this directory may be a good source. However, in some parts of the country (like California), musicians that specialize in weddings are often not members of the local union.

❦ *Agents.* Last but not least, many bands and some DJs are booked through agents. Larger agents may book a wide variety of entertainers that specialize in weddings and receptions. In some cities dominated by unions, agents may be the only way to book a band. There are several advantages and disadvantages to using agents, which we will discuss later in this chapter in our spotlight "Agents: Helping Hand or Scum of the Earth?"

Top Money-saving Secrets

1 GET MARRIED ANY OTHER NIGHT THAN SATURDAY. Okay, we realize that this is not a popular alternative but few people realize bands/ DJs often give a 10% to 20% discount for Friday or Sunday weddings. Given the average entertainment cost of $1000, this could lower the music tab to $800. Total savings = $200.

2 GET MARRIED DURING THE "NON-PEAK" WEDDING SEASON. Obviously, this varies from region to region, but generally entertainers offer discounts for particularly slow months like January. Entertainers that would normally sit idle during these slow times might be willing to knock 5% to 10% off their regular rates. Ask and ye shall receive. Total savings = $50 to $100.

3 DON'T GET MARRIED IN DECEMBER. This is an absolute no-no. Corporate and private Christmas/New Year's Eve parties push up the demand for entertainers and (surprise!) up go the prices. One popular band we interviewed regularly charges $1450 for a typical reception. However, dates in November and December go for $2500 and (are you sitting down?) New Year's Eve goes for a whopping $4500. Enough said.

4 HIRE A DJ INSTEAD OF A BAND. DJs charge an average of 60% less than most live bands. If your parents can't stand the thought of recorded music at your wedding, a possible compromise could involve incorporating live music at the

ceremony and then a DJ at the reception. We'll examine the pros and cons of bands and DJs later in this chapter. If you go with a DJ, however, the total savings = $600.

5 IF YOU'RE ON A REALLY TIGHT BUDGET, MAKE TAPES TO PLAY AT THE RECEPTION. Many reception sites already have a sound system. By using your own stereo equipment and CD collection (or borrowing from friends and relatives), you can record an evening's worth of entertainment for pennies. Besides your time, the only costs are for the tapes. Total savings = Who knows? Certainly mucho dinero.

6 SELECT A BAND WITH FEWER MUSICIANS. Prices for bands are often scaled to the number of musicians. Fortunately, today's technology enables a four-piece band to sound like an orchestra (or at least a larger band). That's because many synthesizers and drum machines can add a string section to a ballad, a horn section to a Glenn Miller tune or even Latin percussion to a particularly hot salsa song. We met one pianist who uses a computer and keyboard to simulate a several piece band for receptions. Another band we interviewed augments a live drummer with a drum machine to add a complex percussion track to current dance songs. Fortunately, couples today don't have to pay for an extra percussionist or horn section to get the same sound. Remember that every extra musician costs $75 to $175 per hour. For example, choosing a four-piece instead of a six-piece band could save $800 or more on a four-hour reception.

7 IF THE DJ DOESN'T HAVE THE ETHNIC MUSIC YOU WANT, BORROW IT FROM THE PUBLIC LIBRARY. Many public libraries have an extensive collection of music (from polkas to Madonna) all available to the public on loan. This is a cost-effective way of getting the music you want at a price you can afford.

8 USE A BAND MEMBER TO PLAY COCKTAIL MUSIC. If you're having a band at your reception and would like some light background music for the cocktail hour, ask if one of the band members can do this. Since they're already doing the rest of your reception, you might get a break on an hour or two of piano or acoustic guitar.

9 CONSIDER HIRING STUDENT MUSICIANS FROM A LOCAL UNIVERSITY OR COLLEGE. Many charge 20% to 30% less than so-called professional musicians. If you go this route, be careful to audition the musicians before signing a contract. For more on how to do this, check out the following Real Wedding Tip.

Getting Started: How Far in Advance?

Don't leave the music for your wedding and reception to the last minute. For ceremony music, you must give the organist time to learn and practice a special request. Meeting with the organist a month or two in advance will smooth the process.

For reception music, many of the best bands and DJs book up months in advance. In general, three to six months is enough time to book an entertainer in smaller towns and for the "off-peak" wedding months. In the largest metropolitan

---

R E A L   W E D D I N G   T I P :
The Smart Way to Hire Student Musicians

Recent bride Melissa Martinez had a unique perspective to share on how to hire student musicians—she works for the music department at Rice University in Houston, Texas. Here are her thoughts: "I get at least 8-10 calls per month from brides looking for cheap entertainment. It's amazing how abusive some people can be when I say that I can't help them. I am not a booking agent, and I can't make a student take the job offered. I can only pass on information as I receive it. And some people try to take advantage of student labor. One person offered $25 for a six-piece jazz combo to play for a four-hour reception! That's total, not a piece!"

"Our jazz instructor is a professional musician whose talents are well known in Texas. Occasionally I will pass on names and numbers to him to handle, since he knows better than anyone which students can handle a job. Sometimes he offers his own services. Once again, I will get calls asking why I referred them to him, because he is too expensive, or he doesn't play the right kind of music, or he wanted a contract . . . I don't know if many music administrators have the same problems that I have, but it IS a problem. Is there any way that brides can be told not to harass us innocent working types?"

Here's Melissa's advice for brides-to-be: "The couples who have had the best results in my experience have been the ones who come to the music or band department with a printed notice of what they are looking for, with all pertinent information also listed, and a number to contact or a time/location for auditions. Students see these on bulletin boards or on job postings, take them down and photocopy them, and follow through far more frequently than on phone messages."

areas, popular dates (the summer months and December) book up anywhere from six to twelve months ahead.

So what if you only have two months left to plan? Don't panic. You may get lucky and find a good band or DJ with an open date. It just may take a little more legwork.

Biggest Myths About Entertainers

Myth #1 *"I'd never consider having a DJ at my wedding. All DJ's are unprofessional, dress sloppily and play disco music. Yuck."*

We often hear this refrain from parents. Yes, its true that most DJ companies owe their entire existence to John Travolta and his infamous white suit. The good news is that most DJs have moved beyond disco and, with sophisticated equipment and a broad music repertoire, have become a credible threat to live bands. We'll discuss the pros and cons of DJs later in this chapter in "Canned vs. Fresh: Should you have a DJ or a band at your reception?"

Myth #2 *"For our reception, we've decided to hire a great band that plays in several local clubs here. Is this a good choice?"*

Be careful. A great club band does not necessarily make a great wedding reception band. The main reason is variety. Playing a wedding reception requires musicians to be "jacks of all trades." Not only must they play Blues Traveller and Janet Jackson for the bride and groom but they must also satisfy Mom's and Dad's request for Elvis and Grandma's request for Glenn Miller. Switching between the Rolling Stones and Benny Goodman can be vexing for even the best bands.

While good club bands may feature competent musicians, they often play to a narrow audience. For example at one wedding, we saw one great club band that did excellent covers of 60's standards. While the bride and groom and their friends loved this music, the parents and grandparents stood in the back of the room for most of the evening.

Of course, you can't please everyone all the time. However, bands should play music for all the generations present at a wedding. Before you hire that great club band, make sure they have a wide repertoire encompassing many musical eras.

Step-by-step Shopping Strategies

CEREMONY MUSIC
❧ **Step 1:** Find out your ceremony site's policy about wedding music. Realize that houses of worship often have varying policies about what is considered "acceptable" wedding music. For example, music like the

"Wedding March" is not allowed at some sites because it's deemed too secular.

❦ Step 2: Meet with the music director of your ceremony site several weeks before your wedding. If you need to bring in musicians, use our sources to find three good candidates. Interview the musicians and discuss your ideas for the ceremony site music.

❦ Step 3: Ask to hear samples of various selections. If you're getting married at a church, ask the music director if you can attend a wedding ceremony. Listen to how certain pieces sound on the organ or other instruments.

❦ Step 4: If you hire outside musicians, get a written contract specifying the date, time, place and selections of music. Find out if the musicians/organist will come to the rehearsal (and if there is any fee for this).

RECEPTION MUSIC

❦ Step 1: As soon as you have your wedding date confirmed, start your search for an entertainer. Decide what type of music fits your reception. Some important considerations include:

- ❦ The time of day of your reception—For example, in the afternoon, most people do not feel like dancing. Perhaps a good choice here would be a guitarist to play soft background music. But, hey, its your reception so choose the music you want.

- ❦ The ages of the guests—You can't please everyone but selecting a band/DJ that plays a wide variety of music will help keep everyone dancing.

- ❦ The size of the reception—Typically, the "reception music axiom" says the larger the crowd, the bigger the band you need to keep the event hopping. In reality, a four or five-piece band can play a reception of 500 guests as easily as 200 guests. Do what your budget allows and don't get talked into a certain size band because you have X number of guests. For DJs, the size of the crowd may determine whether extra speakers/amplification are needed.

❦ Step 2: After deciding on the type of music you want, identify three good bands/DJs using our sources list. Call each of them on the phone and ask the questions we outline below. Ask to see them perform at an upcoming reception.

❦ Step 3: When you visit the reception, don't go during dinner time. Instead plan to stop in later in the evening around

10:30 when the dancing gets going full swing. Dress appropriately for a wedding and stand in the back of the room. Look for three key factors:

1 Is the band/DJ correctly reading the crowd? In other words, are they playing the right music for the guests at the wedding? Is anyone dancing? Are they ignoring one generation?

2 How much talking does the band leader/DJ do? Is this amount of chatter helping or hurting the reception? Do you like their announcing style?

3 Is the band/DJ professional? Are they dressed appropriately? Is the volume at a good level or a deafening roar? Is the entertainer varying the tempo, mixing fast and slow selections?

❦ *Step 4:* After you preview as many entertainers as time allows, select the band/DJ you want. Get a written contract that includes the specific date, hours and place as well as the price and overtime charges. Also get the names of the exact musicians who will be there and the instruments they will be playing. If you want, specify what dress you want the band members/DJ to wear. Finally, have specific sets of music written out such as your first song, special requests, etc. You may even want to attach a song list to the contract.

❦ *Step 5:* Remember that the better you specify the music, the more likely you'll get the music you want at your reception. Don't be ambiguous here by saying you want just "rock" or "dance music." Identify specific artists and songs and then star your favorites. For some artists, specifying a certain time period may be helpful (do you want old Elton John or the more current Elton songs?). Don't forget to clearly mark the song you want for a first dance.

❦ *Step 6:* Meet with the band leader or DJ a couple of weeks before the wedding to go over the evening's schedule and any last minute details. Meet them at the site if they're unfamiliar with it to gauge any needs or problems.

Questions to Ask an Entertainer

CEREMONY MUSIC

1 WHAT IS THE CEREMONY SITE'S POLICY ON WEDDING MUSIC? Does the church or synagogue have staff musicians or soloists? What is their fee? Don't assume anything is free.

2 DOES THE CHURCH HAVE ANY RESTRICTIONS ON THE MUSIC I CAN HAVE AT MY CEREMONY? This is a particularly sticky area since some sites may have numerous restrictions on what is deemed "acceptable."

3 DO STAFF MUSICIANS REQUIRE EXTRA REHEARSALS if I bring in outside musicians too? Will there be an extra charge for rehearsals?

4 WHO EXACTLY WILL BE PERFORMING AT MY CEREMONY? Especially when you hire outside musicians, confirm the exact performers who will be at your wedding.

5 HOW FAMILIAR ARE YOU WITH MY CEREMONY SITE? Obviously this question is only for outside musicians. Inform them of any restrictions the site has on music. A pre-wedding meeting at the site might be a good idea in case there are any logistical questions (electricity, amplification, etc.)

RECEPTION ENTERTAINMENT:

1 WHO EXACTLY WILL BE PERFORMING AT MY WEDDING? Be very careful here. The biggest pitfall couples encounter with bands/DJs is hiring one set of musicians/DJs and getting another set at your wedding. See the Pitfalls section later in this chapter for strategies to overcome this problem.

2 FOR DISC JOCKEYS, DO YOU HAVE PROFESSIONAL EQUIP-MENT? Novice DJs are most likely to use home stereo equipment from Radio Shack. While that's nice for a living room, it may not work in a large reception site. Experienced DJs have professional equipment (amplifiers and speakers, especially) that produces crisp sound and have enough power to fill up the largest ballroom.

3 HOW DO WE CHOOSE THE MUSIC? A simple but critical question. How open is the band leader/DJ to letting you select the evening's music? Do they want you to submit a song/artist list? Some bands/DJs will interview you and your fiance to find out your musical preferences. If the entertainer is evasive about this question or replies that they "have a standard set they always play," you may want to look elsewhere.

4 CAN WE SEE YOU PERFORM AT A WEDDING? The best way to gauge whether a band/DJ is worth their asking price is to see them perform live. Most entertainers should let you attend an upcoming reception, with the permission of that bride and groom, of course. We've talked to some couples

who feel uncomfortable attending a stranger's party—our advice is don't sweat it. No one will recognize you. If you can't see the band/DJ live, you might be able to view a video or listen to a demo tape (see the pitfalls section for drawbacks to this suggestion). Another smart idea is to call a few recently-married couples for references. Ask the reference if there was anything they would have changed about the evening's entertainment.

5 HOW MANY BREAKS WILL YOU TAKE? Will you provide a tape to play during those times? Instead of having silence during a band's breaks, consider playing a tape of dance music to keep the reception hopping.

6 DOES THE PRICE INCLUDE BACKGROUND MUSIC DURING DINNER OR COCKTAILS? Some bands and DJs throw in a free hour of background music during dinner or cocktails. One band leader we met said he always throws in a free hour of cocktail music. Besides being a nice freebie for the bride and groom, this gives the entertainer an opportunity to scope out the crowd. Then, when the dancing begins, the band is better attuned to the music the guests want.

Helpful Hints

1 FOR THE CEREMONY MUSIC, REMEMBER THAT SHEET MUSIC IS OFTEN WRITTEN FOR ANOTHER INSTRUMENT THAN THE ORGAN. Hence, give the organist plenty of time (several weeks perhaps) to transpose and rehearse the piece so it's perfect by the wedding day.

2 SHOULD YOU FEED THE BAND/DJ? Obviously, this is up to you. You may not want to provide a meal to each band member at a $50 per plate sit-down dinner. However, at least try to arrange with the caterer to provide them with some snacks or sandwiches. Remember that bands/DJs have to be at the reception a long time, and a well-fed entertainer performs better than one with an empty stomach. Whatever your decision, inform the band leader/DJ about food arrangements before the wedding.

3 TRACKING DOWN OBSCURE ETHNIC MUSIC. Unfortunately, the mall record store rarely stocks ethnic music today. Hence, DJs may find it challenging to locate certain songs. A better solution may be to let them borrow your family's records or tapes. Specifically point out the songs you want.

Pitfalls to Avoid

Pitfall #1
BAIT AND SWITCH WITH BANDS AND DISC JOCKEYS
"My fiance and I saw this great band perform at a friend's wedding so we hired them for ours. At our reception, different musicians showed up and it just didn't sound the same."

This is perhaps the #1 problem brides and grooms have with their reception entertainment. We've known some agents and band leaders who play "musical chairs" with backing musicians—sometimes known as "pick-up bands." Here a group of musicians are thrown together at the last moment ... and the lack of rehearsal shows. You might hire a certain "name brand" band but then the band leader substitutes some different (and possibly inferior) musicians at your reception. Hence, you don't get what you paid for, that is quality entertainment. Large DJ companies with several crews are also guilty of this tactic. You can prevent this deceptive practice by specifying in a written contract the exact musicians/DJ you want at your wedding. Stay away from agents, band leaders or DJ companies who won't give you a straight answer.

Pitfall #2
CHATTERBOX BAND LEADERS AND DJs
"We recently attended a wedding where the band leader incessantly talked to the crowd. No one found this constant chatter amusing and it detracted from the elegance of the reception."

Band leaders and DJs often have their own "schtick"—a certain routine they do at a wedding. How "energetic" you want the band to be is your call since, of course, it's your money. Don't be surprised by a chatty band/DJ. See them perform at another reception before you sign that contract. If you have any doubts, ask them about the amount of talking and tell them what you believe is appropriate for your reception.

Pitfall #3
DECEPTIVE DEMO TAPES.
"We heard a demo tape from a band that sounded great. But later we saw the same band and boy was it disappointing! What happened?"

Some demo tapes are produced in studios where a battery of sophisticated electronic equipment can make the weakest band sound like a stadium headliner. Add a little reverb to the vocals and clean up the guitar with some equalization and

poof! Instant superstar band! In the harsh reality of a live performance, however, none of these studio tricks can save a
lousy band. Listen to the demo tape for "style," not production quality. Beware the slick demo tape and try to see the
band perform in person.

We heard about a twist on this scam from a band leader in
Boston. We call it the "Milli Vanilli syndrome." Some bands
don't just "clean up" their demo tape in a studio, but use
entirely different musicians to record the tape! That's right,
the band pictured on the video tape is *not* the one that has
recorded the soundtrack, just like the infamous singing duo
Milli Vanilli that were exposed as fakes.

Pitfall #4
KICKBACKS AND "REFERRED" LISTS.

*"My wedding site recommend a musician who turned out
to be lousy! Meanwhile, several great musicians in my town
are nowhere to be found on their 'recommended list.' What's
going on here?"*

A problem with some wedding site coordinators (as well as
catering managers at reception sites) is the question of kick-
backs. Believe it or not, some of these folks demand fees (we
call them kickbacks) to be listed on the site's "recommended
list" of musicians. A harpist in Northern California told us
this unscrupulous practice is rampant there. Ask the coordinator if they take fees from recommended musicians. If you
don't get a straight answer, be careful.

Trends in Wedding and Reception Music

So what's hot with wedding and reception music?

❦ **New technology.** Compact discs have enabled DJs to provide
crystal clear sound, replacing scratchy vinyl and mediocre cas-
sette tapes. In the live music world, bands now have access to
increasingly sophisticated computerized synthesizers and drum
machines. With these computers, bands can add a phalanx of
horns or a dash of strings to their "basic" sound, enabling them
to compete better with a DJ in music reproduction.

❦ **DJs are replacing bands at many receptions.** To find out
why, see our spotlight, "Canned vs. Fresh: Should you have a
DJ or a band at your reception?"

❦ **Ethnic music and bands.** Mariachis are chic in the
Southwest, while a good Polka band is still in vogue in the
Midwest. Couples are not only celebrating their own family
heritage but also reflecting a new cultural diversity. One

recently-married Anglo couple in Miami had a Caribbean-flavored reception complete with a hot salsa band. When their caterer asked why they selected this theme, the couple responded that this was the music they grew up with.

❦ *Music from the '50's, '60's, '70's.* Reflecting radio's current fixation on "classic rock," many bands are playing more hits from the "early history" of rock 'n roll. Motown music (à la the "Big Chill") is still popular. You might even find a DJ who leads the crowd in a dance-along to "YMCA."

❦ *At the ceremony, the "Wedding March" is being replaced by a wider variety of classical and modern music.* This is partly due to some churches forbidding this song on religious grounds. To others, the song has become too cliched.

Special Touches to Make Your Wedding/Reception Music Unique

1 PERSONALIZE THE WEDDING AND RECEPTION MUSIC WITH YOUR FAVORITE SONGS. Incorporating special songs that have personal meaning for you and your fiance is a great way to make your celebration unique. Before the wedding, give the band leader/DJ a list of special requests.

2 INSTEAD OF STANDARD ORGAN MUSIC, CONSIDER DIFFERENT MUSICAL INSTRUMENTS. The combinations here are endless. Many couples enjoy harp and flute duos, while others attest to the regal splendor of a single trumpeter. Classical guitar (as well as violin) are beautiful alternatives, too.

3 USE ETHNIC MUSIC TO CELEBRATE FAMILY HERITAGE. Several weeks before the wedding, talk over the possibilities with your band/DJ. Some songs may take a band time to rehearse or DJ time to track down.

4 IF YOU'RE UNSURE ABOUT CLASSICAL MUSIC FOR YOUR CEREMONY, consider ordering "Processionals and Recessionals for Traditional Weddings." This tape has a sampling of 30 different selections, plus a booklet that explains each song. Produced by David Perkoff's Seven Veils Records, it can be ordered by calling (512) 458-3539. The cost is $14.95 plus $2 shipping. Looking for a special song to dedicate to parents? Mikki Viereck of New Traditions Music (800) 447-6647 has crafted "A Song for My Son" from the CD *New Wedding Traditions* in response to requests from couples for a "mother-to-groom" song. The CD includes six more songs (both vocal and instrumental) such as "As We Break This Bread" (for cake cutting) and "A Song for My Daughter."

Spotlight

"Canned vs. Fresh: Should you have a DJ or a band at your reception?"

DJs are often the Rodney Dangerfield of wedding reception music—they just don't get any respect. For example, we've read many other books on weddings that don't even mention DJs as an entertainment alternative. Instead, *Emily Post's Complete Book of Wedding Etiquette* suggests "a full orchestra" complete with a "string section for soft background music before the dancing starts." We don't know about you, but hiring a forty-piece orchestra with accompanying string section was just a teensy bit out of our wedding budget.

According to Emily Post, if you're having a small, informal wedding, "a record player provides adequate and lovely music." Nowhere are the words "disc jockey" mentioned. Even more disturbing is the venerable *Bride's Book of Etiquette (5th Edition)* which, after talking at length about the merits of "small orchestras" at weddings receptions, says "taped, pre-recorded music is a good alternative when live music is not available." Of course, instead of mentioning DJs, the book suggests you "ask a music buff friend to pre-mix your selection on one long-playing tape."

Hey! What's going on here? Do the etiquette fanatics who write this dribble just have their collective heads in the sand or is there a conspiracy to deny the existence of DJs? If all these wedding experts are convinced that only live orchestras are appropriate for wedding receptions, then explain to us why disc jockeys dominate reception music in most major cities.

Well, let's take a look at why DJs are so popular. According to a recent survey in *Bridal Guide,* 64% of all brides choose a DJ—that's much more than those who hire a band (22%) or have no music at all (14%). Of course the number-one reason is cost—DJs cost only $300 to $500 for an evening, compared to the $1000 to $2000 fees bands demand. With the cost of a wedding soaring, couples are obviously opting for the affordable alternative.

Perhaps a more subtle reason may be the state of pop music today. Almost all the music you hear on the radio is augmented by computerized keyboards and percussion tracks. For a live band, trying to reproduce this music is perilous at best and embarrassing at worst. Sure, bands can play Glenn Miller and Johnny Mathis rather realistically, but many reception bands we've heard make every modern song they attempt sound like "New York, New York."

To their credit, DJs have also cleaned up their act in recent years. Many companies are now professionally-run businesses with tuxedo-clad DJs and professional sound equipment. This is a far cry from the late 1970's, when less-formal DJs spun mind-numbing disco hits complete with throbbing disco lights. Of course, disco is still with us (under the new label of "dance music") but many DJs diversified their music collection to include rock, country & western, and rap, as well as the hits from the 50's, 60's and 70's.

In fact, musical versatility is one of the top reasons couples choose DJs. Since most weddings feature several generations of guests, a good mix of music is a must. While some bands play a variety of music, many are most proficient at one or two musical genres. The lack of variety is one of live bands' biggest disadvantages.

Another plus for DJs: they never take breaks. Most DJs play music continuously, unlike bands which need to take breaks every hour. Just when the crowd gets into a particular groove, the band shuts down for five to ten minutes. Obviously, this can kill the mood. With a DJ, the beat never stops until the party ends.

So what does Emily Post suggest if you want continuous music? Hire two orchestras, so one can play while the other is on break. We are not kidding here. That's what she really suggests. Can you believe it?

Of course, we could rattle off a million advantages of DJs over bands but that wouldn't faze those hard-line etiquette gurus. With their noses firmly planted in the air, they'd say something like "only live music such as a combo or orchestra is appropriate for a proper reception."

Still, bands dominate in some areas, especially in cities with a thriving live music scene (i.e., New Orleans, some East Coast cities, etc.). Also, bands are still the most popular choice for those large "society" weddings.

Sure, we admit that watching a live band crank out "Louie, Louie" is more visually interesting than seeing a DJ play the same song via vinyl (or laser with compact discs). All we are saying is don't get bullied by the etiquette police into hiring a band when a professional DJ might fit your musical (and financial) preferences better.

Spotlight

Agents: Helping Hand or Scum of the Earth?

So, what exactly is an entertainment agent? People in these businesses function as middlemen between bands or DJs and consumers. An agent's primary activity is booking bands and DJs at various engagements—in return they receive a commission. The standard commission is 15% of the band's regular performing fee.

Now, the power of agents varies from city to city. In cities with stronger musicians' unions, agents tend to proliferate. In general, we've found agents more likely to dominate older cities such as New York and Chicago rather than sun-belt towns like Atlanta and Dallas.

Agents cite several reasons for their existence. First, they can more effectively market the bands to engaged couples by pooling their resources. Also, many band leaders (who have other daytime jobs) hate the paperwork associated with deposits, contracts, etc. Agents do all the legwork and remove the administrative hassles.

Fine, you say, but what can an agent do for me as a consumer? Well, agents provide "one-stop shopping," enabling you to make one call and get information on a wide range of bands and DJs. If you are in a hurry or just aren't aware of the entertainment options in your area, an agent can certainly help. Agents don't charge you a fee for their services, instead they collect a commission from the bands.

As you might imagine, some entertainers are less than enthusiastic about giving agents a 15% cut of their salary. Many of the entertainers we interviewed for this book held unanimously negative opinions about agents. And, frankly, we've met some agents who could be charitably described as "scum of the earth."

The main gripe we have with agents is their lack of "product knowledge." Too many just book a band or DJ without giving thought to whether their music is appropriate. Other agents deny brides and grooms the right to preview the band/DJ at a wedding before booking—a cardinal sin in our view.

Another major factor in this controversy: many bands say off the record they will give brides and grooms discounts off their regular rates if they book them directly. For example, one band told us they would knock off 15% (which, of course, is equal to the agent's commission) from their $2000 normal reception rate—that's a savings of $300, no small potatoes.

Agents respond to our criticism by claiming they can save brides and grooms money. One agent told us agents "can get a lower price because they do a volume of business with a band, whereas a band leader contacted directly can get very greedy." Furthermore, agents claim that legitimately professional band leaders will keep their prices the same—whether the booking comes directly from the couple or through an agent.

Well, we've "mystery shopped" dozens of bands and DJs and have yet to find any entertainer quoting a fee over their "regular rates." (After we posed as an engaged couple, we later confirmed their rates from agents and other sources). Agents have never quoted us a rate lower than the normal fee, and we often found many professional band leaders who offered a quiet discount when approached directly.

So what should you do? We recommend you try to book a band or DJ directly if you have found them from one of our sources listed above. If you are short of time or can't find any good entertainment options, call an agent. Be careful to check out any band or DJ the agent recommends before you sign that contract. You might even call the local Better Business Bureau to make sure the agent is on the up and up. Most importantly, make sure the agent lets you meet the band to talk over the music, scheduling, and other reception details.

Whether you book a band or DJ directly or through an agent, follow the tips in this chapter to make sure the reception music is everything you've imagined.

Chapter 13

Etcetera

How can you use the Internet to plan your wedding? What the heck is wedding insurance? Do you need a wedding consultant? This chapter gives you advice on these and more topics. Plus, we'll examine limousine services, wedding rings, and all-in-one wedding companies.

Limousine Services: Getting to the Church on Time

What Are You Buying?

 ❦ *The Limousine* A stretch limousine has several basic amenities that qualify it as a limousine. These include an extra long body, plush carpeting, a stereo, possibly a TV, sunroof and telephone, and a privacy window as well. More luxurious models have been known to contain even a hot tub or other interesting amenities.

Non-traditional forms of transportation include horse-drawn carriages, antique cars and even buses or trolleys. These options will probably not include the types of amenities mentioned above, but they will have their own versions of luxury.

❦ *The Driver* Every type of transportation you hire will include a driver. The driver should be dressed appropriately, either in a dark suit and chauffeur's cap or a black tuxedo.

AVERAGE COST: Limousines will cost approximately $60 to $150 per hour. Usually, they have a three hour minimum rental time, with the total cost for the car between $180 and $450 per car per evening. The driver is paid with an additional mandatory gratuity of about 15%. For non-traditional transportation, the cost usually starts at $100 and goes up depending on the vehicle you rent.

Sources to Find Transportation

 Some sources include the Yellow Pages under "Limousines," "Carriages-Horse" or under "Wedding Services." By all means ask a recently married friend for recommendations and look for information about transportation companies at bridal shows.

Top Money-saving Tips

 1 CALL A FUNERAL HOME. Yes, you read right—call a funeral home for a great deal on a limo rental for your wedding. We heard about this bargain from recent bride Stephanie Kampes in Drexel Hill, PA. She priced regular limo companies at $275 for three hours, plus a 15% gratuity. "Then I called a reputable funeral home and was surprised with the price!" Apparently, this funeral home rents out it's standard stretch limos during down times (Saturday night must not be a big time for funerals). The cost? $125 for the evening. "This may sound rather morbid, but it works! While they don't have hot tubs or TV's, funeral homes have lovely vehicles!" While not every funeral home rents out limos for weddings, it's worth a try.

2 FIND A TRANSPORTATION COMPANY WITH A SHORT MINI-MUM TIME REQUIREMENT. Most companies require you to hire them for a minimum of three hours. You may be able to find someone who is willing to require only an hour or two-hour minimum, thus saving 30% to 60% of the cost.

3 RENT A TROLLEY! A bride in Trenton, NJ called in this great idea—she found a company that rents a 30-seat trolley for four hours for $715 (which includes a gratuity for the driver). We found trolley companies in other cities that had even lower rates (look in the phone book under "Weddings Services," "Limousine Rental" or "Buses-Charter/Rental"). If you're having a large wedding and don't want to rent a fleet of limos, this might be a smart idea.

4 CONSIDER A "PICK UP-DROP OFF" SERVICE. Instead of having the limousine driver wait outside the church during the ceremony, simply hire a limo to pick you up after the ceremony and go to the reception (pick-up/drop-off service). Often this will cost you much less than hiring someone for three hours.

5 HAVE YOUR WEDDING ON AN OFF-NIGHT. Some companies offer deals for brides having weddings during the week.

6 Rent a luxury car. Many car rental companies rent Cadillacs and Lincoln Continentals for as little as $50 to $75 per day. While you'll need to find a driver (perhaps a friend or relative), this is a big savings over a limo.

7 Consider hiring a "regular limo." These are regular luxury cars—not the stretch variety. Many limo companies offer these cars at reduced rates.

Getting Started: How Far in Advance?

 For most limousine companies, you may not need to start looking until a month or two before your wedding date. If limos are popular in your area and you have a wedding date in the busy summer months, consider planning three months in advance. For carriage companies, you may also have to plan farther in advance because the demand is greater and the supply limited.

Step-by-step Shopping Strategies

 ❦ *Step 1:* Using the sources mentioned above, find two or three companies you want to talk to.

❦ *Step 2:* Find out what type of vehicle you will be hiring. See if you can visit the company and see the cars or carriages. Get details on available options, minimum required hours and the cost per hour.

❦ *Step 3:* Visit the company. Check to see how clean the cars are and what amenities they have. Find out who will be driving the car and what they will be wearing.

❦ *Step 4:* Consider calling the National Limousine Association to find out if the company you want to hire has adequate insurance and is licensed. These folks can give you that information or at least inform you of how to find it for yourself. Call the NLA at (800) NLA-7007.

❦ *Step 5:* Choose the company you like the best and get a contract detailing the car you like. Make sure the date and time are clearly written. As you get closer to your wedding day, call to remind them of your date and time.

Questions to Ask a Transportation Company

 1 WHAT AMENITIES ARE AVAILABLE?

2 WILL WE BE ABLE TO BRING CHAMPAGNE? Will you provide us with ice and glasses? Some companies will allow you to bring alcohol while others will even supply it. In some areas, it is illegal for the company to provide the alcohol, but they will bring ice and glasses for BYOB.

3 HOW MUCH IS THE GRATUITY FOR THE DRIVER? Typically, you aren't given a choice about how much the gratuity will be. Gratuities range from company to company, so check around before you book.

4 DO YOU HAVE ANY DISCOUNTS AVAILABLE? As we mentioned above, many companies will discount their service for week nights. Other discounts may be available if you hire more than one vehicle or if you hire them for longer time periods.

REAL WEDDING TIP:
The Limo Driver Terrorist

 A bride-to-be in Atlanta Georgia wrote us with this limo scam story—her sister-in-law fell victim to the "early arrival/over-time" surprise rip-off. How does this scam work? First, she wrote, "the limo showed up at the bride's house over 30 minutes early. The driver was insistent that the bride and her mother finish dressing and ride to the church, which they did. After the wedding and after all the guests left the ceremony site for the reception, the driver boarded the wedding party into the limo. He then informed the couple 'the limo is on overtime' and demanded $60 before he would take them to the reception."

"Since neither wedding gowns nor bridesmaids dresses have pockets (another bad idea), the groom and best man frantically scraped together the ransom. The limo company reluctantly refunded part of the additional charges only after several unpleasant telephone calls during the next few weeks." How can you prevent this from happening to you? First, if the limo arrives early, don't get in it, no matter how insistent the driver is. Realize that the moment you step inside, the driver's clock is running. Try to pay any overtime fee or deposit by credit card—then you can dispute the charge later if you feel you were mistreated.

5 DO YOU SPECIALIZE IN WEDDINGS? Those companies that do may have special bridal packages or other freebies.

Pitfalls to Avoid

Pitfall #1
COMPANIES THAT DON'T SHOW UP.

This is one of the biggest problems with limousine companies. We recommend you check with the Better Business Bureau in your area if you have any questions about a limo service. Checking with the city agency that licenses limousines will also determine whether the company you are considering meets local requirements.

Wedding Rings

The good news about wedding rings is you can buy a beautiful band in just about any budget range. Unlike other goods and services you're purchasing for the wedding, there is a plentiful supply of jewelry stores and other sources to find rings. For example, in our town of 90,000 people, we have just two bridal dress shops, but over 40 jewelry sources (from chain stores in the mall to independent shops and custom jewelry makers). The plentiful supply means you'll probably find something to fit your budget and style.

What Are You Buying?

What does a set of rings cost? Couples spend on average $1000 for weddings bands, according to a recent article in *Kiplinger's Personal Finance Magazine*. Yes, that's $500 per ring! Prices range from as little as $50 for a plain ring to $1000 or more for a heavy, ornately finished 18-karat-gold ring.

What does 18-karat mean? That number refers to the purity of gold in the ring—and that's just one factor that influences a ring's value. Here are the four key aspects to keep in mind when ring shopping:

❦ **Gold purity.** The "karat" is a term that refers to the purity of the gold. 24-karat (24K) gold is pure, 100% gold. Wedding rings also come in 18K, 14K and even 10K gold. 18K has 75% gold (25% other metals), 14K is 58.5% gold and 10K has a mere 41.6% gold. Which is best? There are trade-offs to each karat class. While 18K has a higher gold content, it's also softer (and hence it may not wear as well). By contrast, 14K is harder and wears better—and it's less expensive.

❦ *Style.* Color is one factor to consider. While pure gold comes only in one color (yellow, as you might guess), gold can be combined with other metals to form different colors. A 14K white gold ring is a mix of gold (58.5%) plus copper, nickel and zinc. In order to cover over any yellow tints, white gold rings are often coated with rhodium, a metal that's a member of the platinum family. In addition to color, the style of the ring also refers to its shape. Rings can be either flat or half-round—a dome-like or curved appearance.

❦ *Width.* Ring width is measured in millimeters (mm). Most woman's wedding bands are 2-4mm, while men's are 4-6mm. Of course, the wider the ring, the more expensive it is. Other widths are also available.

❦ *Finish.* Just like the icing on a wedding cake, a ring's finish can range from simple to ornate. Like the shiny look? Then choose a high polish ring, instead of a matte finish. Rings can have monograms, diamond cut patterns and other finishes. A milgrain edge is popular today—that's an ornamental border on the edge of the ring that resembles a string of tiny beads. Want diamonds in your wedding ring? You can have stones that encircle the band or are just on top.

Top Money-saving Tips

1 GO FOR A 14-KARAT RING. Yes, it has less gold in it than 18K or 24K rings, but this is also an advantage. 14K gold is harder and wears better than higher-karat rings. And, best of all, it's much less expensive.

2 CHECK OUT PAWN SHOPS. Divorces and other financial mishaps often lead folks to pawn their wedding rings. As a result, pawn shops have an incredible selection of jewelry at very good prices. Another good bet: estate sales (usually advertised in newspapers) often feature rings and other jewelry.

3 COMPARISON SHOP. Which place has the best deals on wedding rings—mall stores or independent jewelers? Well, there is no one answer. Sales, special deals and other events may make one jeweler temporarily less expensive than another. Make sure you're comparing "apples to apples" with rings (the same width, gold purity, etc.).

4 GO MAIL ORDER. See the Spotlight: Best Buy below for a discount mail-order source for wedding rings.

Spotlight: Best Buy

Wedding Ring Hotline
(800) 985-7464 or (908) 972-7777

Tired of the high prices of the mall jewelry stores? Like the prices but not the styles of discount, catalog showrooms? Well, we found a great alternative: The Wedding Ring Hotline of Englishtown, New Jersey.

Owner Mitch Slachman has been in the business since 1983 and has developed a loyal clientele in New York and New Jersey. The Wedding Ring Hotline not only carries Mitch's custom designs, but also the styles of leading designers' lines as well. If you see an advertisement for a name-brand ring or have the style number, you can get a price quote.

And talk about good deals—The Wedding Ring Hotline's prices are 25% to 33% below retail on most designs. Or Mitch can custom design a ring from you for even bigger savings. Their retail showroom (under the name Bride & Groom's West) in Englishtown, New Jersey has over 500 styles on display. If you don't live in that part of the country, you can call for their color catalog. We saw an impressive number of styles, from monogramed bands to diamond-studded rings. A simple 4mm plain band in 14K white or yellow gold starts at $52. Most simple styles in 14K gold are in the $100 to $170 range—call for price quotes on 18K gold and platinum rings.

The Wedding Ring Hotline takes all major credit cards and has a 30-day 100% money-back guarantee if you're not happy. There's also no sales tax if you live outside New Jersey, a big money-savings as well. "In a market full of unscrupulous jewelers and diamond dealers, I pride myself in being trustworthy, honest and fair," Mitch told us. And we have to agree—The Wedding Rings is definitely a best buy.

Further reading

As you've noted above, this section just addresses wedding bands. We assume you already have a diamond engagement ring. Yet, if you're more interested in learning how to purchase diamonds and colored stones, there are two excellent books to read:

• *Engagement & Wedding Rings: The Definitive Buying Guide for People in Love* by Matlins, Bonanno, Crystal (1990, $14.95, Gemstone Press 800-962-4544, 802-457-4000).

• *The Diamond Ring Buying Guide: How to Spot Value & Avoid Rip-offs* by Renee Newman (1993, $12.95,

International Jewelry Publications, PO Box 13384, Los Angeles, CA 90013).

If you have access to the Internet, check out Jim Kokernak's "Frequently Asked Questions (FAQ) about Diamonds". This 16-page guide includes sections on finding a jeweler, the basics on diamonds, how not to get ripped off and more. You can find this FAQ at the soc.couples.wedding home page on the Web. The address (URL) is http://www.wam.umd.edu/~sek/wedding.html. You can also send e-mail to Jim Kokernak at kokerj@rpi.edu.

Brides in Cyberspace

Surf the Web Before You Walk Down the Aisle

Got a personal computer and modem? That's all you need to surf the bridal information superhighway. You can ask a fellow bride for a recommendation of a photographer in your town, view a bridesmaids' dress catalog on-line or even send electronic notes (e-mail) to the authors of this book.

How do you get started? First, sign up with an on-line service. Our favorite is America On-Line (call 1-800-215-0800 for a free start-up kit and 10 free on-line hours). Whether you have a PC or Mac, America On-Line lets you send e-mail, access the Internet and surf the Web.

Once you're plugged in, check out these nifty places:

❦ *E-mail.* Tired of how slow the post office is? Send e-mail to your friends, relatives or vendors with a simple click of the mouse. Our e-mail address is adfields@aol.com (if you use America On-Line, just send your notes to the id "adfields").

❦ *Bridal newsgroups.* Here's a great place to ask a question or get help on a problem. Newsgroups on bridal-related topics are much like bulletin-boards—brides and grooms post questions and others reply. Since tens of thousands of folks read and post messages, you can ask others for a local photographer referral or post a question about etiquette. Sometimes the newsgroups are like group therapy, where brides swap tips on dealing with troublesome in-laws and the like. Unlike the sugar-coated world of bridal magazines, the Internet newsgroups are an uncensored look at what's really on the minds of today's brides and grooms. How do you access these gold mines of information? If you're using America On-Line, go to the Internet Connection and then to the newsgroups. The two bridal newsgroups go under the names "soc.couples.wedding" and "alt.wedding."

❦ *The World Wide Web.* Want to get free updates on this book? Check out our home page on the web (see the "How to Reach Us" page at the back of this book for the address). The World Wide Web is the graphical and information-packed part of the Internet. Businesses and individuals have "home pages" that include pictures, information and more. The newsgroup "soc.couples.wedding" has an excellent home page—it's address (or URL) is http://www.wam.umd.edu/~sek/wedding.html. By clicking on highlighted text words, you can jump to other locations, such as a list of Frequently Asked Questions or commercial home pages like Weddings On-Line (a collection of advertisements for local wedding vendors). You can use commercial on-line servers like America On-Line and Compuserve to access these "web pages."

All-in-one Companies

Wedding-in-a-box or Time-saving Convenience?

All-in-one companies are difficult to describe because they encompass a wide range of businesses. The term "all-in-one" itself may be rather misleading, since we are referring to any bridal business that combines two or more elements involved in a wedding. For example, an "all-in-one" could be merely a florist combined with a caterer. More often these businesses provide a wider range of services such as photography, flowers, catering and even a reception site. Of course, there are those few businesses that literally take on everything imaginable: apparel, invitations, cakes, videography and so on.

Many all-in-one wedding companies are trying to provide brides with a "one-stop shopping" alternative—almost like a wedding mall. On the East Coast, some reception sites offer "complete wedding service:" flowers, photography, videography, catering, limos, cakes, favors, tuxedos, gowns and even furniture. Just add a groom and poof! Instant marriage!

Problems with All-in-one Wedding Services

1 SPREADING THEMSELVES TOO THIN. Instead of doing one service well, many all-in-one companies do several services poorly. For example, we met one caterer who also offered floral arrangement services. While the food looked great, the flowers weren't impressive.

2 MASS-PRODUCED WEDDINGS. Because these companies offer so many services, they often "standardize" their options. While this streamlines their business, it makes for weddings that have all the appeal of a fast-food burger. Instead of having your wedding reflect your personal tastes, all-in-one companies tend to fit all brides and grooms into one mold.

OUR RECOMMENDATION: Use an all-in-one company for just one or two of their services. You don't have to hire them for the whole package.

Bridal Accessories and other details

What's the silliest bridal accessory we've discovered? Would you believe lucky pennies for $5 each? Yes, that's what a company in Texas was selling—a penny wrapped in tulle and tied with a ribbon. If that wasn't enough, we found other catalogs selling "lucky six-pence" for $12. Last time we checked exchange rates, a six-pence was worth, say, ten pennies. What a deal, eh?

As you can see, when it comes to accessories, it pays to think rationally. And compare prices at local stores with mail-order catalogs. One good source is the M-R Wedding and Party catalog ($3 cost, which is applied to your first order, 812-282-1055).

Even with a lucky penny in your shoe, there's no guarantee you will be Fred Astaire and Ginger Rogers at your wedding reception. If you're in need of dance lessons, Blanche and Emilio Liberero, dance teachers in Tampa, Fla., have come to your rescue. They put together "Waltz at Your Wedding " ($29.95 plus shipping), a 35-minute tape that teaches you how to box step, turn, promenade and more. Call (800) 443-5641 to order.

Do you need wedding insurance? Fireman's Fund (800) 428-1419 offers a policy that protects you in case of cancellation of the wedding, lost wedding photos, damaged wedding attire, lost gifts and personal liability for bodily injury or property damage at your wedding and reception. Premiums start at $95. So, should you buy? Well, *Money Magazine* picked wedding insurance as a great example of insurance you really don't need, pointing out that the skimpy coverage didn't justify the hefty premiums. We have mixed feelings about this insurance— if your reception site requires you to purchase liability insurance, this might be an affordable alternative. If your spouse is in the military and you worry a surprise overseas deployment may scuttle the wedding plans, this insurance may also help. Of course, read the policy carefully to catch all the fine print.

Are you tearing your hair out trying to find a nice gift for the bridesmaids and groomsmen? Tired of the standard earrings or money clip? Here are some gift catalogs that may be able to solve this dilemma:

Anticipation	(800) 556-7376.
Attitudes	(800) 525-2468.
Coldwater Creek	(800) 262-0040.
Hammacher Schlemmer	(800) 543-3366.
Hold Everything	(800) 421-2264.
Potpourri	(800) 388-7798
Smithsonian	(800) 322-0344.

Bridal Shows:

Fun Afternoon or Highway to Bridal Hell?

If you need a good laugh, attend a local bridal show in your town. If you aren't convinced that the wedding "industry" is a joke, this is the place to give your cynical side a booster shot.

Basically, most bridal shows attempt to stage a fashion show (we use the word "show" here very loosely) and a trade fair. The latter consists of various booths with displays from merchants with names like "Brides 'R' Us" and "Fred's Professional Wedding Photography." Like sharks smelling blood in the water, these merchants crawl out of their subterranean homes and swim circles around brides, passing out little gifts like potpourri balls, which will emit such a pleasant perfume that it will take you three months to get the smell out of your purse.

The fashion show is the alleged bait to get you (the consumer) into their (the merchants') clutches for two hours of unabashed commercial plugs. During this fashion show, you will actually see live and in person many of those hideous bridesmaids gowns that you only thought existed in the bridal magazines and in the backs of closets.

After hearing the announcer say for the twentieth time, "Here's a lovely taffeta design with PUFF SLEEVES" you'll probably be able to actually feel your teeth grind.

What's most interesting about these runway shows is the realization of how far removed the bridal apparel industry is from reality. If you look closely, you'll notice the "new design for this year" looks suspiciously like one from a wedding you attended in 1989.

After the show and the non-stop commercial plug-a-thon (yes, Bob, we'd love to thank Burt's Wedding Chair Rental for providing the chairs you're sitting in today! Aren't they just lovely! And they're just $3.95 plus deposit!), you have time to walk around the booths and chat with local merchants. Many of these merchants will lunge at you from their booths and shove a brochure in your hand while simultaneously complementing you on how LARGE your engagement ring is—all with a look of sincerely feigned sincerity. While visiting a recent bridal show, we were struck by the sheer ingenuity of wedding entrepreneurs who have invented brilliant ways to separate you from your money.

Perhaps the best known bridal show operator is Bridal Expos, based in that state known for bridal bliss, New Jersey (just ask Bruce Springsteen). Bridal Expos mounts this massive multimedia show that admittedly is much more polished than the typical dog-and-pony show put on by locals. Slickly choreographed, the Bridal Expos are thick with plugs for the Official Sponsors.

What's most hysterical about the Bridal Expos is that these folks from New Jersey think that the world is simply dying to see what newest horror the New York bridal designers are trying to heap on us consumers. At one show in Denver, we couldn't help but notice the crowd audibly guffawing at several bridal gowns that some designer must have dreamed up in his Manhattan office during a bad acid trip.

The biggest scam at all these bridal shows are the so-called door prizes. As you enter, most bridal shows will ask you to register for A FREE EXCITING HONEYMOON TRIP TO NEPAL. Of course, besides your name and address, the "registration card" will ask for your phone number, fiance's name, yearly income, birth place, blood type, and so on. As you wander around the booths, the wedding merchants will ask you to fill out entry forms for such tantalizing door prizes as "A FREE NAPKIN (WHEN YOU PURCHASE $1000 WORTH OF PICTURES)!"

As you fill out the forms, you'll noticed the merchants and show organizers will barely be able to keep the drool from dripping down their shirts in sheer excitement. That's because this whole thing is a big sham—what these bridal shows really want is your phone number and address. Then they can call you frequently at dinner time to inform you that they have a BIG SPECIAL this month and that if you sign up NOW you won't be killed by their bridal death squad.

Yes, bridal merchants pay hundreds of dollars to do these shows and THE BIG REASON is that list of brides, all neatly alphabetized with their home phone numbers, wedding date, bank account numbers, and more. Many brides are alarmed to find after they've attended a bridal show that they must buy a six-foot mailbox with forklift to handle the volume of mail that will give new meaning to the word junk.

The lesson? If you've got an afternoon to kill and would like to overdose on sugar from 67 cake samples, then a bridal show may be for you. But, if you value your privacy, be careful out there.

Wedding Advertising Publications

It takes approximately six to eight seconds from the time you get engaged until you get deluged with advertising publications that pretend to help you plan your wedding. Let's take a second to look at these local bridal "books" and "magazines."

We use the words "books" and "magazines" liberally here because what these things are are pure advertising masquerading as "helpful information." For example, some company in Texas actually published a "bridal resource guidebook" that claimed to be an "independent" survey of the area's best bridal merchants.

What the publisher forgot to mention was that they insisted bridal merchants pay a $200 "service fee" to be included the book. The book does say, and we quote, "many other quality and 'excellent-rated' businesses were invited to participate in our first edition. However their consent may not have reached us by the publishing deadline or they may have chosen not to be listed." TRANSLATION: the best merchants in town refused to pay our ad fee so we left them out of our "independent, unbiased" survey. Only the merchants that coughed up $200 are in here.

Of course, the publisher also forgot to say that the merchants wrote their own descriptions in this book. And that's the way it goes in bridal land—the lines between editorial and advertising are often nonexistent. Of course, considering how "ethical" the big bridal magazines are, you can understand why local publishers have no scruples.

Here are a few publications that you may come across (or have shoved in your face) during your bridal journey:

1 ***The Wedding Pages.***
This Omaha, Nebraska company claims to produce the "yellow pages of the bridal industry." This slick planner is packaged in a work-book format. Over 90 versions of the book are produced for different cities. Graphics and such insightful bridal advice as "weddings often include dancing as part of the reception festivities" are interspersed with ads for local wedding merchants.

Perhaps the best thing that can be said about *The Wedding Pages* is that it's free. Of course, there's a catch. You must fill out a card at a local *Wedding Pages* dealer (typically, a jeweler or bridal shop) and then wait a few weeks for delivery. The catch is your name (and address, phone number, wedding date and birth date) then goes on a mailing list which is sent faithfully by the company to local wedding merchants. Soon, you'll receive little love notes from such companies as "Bill's Wedding Candles" and other firms that want to sell you customized cake knife corsages. Your only clue about this comes in a sheepishly worded disclaimer at the bottom of the order form: "acceptance of this Wedding Planner may subject your name to other solicitations."

A darker side to the *Wedding Pages* is their attempts to block discounters from advertising in their book. We spoke with a Discount Bridal Service rep in one city who was blocked from advertising in the local *Wedding Pages*. Why? Well, the publishers don't want to offend those full-price bridal retailers by accepting the discounter's ads.

We spoke to Doug Russell, the VP of Marketing for the *Wedding Pages*, who said they have no official policy on discounters and "let the franchisee make the decision on who can be a *Wedding Pages* sponsor in their respective markets. The franchisee has the right to do business with whom ever they feel will benefit them the most." In one city, after they let a discounter advertise, eight other bridal shops boycotted the *Wedding Pages*, pulling their ads. Obviously, the *Wedding Pages* is letting full-price retailers censor their publication—a practice we find disgusting, in our opinion. And the fact that the *Wedding Pages* lets their local franchisee make the decision on discounters is a cop-out. But, there's big bucks in those ads.

ONE TIP: *The Wedding Pages* asks for your phone number on their order form. Our advice is don't give it. They don't need it to send you a copy and you don't need the invasion of privacy.

2   The Wedding Guide.

This is the other big bridal advertising publication. Unlike the *Wedding Pages*, the *Wedding Guide* is less of a fill-in-the-blank planner and even more of an advertising vehicle for its sponsors.

In a smaller, stapled format, the *Wedding Guide* is more transportable than the *Wedding Pages*, but that's the best we can say about it. The gimmick here is the same: the Denver-based company produces a generic advice book with local ads. Merchants who advertise in the guide are provided copies to give away free. Before you can take one, however, many ask you to fill out a card to win some "prize giveaway." Don't be fooled, they want your address for the same reason the *Wedding Pages* wants it: to put you on a mailing list.

On the upside, the *Wedding Guide* has a center section of coupons that offer discounts. On the down-side, the advice in the *Wedding Guide* is predictably schmaltzy. In an article titled, "Building a Healthy, Vital and Loving Marriage," the book says "lovely gowns, champagne bubbles, stolen kisses and parties in your honor currently fill your life and it feels wonderful." Ugh.

3 *Other Local Magazines and Books.*
A few cities have local bridal magazines. *Best Weddings* is a slick magazine that includes ads and listings for local bridal merchants. Editions are available for Washington DC, Atlanta, Denver, Nashville, Boston, Miami, Tampa, Dallas, Houston, Chicago, Detroit, St. Louis, Baltimore, Los Angeles and Philadelphia.

What about local bridal books? In Chapter 14, Weddings Across America, we list local resources for wedding planning. Check the section on your region of the country or pop into our home page on the World Wide Web for the latest information (see the How to Reach Us page at the end of this book).

Wedding Consultants

The last decade saw a return of a member of the wedding not seen for thirty years: the professional wedding consultant. Once a fixture of weddings in the 1950's, wedding consultants were hunted to near extinction in the 1970's when weddings were less formal affairs usually held on a beach.

As weddings have become more complex and formal events, professional wedding consultants have made an impressive comeback. We should note, however, that there are several types of wedding consultants. Many people who work at bridal shops or retail florists call themselves "wedding consultants." In addition to helping the bride with their own specialty, these folks pass along referrals of other bridal professionals. While they may be helpful, these are not the wedding consultants we are referring to in this section.

We define a "professional wedding consultant" as an independent business person who, for a fee, helps plan and coordinate the entire wedding. They don't actually bake the cake or sew the gown—this is done by outside suppliers. In a sense, a wedding consultant is a like a personal shopper. Or as some planners have discovered, like a low-paid waitress.

So How Much Do Wedding Consultants Cost?

Most charge an hourly fee or a percentage of the wedding budget. For example, one consultant we met charges a 15%

fee on the wedding expenditures. So, if you spend $10,000 on a wedding and reception, you then write out a check for $1500 to the consultant. Other party planners we met charge a flat hourly fee ($75 per hour, for example) no matter what your budget. Many consultants offer different levels of help—coordinating just the rehearsal and wedding ceremony costs a small fee, while planning the whole affair from "ground zero" will run you much more.

Sources to Find a Consultant

 ❧ **Call a professional association.** June Wedding (415) 252-9195 will give you a referral to a local bridal consultant (their membership is mostly in the Western U.S.) Two other groups with a nationwide database of wedding planners include the Association of Bridal Consultants (203) 355-0464 and the Association of Certified Wedding Consultants (800) 520-2292, (214) 596-7450.

❧ **Ask your friends.** The best wedding consultants work by word-of-mouth referrals.

Questions to Ask a Consultant

 1 EXACTLY HOW DO YOU WORK YOUR FEES? Do you accept commissions or finder's fees from other bridal merchants? See the Pitfall section below for more information on this practice. Ask the consultant to clearly explain his/her fee schedule.

2 HOW WILL YOU INCORPORATE MY TASTES INTO THE WEDDING? If the consultant will be doing the majority of the legwork, ask them how they will account for your tastes. Will they get your approval at various stages in the planning process?

3 HOW LONG HAVE YOU BEEN A CONSULTANT? HOW MANY WEDDINGS HAVE YOU PLANNED? This is a key question. Many "consultants" we've talked to were far too inexperienced to trust your wedding to. Some have been in business for less than a year or so. We recommend you trust your wedding only to a seasoned professional with at least three years minimum experience. Sure, consultants with less experience can still plan and coordinate a beautiful wedding—but be careful. You don't want someone "learning the ropes" on your big day.

Pitfalls to Avoid

Pitfall #1
KICKBACKS AND VENDOR REFERRAL FEES

"I visited a wedding consultant who recommended I buy my wedding gown from a particular bridal shop. Later, I learned the shop paid her a commission for recommending me. Is this legitimate?"

Well, it certainly isn't ethical. This points up a central problem we have with some less-than-professional consultants. In a clear conflict of interest, some consultants collect "finder's fees" or "commissions" (read: kickbacks) from other bridal merchants on the products and services they recommend to brides. So who are they representing—the bride or the businesses? We don't believe a consultant can negotiate effectively for the bride when they receive a kickback from bridal merchants. If you use a consultant, make sure the consultant clearly identifies how they get paid.

Pitfall #2
PERCENTAGE-BASED FEES MAY ENCOURAGE GREED.

"One bridal consultant told me she could save me hundreds of dollars. However, her fee is based on a percentage of the money I spend. Where is her real incentive to save me money?"

Of course, a professional consultant relies on word-of-mouth referral for new clients. If they don't deliver what they promise, word will spread quickly. However, we do agree that a conflict exists here: when their income is based on how much money you spend, less-than-ethical consultants may feel the temptation to encourage lavish spending. Or at least, the incentive to save you money comes in conflict with their bottom line. Realize that all consultants do not charge a percentage-based fee—others charge flat fees or hourly rates. This might be a better alternative.

Pitfall #3
COUNTERFEIT CONSULTANTS.

"I called a so-called 'wedding consultant' from the phone book. Instead of offering a consulting service, she pitched me on her wedding chapel and reception site."

Yes, many "all-in-one" wedding companies deceptively advertise themselves as wedding consultants. Don't be fooled—these businesses aren't interested in consulting on your wedding. They just want you to book their wedding and reception site, photography and so on.

Pitfall #4

LACK OF REGULATION.

"I contacted a wedding consultant to talk about my wedding. Boy was I surprised! This person knew nothing about weddings. Aren't these guys suppose to be licensed?"

Unfortunately, very few laws regulate wedding consultants. When you think about it, wedding consultants are quasi-financial planners—they advise people on how to spend money. Unlike other financial planners, however, there is very little regulation. Anyone can call themselves a wedding consultant—and sometimes it seems like everyone is. Some cities do require wedding consultants or party planners to be licensed. In most areas, however, the industry is left to police itself. Consider hiring a consultant who is a member of a professional association. Many require the members to subscribe to a basic ethics pledge. Other groups offer on-going training through seminars and workshops.

Advantages of Consultants

❧ *Bridal consultants can save you time.* If you and your fiance are working too many hours to plan your wedding, you may find a wedding consultant to be worth the expense. Frankly, planning a wedding is very time-intensive. Realistically evaluate your schedules and time commitments to decide if you can handle it alone. Brides planning large and expensive wedding may find consultants a necessity.

❧ *Long-distance weddings may require such help.* Planning a wedding in another city is quite challenging. Having a local bridal consultant to coordinate the details may be prudent.

❧ *Seasoned experts may be able to negotiate more effectively, getting you a better deal.* Now we aren't talking about novices here but wedding consultants with years of experience. These people are on a first-name basis with catering managers and other bridal professionals. Some consultants are tough negotiators who can make sure you get the best price. Other consultants claim that other bridal professionals have a vested interest in doing their very best work for their clients—if they don't, they may lose future business. We are not sure to what extent these claims are true but we do believe one thing: a talented, experienced consultant may be worth the extra expense.

So You Want to Be a Bridal Consultant?

The other day we got a mighty strange call here at the home office. On the other end of the phone was a wedding consultant from Illinois who was upset about the advice on this chapter.

Now, that's not terribly unusual—to some wedding planners, this book might as well be *Satanic Verses*. Nope, the real strange part came when the wedding planner started telling us about herself and her business.

It turns out she's sixteen years old.

That's right, we had a hopping mad wedding planner on the other end of the phone who just last week got her driver's license. She said she doesn't like our advice to hire only *experienced* planners—she's only been in business for a month and doesn't need some know-it-all book scaring away customers. Click.

After that call, it dawned on us how this wedding planner-career bug has apparently afflicted several generations of otherwise normal folks. Not a week goes by when our phone doesn't ring with a person who's convinced this is the career for them. And they'd like to know what advice we have for aspiring bridal consultants.

Well, you asked for it.

Admittedly, the advice we give usually doesn't inspire wild applause from the other end of the phone. While we don't ever want to discourage anyone from living out their entrepreneurial dream, the Hollywood image of a wedding planner and the gritty reality are worlds apart. So if you're one of those aspiring bridal consultants, here are our five pieces of unsolicited advice:

• *Prepare to work like a dog.* Forget everything you've seen in movies or read in those sugar-coated bridal magazines—a wedding planner's life is hardly glamorous. Experienced planners often burn out from the 70-hour weeks and no free Saturdays. Even those who love the business point out their

Disadvantages of Consultants

❧ *The "professional organizations" for bridal consultants aren't that professional.* Unlike other fields, most bridal consultant groups don't have rigid standards for membership. Printed up business cards that say you're a wedding consultant? Have a pulse? That's enough for the Association of Bridal Consultants (ABC), the group that has come in for the most criticism.

Anyone can join the ABC, although the group points out that members must subscribe to an ethics pledge. Critics slam their home study courses as "simplistic" and claim their job is really nothing more than being a glorified waitress—they fetch items for a bride, instead of a group of bar patrons. "Politeness-challenged" mothers-of-the-bride and budget-conscious couples ratchet up the stress level and squeeze profit margins to the breaking point.

• *If you still want to be a planner, apprentice with a pro.* That's right, go to work one summer for a bridal planner as an unpaid intern and learn the ropes. Call a local wedding consultant and offer to work as slave labor.

• *Work in a wedding-related business.* Spend a few months in a bridal shop and you'll get a real understanding of what this business is like. Another great place: catering halls or hotels. Since the reception is where the big bucks are spent, understanding this aspect of the wedding inside and out will help you in the long-term.

• *Plan friends' weddings for free.* And we mean more than just one friend—try five. You'll get a candid picture of how much work this job entails. Of course, going from giving away your services to charging potential customers is a big leap.

• *Pick up business skills.* Being a wedding planner is no different than starting any other business. You don't need an MBA, but some basic business skills like marketing and accounting will be invaluable (and perhaps the difference between success and failure). Take a community college course on how to write a business plan.

One key point: research the market and decide if there is demand for your service. Notice we didn't say a "need" for your service. One of the biggest mistakes a wedding planner can make is assuming, "Well, there are so many brides out there, there must be a need for bridal consultants." Sure there is *need*, but does anyone care? Do brides want to part with hard-earned cash to get your help? We can only assume the high failure rate for bridal consulting businesses is the result of a "no" answer to that last question.

workshops are more applicable to the Northeast (the ABC is headquartered in Connecticut.) We've also been disappointed with the ABC for not taking a strong position on the kickback/vendor commission issue.

Other groups are better—June Wedding (817) 983-3596 is probably the best-run professional organization of the bunch. Director Robbi Ernst has crafted an excellent home-study course and has taken a strong position against kickbacks.

So what does this mean for you? While it's a good sign if the bridal consultant you've discovered is a member of one of these groups, don't assume they are all-knowing "experts." Check references and ask some tough questions to weed out the amateurs.

PART III

Weddings
Across America

Chapter 14

Weddings Across America

Here's a quick quiz. If you are at a wedding and encounter a Mandelringstarta, what would you do? If you answered "run like hell," guess again. The correct answer: eat it. That's because a Mandelringstarta is a Swedish wedding cake made from rings of almond pastry. If you don't live in Minnesota (with its large Scandinavian population), you probably have never come to face to face with a Mandelringstarta. Which brings up a point: weddings in the U.S. are anything but uniform.

Weddings vary greatly from region to region, state to state and even city to city. What's a time-honored tradition in one town is a major social gaffe in another.

Take the relatively straight forward concept of a "wedding reception," for example. In the Northeast, this means a formal sit-down dinner. Suggest such a reception in Texas (or for that matter, anywhere in the South or West) and you'll get weird looks from caterers. Cocktail receptions with "heavy hors d'oeuvres" are the norm in those regions.

You get the idea. While the "wedding press" often reports on nuptial traditions in New York or Los Angeles, there's nary a word on wedding customs in places like Memphis, Denver, or Seattle. We wondered, hey, how are couples tying the knot in the U.S.?

In order to find out, we conducted telephone interviews with nearly 30 bridal consultants across the country. What follows is a region-by-region look at weddings in the U.S.

The West Coast

Western brides and grooms definitely like to bring in the beautiful scenery into their weddings and receptions. You'll find more outdoor weddings here than anywhere else in the U.S.

Of course, with a region as large as the West Coast, you'll find just about every bridal trend under the sun. Or the clouds—in the Pacific Northwest, the weather greatly influences which months are most popular for nuptials.

For example, don't go to **Seattle** in June and expect to see many weddings. Unlike the rest of the country, June is not the most popular wedding month in Seattle, thanks to that month's usually wet weather. Instead, dryer August is the number-one choice.

Seattle brides spend $10,000 to $20,000 on an average wedding. That number is about the same in Portland, Oregon as well. Of course, more rural areas of the Pacific Northwest are usually less expensive; bride typically spend just $5000 or less in smaller towns.

"People like to plan outdoor weddings here," said a Seattle bridal planner. Favorite reception sites in Seattle include the famous Space Needle and several restored mansions. "Another popular site is the Kiana Lodge, which is noted for its beautiful salmon barbecues and surroundings with native American carvings," she said. If you want to wed at sea, over 15 charter boats are available for wedding cruises. One boat can hold 600 people on three decks with dancing and dining!

Northwestern wines and foods are popular at weddings in Seattle. For example, salmon is the most popular dish at wedding receptions, as are other seafood dishes. Buffets with pasta stations are common sights.

Seattle's large Filipino community has their own wedding traditions, including a roasted pig for the buffet and a "money dance," where guests pay to dance with the bride and groom. This money helps pay for the honeymoon, etc.

Down the coast in **Portland,** May has almost replaced June as the most popular month to wed according to Melanie Perko (503) 291-1070, a bridal consultant and Portland native. And, while Portland weddings are large (averaging 250 guests), the cost is somewhat more affordable than national averages. Melanie told us the average wedding in Portland costs $13,000.

Portland also boasts several unique wedding sites. "Local vineyards west of Portland are popular reception sites," Melanie said. Other popular sites include local hotels and several area private clubs.

Most Portland wedding receptions feature heavy hors d'oeuvres. "Quite a few weddings I've seen are staying away from the sit-down dinner. The food is more healthy—lots of pasta, fresh fruit, shrimp, and chicken wings. Since we're close to the coast, there are always quite a few seafood dishes, too," Melanie said. Cappuccino bars are hip, of course, in a city that has drive-through coffee shops.

For dessert, "wedding cakes are going toward the real unusual," she said. "I've seen many French cakes with Marzipan icing and layers of flowers and icing ruffles."

Banana, chocolate and poppyseed are the most popular flavors for wedding cakes in Portland.

Melanie also told us couples in Portland are breaking with tradition in one way—most see each other before the ceremony to take all the formal photographs. Of course, that doesn't mean weddings there are informal by any means. "In fact," Melanie said, "quite a few weddings are optional black tie."

California brides and grooms face much higher prices than couples in other parts of the West. A reader in **San Francisco** pointed out that the total for her wedding for 125 guests was nearly 20,000. Wedding cakes run nearly $4 per slice, receptions are $60 per guest for the food and photography will set you back at least $1500 in the Bay Area.

Although the cost is high, San Francisco-area mansions like Ralston Hall and the Flood Mansion make for spectacular reception sites. As for the food, brides and grooms are choosing "seated buffets," a cross between hors d'oeuvres and seated dinner receptions. Popular dishes include pasta bars, cracked crab and many other varieties of fresh seafood.

Favors are a common sight at Bay area receptions. A Bay Area wedding consultant told us one popular favor is a chocolate truffle in a small box. The box, which is colored in the same motif as the wedding party, is wrapped with a ribbon that has the couple's names imprinted on it.

San Francisco's large ethnic communities have their own wedding traditions. For example, Asian brides often wear more than one gown during their wedding day, changing into two or three gowns that are sewn by various family members. Of course, ethnic foods and family traditions also play a big role in Asian weddings in San Francisco.

While brides in **Sacramento** and Northern California don't have to pay those high prices, planning a wedding in the valley can still set you back $10,000 or more. Outdoor weddings are all the rage here, according to bridal consultant Lorie Worman (916) 486-0909. "We have many parks in Sacramento that have specific areas set aside just for weddings," Lorie said. McKinnley Park Rose Garden is particularly popular.

With all those outdoor weddings, August and September (instead of June) have become the busiest months for weddings in Sacramento since the weather is predictably nice then. For receptions, the Delta King, a newly restored paddleboat on the Sacramento River is extremely popular. "For one fun wedding, we decorated up a speed boat that the couple used as their get-away after the reception," Lorie said.

Other popular sites include restored mansions like the

Grand Island Mansion and the Sterling Hotel. At the Sterling, a European-imported glass conservatory is a unique ceremony or reception site. Best of all, Sacramento brides have a wide variety of choices: both the beach and mountain sites are relatively close by.

Availability and prices of flowers are excellent, thanks to Sacramento's close proximity to California's big flower growers. Also, Lorie told us that flowers as table centerpiece decorations common, while some couples choose balloons to fill up a cavernous reception site. Overall, "jewel tone" weddings are definitely in vogue.

Wedding favors are big in Sacramento— "especially items with potpourri instead of almonds," Lorie said. Another unique trend: after the reception, many couples have a portrait taken in one of Sacramento's parks, sitting on the grass with the river in the background.

Like their northern neighbors, Southern Californians love those outdoor weddings too. In **San Diego**, two popular ceremony sites are Balboa and Presidio Park.

Expect to spend $13,000 to $17,000 for a wedding with 200 guests in San Diego—in **Los Angeles**, those costs easily can be double.

"Brides are choosing very simple but elegant gowns. They are really into long trains," a Southern California bridal consultant said. Preferred designers include Galina and the Diamond Collection. White roses and lilies of the valley are chosen for the bridal bouquet.

Receptions are often elegant, three course sit-down dinners. Buffets are popular for afternoon wedding receptions or for smaller weddings. For the wedding cake, a white cake with lemon or strawberry filling is decorated with white chocolate shavings.

❦ Local resources

For brides who are planning in the Bay Area, *By Recommendation Only* (415) 494-8719 includes information on a wide variety of wedding businesses. Separate editions cover San Francisco/Marin, the East Bay and the Southern Peninsula.

Here Comes the Guide (510) 525-3379 are books that extensively cover California's wedding and receptions sites. One edition covers Northern California and the Bay Area, while a second does the job for Southern California.

Speaking of LA, check out the Wedding Library in Orange, CA (714) 997-1579. It's a free service for brides— you can get information on reception sites, photographers, caterers and more in the LA metro area.

Gerri Samuels of "I Do" Publishing (800) 392-9039 publishes *San Diego Weddings*, a local guide book with reviews of bridal merchants.

The Rockies/Southwest

As you'd expect, weddings in Colorado are closely entwined with the beautiful scenery. Carla Harbert, a **Denver** wedding planner, told us that while "most of my brides want to go to the old mansions," they often schedule a half hour between the wedding and reception to have pictures taken in a local park. Equally popular among Carla's brides are weddings in the foothills and even in mountain towns like Vail or Aspen.

Colorado weddings are smaller than the national average with 100 to 125 guests—in more informal places like Boulder, the guest count might be just 50 or less. "September is usually one of the nicest months," she told us because the weather is at its best. August is another popular month.

Brides in Denver also tend to prefer heavy hors d'oeuvres for reception food rather than sit-down dinners. Sliced beef with rolls, poached salmon, crab wontons and shishkebobs are among the more popular items served. The bridal planner mentioned Denver brides are trying to offer more healthy foods instead of the typical meatballs in sauce.

Even though they are next door neighbors, the wedding scene in Utah is quite different from other mountain states. Credit the state's large Mormon population for blazing their own nuptial trail.

Wedding breakfasts are "what's in" in **Salt Lake City**, according to a wedding planner with Danielle's Bridal Shop (801) 272-1146. She explained that many Mormon ceremonies are at 9:00 or 10:00 in the morning. Following the ceremony, a wedding breakfast is held for the immediate family and the bridal party. Later in the evening, a reception is held for all the guests.

"As far as receptions, there are quite a few reception centers in the Salt Lake Valley that cater to weddings," the planner said, adding that "in the summer, we are seeing a trend toward garden weddings in a home." Several popular reception sites that also have a gazebo for ceremonies include the McCueon Mansion, the Murray Mansion, and the Old Meeting House Chapel.

June is still the biggest month for weddings in Salt Lake City. The average wedding in Salt Lake City costs between $7000 to $12,000. The wedding breakfast or brunch (traditionally paid for by the groom's family) is followed in the evening by a larger reception, which typically features a light buffet. "Little finger sandwiches, fruit kabobs and pastries are the most popular foods at Utah receptions," the planner said.

And those receptions are big. "On the average, 500 invitations go out for a typical Mormon wedding," she said. "We're a little more conservative here in Utah with wedding (spending). The contributing factor is because the average family has at least four or five children. Some have as many as eight or nine children. And that's a lot of weddings to pay for."

Another unusual feature of Salt Lake City weddings: taffy wedding cakes. "The cake is also covered with taffy flowers, for a unique look." Other unusual wedding cakes include a replica of the L.D.S. temple. With the preponderance of Mormon weddings, liquor is virtually non-existent at Salt Lake wedding receptions.

"What used to be big were those invitations with a picture of the bride and groom. Now, its definitely out," the planner said. Dancing is not as big for receptions, with less than half of the couple's opting for a band as entertainment. Instead of musical entertainment, a video is often played that chronicles the couples' childhood.

Believe it or not, weddings and receptions in **Phoenix** are much more like those on the East Coast than the Western U.S.

"Most of the people who live in Phoenix are not from Phoenix—many moved here from the East Coast and Midwest," Jacque Carman, a former wedding planner in Phoenix, said. "Most of the couple's relatives don't live in the Phoenix area and must fly in. As a result, I don't think weddings here are as large as other areas of the country where people have lived (in one city) all their lives."

Jacque said most weddings and receptions cost $6000 to $15,000 with 125 to 150 guests. "The largest wedding here I have ever seen was 300 people." The exception to this rule is Phoenix's large Hispanic and Indian communities, who generally have larger weddings and receptions.

The extreme summer heat in Phoenix dictates some changes in wedding traditions. For example, unlike the rest of the country, the summer is not the most popular time to tie the knot in Arizona. "March, April and May are the most popular months to get married," Jacque said. "When its 118 degrees (in June) and you got Grandma and Grandpa in from Detroit passing out—it's not a pretty scene."

One recent change Jacque has noticed is a shift from Friday and Saturday night weddings to Saturday afternoon. "Most couples now get married at 11 or noon on Saturday with a luncheon reception following," Jacque said.

Next to churches and synagogues, the most popular wedding and reception sites in Phoenix are the area's many resort hotels. "Some of my clients don't want to get married in churches anymore," she said. "First of all, they're expensive. Also, most Phoenix churches require engaged couples to take classes. Couples simply don't want to be bothered." Instead, the Camel Back Inn and La Posada are two popular sites, as well as an historical district in downtown.

Most receptions start with a cocktail hour with hors d'oeuvres "served Butler style." Perhaps due to the influx of Easterners and Midwesterners, the sit-down dinner (or luncheon) is most popular. "Also, buffets (in Phoenix) are more expensive, believe it or not," Jacque said.

Fresh flower decorations are the most popular cake toppers. Since they have to be flown in to Phoenix, flowers in general are quite expensive. "Of course, roses are always popular. I'm seeing a lot of pink tiger lilies (alstroemeria)." As you might expect, flowers that aren't as heat-sensitive (carnations and daisies) are also common.

Planning in advance is critical for Phoenix brides. "A year is good since the hotel resorts book up very fast. This is a convention center town. They don't want to fool around with a wedding for 150 guests when they can book a big convention for thousands."

The biggest time for conventions in Phoenix is November and December. During those months, "you can hardly find a place," she said.

The Northeast/Mid-Atlantic

If there's one common denominator to weddings in the Northeast and Mid-Atlantic part of the country, it's money—weddings there are darn expensive.

Boston is a typical example. Estates and hotels are the most popular places to tie the knot in Boston, says consultant Elizabeth Gemelli of Weddings by Elizabeth, a Boston-based wedding consultant.

Weddings in Boston are somewhat smaller than in other cities, averaging about 150 guests. Nevertheless, Elizabeth said her clients spend $20,000 to $30,000 for a wedding reception. While Bostonians invite fewer guests, they tend to spend more per guest for the reception, according to one hotel catering manager who worked in Boston for eight years. While Bostonians still adore June weddings, October is quickly gaining in popularity.

A large part of the wedding budget is for a sit-down dinner, still the mainstay of receptions on the East Coast. However, Elizabeth told us she's noticed a new trend.

"Many of my clients don't want that typical, sit-down boring dinner," she said. "Now, they're doing cocktail receptions where they have heavy hors d'oeuvres and food stations. They might have a wok station, a pasta table, a roast beef station and so on," she said.

For apparel, brides in the Northeast are still wearing traditional gowns "no matter how young or old they are," Elizabeth said. Popular designers include such hometown favorites as Bianchi and Priscilla.

Wedding photographers in Boston are doing more candid and creative pictures than posed shots, she said. Bridal portraits are rare but wedding videos that cost $900 on the average are quite popular.

While weddings in the major cities of the Northeast and Mid-Atlantic are pricey, there are areas that are more affordable. For example, we spoke to Jeannie Greene of the Party Planning Service (914) 462-4858 in **Poughkeepsie**, New York, who said the average wedding in her area has 150 to 200 guests and costs between $8,000 and $13,000. The Hudson River Valley is blessed with many unique wedding and reception sites—the area's many mansions and hotels are popular picks.

Among the best sites are the Hotel Thayer at the West Point Military Academy, the Troutbeck Mansion (in Anenia), the Valeur Mansion and the Bear Mountain Inn in Bear Mountain State Park. The area also boasts the oldest inn in America, the Beekman Arms in Rhinebeck, NY, which is a popular spot for receptions.

Local wineries are also a favorite choice for weddings and receptions. Among the best are the Regent Champagne Cellars, the Cascade Mountain Winery, and the Westpark Wine Cellars on the Hudson River. If that isn't enough, brides and grooms can celebrate their wedding on a river cruise. May and October are the most popular months to tie the knot in the Hudson River Valley.

"Chicken and prime rib are the popular dishes here in the Hudson Valley," Jeannie said. A several course sit-down dinner with wine starts at $30 and can go up to $75 per person. For entertainment, "disc jockeys are being used here instead of expensive bands. The advantage is that they play continuously and also provide the special dances like the circle dance, the limbo, the conga and many ethnic dances."

In fact, ethnic weddings are quite big in Poughkeepsie. "We do have Hungarian, Italian, Jewish, Polish, German, Greek and Russian weddings—it's a melting pot here since we are so close to New York City. So, ethnic foods are big. Usually the grandmother will bring in special breads and cakes for the reception," the bridal planner said.

Down the Hudson river from Poughkeepsie, brides in that tiny burg called **New York City** would love to find receptions for $30 per guest—most are triple or four times that amount. One New York City bride called us with a great money saving tip to beat the high prices—get out of town. She found vendors outside the city are much more affordable. A photographer in Larchmont was just $1300 for a complete wedding package. She was quoted prices that started at $2200 for wedding photographers in Manhattan.

Another bargain tip for New York brides: Michaels bridal consignment on the upper east side (Madison and 79th, 212-737-7273) has 80 to 90 gowns in stock for $800 to $1000. These are fancy label designer gowns that originally cost $2800-$5000!

A trend toward spring and fall weddings (instead of the summer) is the latest news in **Pittsburgh** weddings. A veteran bridal planner in the Steel City told us "many of the older churches in Pittsburgh, which are most popular for weddings, do not have air conditioning. This probably accounts for the shift away from the summer." One result: Memorial and Labor Day weekends are the most popular times.

Most weddings in Pittsburgh are held on Saturdays at 4:30 PM. For receptions, "what's becoming more popular in Pittsburgh are restored estates. The only problem with estates is they will only accommodate 100 people," the planner said. The average wedding in Pittsburgh is 175 guests.

Wedding receptions in Pittsburgh are typically sit-down dinners with open bars and dancing. Most menus feature a chicken dish and a meat dish. For dessert, the wedding cake is traditionally served with French vanilla ice cream.

"A lot of people this year have gone with fresh flowers on the wedding cake. A simple icing like basketweave is popular. I've even seen a few wedding cheesecakes," she said.

Disc jockeys are the most favorite entertainment at receptions. "Another popular musical choice here is to have a strolling violinist during dinner," she said. Favors are still popular with Pittsburgh's large Italian community.

"One tradition we have up here that is so popular is the balloon releases. Couples will have these instead of throwing rice since most churches prohibit it. The balloons are usually ordered in the same color as their wedding party. There is usually a separate, heart-shaped balloon for the bride and groom. In other cases, there is a little paper attached to the balloon so everyone can write a wish to the bride and groom."

❧ Local resources
Places (212) 737-5536 is a book with site information for major metropolitan areas, with an emphasis on the

Northeast. For New York brides, the *Down the Aisle Directory* (212) 779-4219 provides information on the Tri-state area. *Great Locations II* is a videotape of sites in the New York City metro area. Call (212) 727-2424 to order.

If you're a bride in the New York Tri-State area, check out WeddingFone (212) 395-WEDD. This free, 24-hour information service gives you information on local bridal businesses.

In New England, check out *New England Bride Magazine* (508) 535-4186 on local newsstands. The *Wedding Directory* (617) 878-5931 focuses on receptions sites and wedding services in Massachusetts.

Unique Meeting Places in Greater Washington (800) 289-2339 is a book that provides site information. The same company offers a similar book for Baltimore. Also, *Washingtonian Magazine* has an annual wedding planner issue in January. Call (202) 296-1246 for the latest information.

The Midwest

Ethnic traditions play a big role in weddings in the Midwest. If you walked into a wedding reception in **Minneapolis-St. Paul**, you might marvel at the wedding Kransekaki or Mandelringstarta.

Perhaps you're saying right now, hey what are those things besides the ultimate spelling nightmare? Well, quite simply, Kransekaki (as the Norwegians call it) or Mandelringstarta (as the Swedes refer to it) is a traditional Scandinavian wedding cake. With its large Scandinavian population, Minneapolis (and the rest of Minnesota for that matter) sees a lot of these cakes. Taking their inspiration from the French croquembouche, these cone-shaped cakes are stacked layers of almond pastry rings topped with powdered sugar. In addition to a standard, traditional cake, couples often have this almond ring cake too.

We spoke to Joan Kalpiers, a former Minneapolis consultant who had been in the wedding business for 20 years. Besides providing the spelling for those Scandinavian cakes, Joan told us the average wedding there costs $12,000 to $16,000 with an average of 200 guests.

"The Twin Cities are a very traditional and conservative area for weddings. We are seeing larger weddings than in the past and less 'nuts, mints, very small church receptions.' Now there are more elegant hotel and country club receptions," Joan said.

The area's many lakes are a popular backdrop for local weddings and receptions. The "Outdoor Chapel," in a wooded area with a pond and waterfall is a popular site, as is the

Jonathan Padelford Paddleboat on the Mississippi River. Edinborough Park is an "outdoor facility that is inside: its a completely enclosed park with trees, indoor pool, ice rink and amphitheater," Joan said.

In the past few years, several unique wedding sites have become available. Now Minneapolis brides can get married or have receptions at a restored movie theater downtown or on the Minnesota Zephyr train. You can even have a wedding and reception at the Mall of America, the country's largest shopping mall.

In the Midwest, the buffet dinner is king of the wedding receptions. Minneapolis is basically a meat and potatoes town—beef, turkey, chicken, potatoes and salads are common sights on the buffet table. The Twin Cities ethnic communities often add their own favorites: the Polish favor sausages and sauerkraut, the Italians like pasta and the Swedes prefer, of course, a smorgasbord.

Ethnic foods play a big role in **Cleveland** wedding receptions as well. Thanks to the large Polish, Slovenian and Italian populations in the area, you might find dishes like pieroghis (potato or sauerkraut filled pastries), keifles (rolled dough filled with nuts and fruit) or cannolis (Italian pastries filled with cream). Sausages and stuffed cabbages are other favorites that might appear.

Many weddings take place in reception halls rather than in restored homes or hotels. One such hall is the American Slovenian Hall; another is De Luca's Place in the Park. Weddings are usually rather large, topping 250 to 300 guests. But what most surprised us were the bridal showers. Local bridal planners told us many brides invite 100 to 200 guests to their showers! And every guest takes home a plate of pastries and cookies from the shower.

The beautiful fall foliage makes September and October very popular months to tie the knot in **Indianapolis,** local bridal planners told us. The average wedding has 125 to 150 guests and is a bargain compared to most cities—brides spend $4500 to $7000 for a typical wedding.

While Indianapolis has few outdoor locations for weddings and receptions, several restored homes and mansions are popular. One local favorite, the Schnull-Rauch House, is booked up to a year in advance. Eagle's Crest and Hideaway at Eagle Creek Reservoir are two other popular spots.

Indianapolis wedding receptions are most often light buffets that feature hors d'oeuvres, regardless of the time of day. Traditional selections like Swedish meatballs are crowd pleasers.

❦ *Local resources*

For Midwest brides, *Planning Your Chicago Wedding Magazine* (914) 347-2121 gives info on the Windy City. *Chicago Special Occasion Sourcebook* (312) 828-0350 focuses on ceremony and reception sites. Iowa brides can find bridal information in the book *Des Moines Weddings* (515) 224-1358.

The South

What one word sums up Southern weddings? "Big" comes to mind.

While folks in other parts of the country think a large wedding has 200 guests, that's on the smallish side for brides and grooms in Texas.

"The average wedding in Texas has between 200 to 300 guests—and weddings with over 500 guests aren't uncommon," said a local bridal expert from the Lone Star State.

In the state's capital, **Austin**, brides have several lovely reception sites to choose from. The Caswell House is a beautifully restored Victorian home built in 1900. Another popular spot is the Texas Federation of Women's Club, an elegant mansion that oozes Southern hospitality. The Green Pastures Restaurant and Four Seasons Hotel are two other favorite sites.

Elegant hotels are popular for receptions in the **Dallas/Fort Worth** Metroplex. Among the best include the Crescent Court, the Grand Kempinski and the Mansion on Turtle Creek. Another favorite site in Big D is the Camp Estate at the Dallas Arboretum, a beautiful home that overlooks White Rock Lake. Of course, you can even get married at the famous Southfork Ranch.

In **Houston**, brides prefer to have receptions at many of the city's beautiful country clubs and restaurants. The Junior League Tea Room and the River Oaks Garden Club are two standouts, as well as the lush grounds at the Rainbow Lodge restaurant.

Most wedding receptions in Texas feature hors d'oeuvre buffets; sit-down dinners are rare. As one caterer in Dallas told us, Texans like to eat things they can identify. Hence, barbecue and Mexican food is "in"; gourmet dishes with French names are "out." "The most popular wedding cake flavor in Texas has to be Italian Cream," an Austin baker told us, adding that chocolate groom's cakes are a staple at receptions. To match those big weddings, Texas bakers are often called upon to create cakes that tower six feet in the air. A Taste of Europe in Fort Worth, for example, has a seven-foot cake that serves 500 people! Covered in hand-sculpted hard-sugar flowers, this cake costs $1250. Whoa—time to hock the ranch.

June is still the biggest month for tying the knot in Texas, despite the summer heat. December and October are a close second, however. Christmas and New Year's Eve weddings have become increasingly popular over the last few years.

The cost for a wedding in Texas varies from city to city. In smaller metro areas like Austin and San Antonio, most weddings cost $7000 to $13,000. Those costs can soar to more than $15,000 and $30,000 in Dallas/Fort Worth and Houston.

Not to be outdone by Texans, brides in Georgia know how to throw a party as well.

Spring is the most popular time to tie the knot in **Atlanta**. "In April, the blooming dogwood trees, tulips and azaleas make this an extremely impressive time of the year, especially for out of town guests," said Michele La Motte, (404) 299-6091 a wedding consultant in Atlanta.

"A real highlight of Atlanta weddings are all the unique sites to have wedding ceremonies and receptions," Michele said. Among the top spots is the Callanwolde Mansion. Also known as the Coca Cola Mansion because it was built by the family that founded that little soft drink company, the Callanwolde is a Tudor-style mansion that has beautiful gardens as well as a rare organ inside. The site is so popular that it books at least a year in advance.

Another popular spot is the Atlanta Botanical Gardens. After getting married in the gardens, you can have a reception in the large exhibit hall which holds 350 seated. The large, beautiful room has huge windows that look onto the gardens.

Atlanta is blessed with many Antebellum homes that can be used for ceremonies and receptions. Popular Bulloch Hall is where Teddy Roosevelt's mother was born and raised. Other homes "are loaded with history from the Civil War," she said.

"We're suggesting that families totally budget $140 to $170 per guest for a wedding in Atlanta," said Sue Winner (404) 255-3804, another Atlanta bridal consultant who has done many Jewish weddings in the area. Hence weddings cost anywhere from $18,000 to $35,000 with an average of about 150 to 225 guests.

There is good news on the cost front: our sources in Atlanta say that many sites are willing to negotiate on prices for weddings during "off-peak times." Examples include weddings at noon, Sundays and slower months like January, February, March and July. For those off-peak weddings, hotels often throw in extras like complementary honeymoon suites or hospitality rooms.

Receptions in Atlanta feature buffets with carving stations of country ham or roast beef. Cheese straws, a Southern favorite, are perennial hors d'oeuvres. Other popular buffet dishes include Greek phyllo pastries (perhaps because of Atlanta's large Greek community) and various fish and salmon dishes.

Sit-down dinners at local hotels are a close second in popularity. "We are very much into the nouvelle cuisine," Sue said. "There is a lot more fish being served but we still see a fair amount of chicken."

At the ceremony, "programs are real popular. These list who's who in the wedding party and a background of how the couple met each other." Also at the ceremony, Michele told us that the father of the groom is the best man at the majority of weddings. Large wedding parties are currently in vogue. "It's not unusual to see eight bridesmaids and twelve to fourteen groomsmen at an Atlanta wedding," she said.

"Weekend weddings, with events arranged from Thursday evening to a brunch on Sunday morning, are quite popular today," Michele said. Since there are so many things to see in Atlanta, out-of-town guests are often given a hospitality bag with brochures and maps for sightseeing.

A trend in rehearsal dinners is toward a casual picnic that features Southern fare: fried chicken, barbecue, and biscuits. And for dessert? Pecan pie, of course.

"Shagging and Pig Pickin'" are what's hip for weddings in **Raleigh-Durham**, North Carolina. So says Marci Fricke, a local wedding consultant.

So, what are shagging and pig pickin'? Marci told us shagging is a popular dance at wedding receptions that resembles the jitterbug. Pig pickin' is the time-honored North Carolina tradition of having a roasted pig at the rehearsal dinner, which is more a picnic than a dinner.

June is the most popular month to get married, though Christmas is also a favorite time. "The big tradition here is that at most weddings the father of the groom is the best man," Marci said. A late afternoon ceremony on Saturday is the most popular time of day.

Many weddings and receptions in Raleigh-Durham are held either in a church or in a relative's home. Other interesting sites include the historic Arrowhead Inn, the restored Nello Teer House and the elegant Fearrington Restaurant. For those alumni of Duke University, the campus gardens and the beautiful Gothic chapel are quite popular.

"The tradition here is to wear your mother's gown," Marci said. If the mother's gown is not available, simple, classic styles by designers like Priscilla are in vogue. For flowers, daffodils, iris, gardenias, white roses, and stephanotis are popular choices.

Brides in Raleigh-Durham also stay close to traditional food choices at the reception. A white bride's cake and a chocolate groom's cake are standard. "Fruit fillings and carrot cake are starting to make inroads here," she said. Icing flowers are a popular decoration for the bride's cake while groom's cakes normally reflect the area's passion for basketball. "At many weddings I've seen, the groom's cake is (decorated like) a basketball court," she said.

Most receptions in North Carolina feature hors d'oeuvres; sit-down dinners or buffets are rare. (The exception are Jewish weddings that often feature a sit-down dinner reception at a local hotel.) After dinner, the guests usually dance to "beach music," Marci said, "which is more like the Four Seasons and the Four Tops than the Beach Boys or Jan and Dean."

At rehearsal dinners, chopped barbecue and Brunswick stew (a popular regional dish with beef, chicken and vegetables) are common sights. The average wedding in Raleigh-Durham, North Carolina has 150 guests and costs $7000 to $13,000.

Even though Florida is technically in the south, it has more in common with weddings in, say, in New Jersey than Georgia.

Typical of this trend is **Boca Raton**, where the average wedding could set you back $25,000 or more. The most common reception is a formal sit-down dinner like those in the Northeast.

"The winter months are quite popular for weddings," a local wedding consultant said. "When you're inviting many out-of-town guests its wonderful to bring them from the cold climate" to sunny Florida. Unlike the rest of the country, summer weddings are not as popular because of the summer heat.

The "in" reception sites? The Boca Raton Hotel and Club (a five star hotel) is popular as well as the Count Hoernle Pavilion, a restored train station. Other favorite sites include the tony Polo Club and Addison's, a local restaurant. Yachting receptions at sunset are quite popular alternatives to hotels.

Whether on land or at sea, black-tie, sit down dinner receptions are the norm. Popular dishes include exotic veal, chicken and fish entrees. Besides a dessert like chocolate mousse, the wedding cake is typically a stacked confection covered with fresh flowers. After dessert, guests dance the night away to five or six piece orchestras.

Kentucky weddings are an interesting blend of Southern and Midwestern traditions. For example, June, August and September are big wedding months (like their neighbors to the North) but many foods at the receptions are decidedly Southern in character: groom's cakes are a common sight, especially in the southern part of the state.

Buffet receptions are standard for most Kentucky weddings, according to Jo Ann Smith, a wedding consultant in **Louisville**. "Rumaki (an interesting combination of chicken liver and water chestnut wrapped in bacon) is a popular hors d'oeuvre," she added. Other popular dishes include, of course, Kentucky ham served on biscuits, various pâtés, miniature quiches and pastry shells filled with chicken salad.

Jo Ann told us the typical wedding in Louisville costs $10,000 to $12,500, with an average of 200 guests. Saturday afternoon weddings from 4:00 to 6:00 PM in a local church are most common, with a reception following in a local hotel. Other popular reception sites include the Star of Louisville (a cruise ship on the nearby Ohio River) and the Water Tower Association (run by the Louisville Visual Arts Foundation), which offers a beautiful view of the city. Several other restored homes of Victorian architecture are choice spots. In nearby **Lexington**, the Marriot's Griffin Gate Resort is the quintessential Southern Mansion.

Oklahoma has one of the highest divorce rates in the country, but that hasn't deterred couples from taking the plunge again.

"Second weddings are big here—especially from Thanksgiving to Christmas," said Felicia Moghbel, a bridal consultant in **Oklahoma City.**

A typical wedding costs $10,000 and has between 200 to 250 guests, she said. "Although traditional June weddings are most popular, August and September are real close," Felicia said.

Thanks to the unpredictable Oklahoma weather, most weddings are indoors. Popular reception sites include the Renaissance Building and the Botanical Gardens downtown. The Myriad Gardens Convention Center is also a favorite. Next in popularity are many area restaurants that have banquet rooms.

Ethnic weddings are on the rise in Oklahoma City. Besides the city's large Hispanic community, Lebanese, Iranian, Greek and Vietnamese weddings have mixed their customs with American traditions.

"Big Iranian weddings are grand scale here, " Felicia said. "Couples are married on a sophra, a satin cloth. The women then gather around the couples and rub sugar cones together—similar to our tradition of throwing rice."

Vietnamese brides will wear a white gown to a morning ceremony and then change into a red gown (their color for formal weddings). "All of the ethnic groups here have introduced something new to Oklahoma City—the sit-down dinner reception," she said.

"The traditional Oklahoma reception is just cake, nuts, mints and coffee," Felicia said, adding that "in the last five years we have seen a new trend toward hors d'oeuvre buffets." Another unusual aspect of Oklahoma City weddings is the Friday night ceremony. Why not Saturday night? Felicia explained that "churches here don't allow weddings on Saturday evenings to make sure the sanctuary is cleaned up for Sunday services." Hence, formal weddings in the evening must be on Friday night (if they want a church wedding). In the summer, 2 PM Saturday weddings are common, too.

Folks in Oklahoma City have discovered a unique solution to the alcohol question. To keep guests from overindulging, many restaurant banquet halls now give guests who want to drink two tickets that can be redeemed at the bar. Hence guests are kept to a two-drink limit. In rural areas, alcohol is nonexistent at receptions since churches (where most receptions are held) prohibit it.

❦ Local resources

Gerri Samuels of "I Do" Publishing (800) 392-9039 produces a series of popular wedding guides to Dallas, Houston, and Austin. These books review and rate local bridal merchants and contain no advertising. We've also seen several other local wedding books for Texas and other southern states—check your bookstore to see if there is one in your area.

Chapter 15

Last Minute Consumer Tips

O kay, let's assume you're the perfect consumer. Instead of using cash or a check, you've put all the deposits on a credit card. All the agreements with each service are in writing. You've dotted all your "i's" and crossed all your "t's."

But what if your wedding day arrives and, for example, the florist delivers dead flowers? Or the photographer sends a last-minute "stand-in"? Or the wrong wedding cake is delivered? What can you do to prevent this?

Meet the Surrogate Bad Cop

No matter how careful you are, things can still happen at your wedding and reception that are not according to plan. That's why you need a Surrogate Bad Cop as an "enforcer" to fix last minute problems and correct wayward merchants.

Who can be a surrogate bad cop? Anyone you believe is trustworthy and reliable. This can be your best friend, your mother or a close relative. Of course, if you're hiring a professional wedding planner, they would play this role typically.

What does the surrogate bad cop actually do? *Their job is to make sure you enjoy your wedding.* While you're greeting guests and having fun, it's the surrogate bad cop's role to tell the florist to fix the flowers. Or track down the photographer who is running late. Or find out why the wrong wedding cake was delivered and see if it can be fixed.

In addition to major problems, the surrogate cop also handles any minor situations. One bride told us she was upset with the band she hired when the musicians launched into an unscheduled set of heavy metal music. While she was taking pictures, she had her surrogate bad cop (her sister) talk to the band leader. She informed him of the band's mistake and said the bride had requested they change the tempo. And the band complied.

The Surrogate Bad Cop's Bag of Tricks

Any good enforcer needs the right tools at their disposal to do their job effectively. Here's a look into their "bag of tricks," a special folder or notebook that you give to them on the wedding day (or shortly before):

1 PHONE NUMBERS OF EVERY SERVICE (HOME, BUSINESS, MOBILE/CAR PHONE). Okay, it's Saturday night, the wedding is in one hour and the florist is nowhere to be found. You call the shop and, of course, it's closed. Now what? That's why you also need a home phone number for the key contact at every service. Even better: get the car/mobile phone number and/or a pager number as well. These numbers will be crucial if your surrogate needs to track down an errant florist, photographer, DJ, etc.

2 COPIES OF EACH CONTRACT AND PROPOSAL. Let's say the florist has shown up, but she's missing several arrangements. Or a special orchid corsage for your grandmother. But the florist claims you never ordered that. What can you do? Well, if you're smart, you'll put copies of every contract and proposal into your surrogate cop's bag of tricks. That way she can whip out the florist proposal and tactfully point out that, yes, there is suppose to be an orchid corsage. Usually, florists carry a few extra flowers with them (or they can perhaps pop back to their shop and pick up the missing pieces). One hopes that you won't have to resort to producing written contracts to correct problems, but it's a nice back-up just in case. Also, it helps the surrogate bad cop figure out just what you ordered.

3 AUTHORITY TO ACT ON YOUR BEHALF. This "invisible" tool is important. You must tell each service (photographer, florist, caterer DJ, band, etc.) that this special person will be acting on your behalf during the wedding and reception. If they come to them with a request, they should know it is your wishes.

The Final Check-Up

A week or so before your wedding, you should set up a "final check-up" with each merchant and service. Whether it is an in-person meeting or a telephone consultation, you should discuss the following:

❦ *Confirm all dates, days, times and locations.* You need arrival or drop-off times from such services as the florist and baker. Be careful if you're not getting married on a Saturday—make sure the merchant knows your wedding is a Friday or Sunday, for example. We've heard stories of "no-shows" since the merchant assumed all weddings are on Saturday. Don't forget to call the officiant—you can't get married without him.

❧ *Get all the phone numbers we mentioned above.*

❧ *Tell them the identity of your "surrogate bad cop."* While you may not use those words exactly, let the companies know that this one special person will be helping you that evening. They should treat any request from this person as your direction.

❧ *Confirm the order.* Now is the time to make sure that the florist can do bird of paradise flowers in your bouquet. Or that the wedding cake will be a certain flavor. Go over the menu with the caterer and fix any problems. Make sure they have your special requests in writing in their file.

❧ *Pay the Balance.* Many services and merchants will require the payment of the balance due at this time. Try to pay by credit card.

Strategies for Dealing with Problems that Crop up on the Wedding Day

We find these problems fall into one of three categories.

1 IMPROPER DELIVERIES. What can you do if the wrong cake is delivered or the caterer serves the wrong main course? While you (or your surrogate cop) may be able to contact the company before the start of the ceremony, there may not be enough time to fix the problem. Solution: Ask the company to make an "adjustment" in your final bill. This doesn't mean you get the item for free—but a discount or partial refund may be in order.

2 NO SHOWS/LATE ARRIVALS. If the photographer is late, use the contact phone numbers to track him/her down. Solution: anyone who charges by the hour should make an adjustment in their bill if they run late. Or they may be able to make up the time by staying later.

3 INFERIOR QUALITY. You were promised big, beautiful roses, but the florist has delivered half-dead, miniature roses. The DJ said he had an extensive collection of country music, but it turns out that it's just one Garth Brooks album. Honestly, there isn't much you can do on the day of the wedding if a company has deceived you about the quality of their products or services. However, after the wedding, you may want to dispute the charge on your credit card (which you used for deposits and final payments) if what was delivered didn't live up to the promises. If you paid by check or cash, you may have to take the merchant to small claims court to

recover your money. Document the problem with pictures or video. Also, complain to the Better Business Bureau and your city/county's consumer affairs office.

Many so-called wedding "disasters" are due to the lack of written agreements or ambiguous contracts. You can stop this problem by simply getting everything in writing.

Another source of problems are "early deliveries." One bride in Texas told us about a wedding cake that was delivered *six hours* before her reception. As the hotel was setting up the ballroom, someone with a ladder whacked the cake. The lesson: don't have the flowers, cake or other items delivered *too early*. There's just too much of an opportunity for problems.

Finally, some goofs are due to a lack of organization on the businesses' part. Whether the mix-up is an honest mistake or an intentional fraud, it doesn't matter. As a professional, the service should act to correct the mistake or give you a refund. Sadly, not all wedding merchants are professionals and you must take steps to protect yourself as a consumer.

The Bottom Line

While there's no such thing as a perfect wedding, there is such a thing as a consumer-savvy bride and groom. With credit cards, complete written agreements and a well-armed surrogate bad cop, you can get the quality that you're paying the big bucks for at your wedding and reception.

Chapter 16

What Does It All Mean?

After reading through all the tips and advice in this book, your first thought may be "Let's elope!" And, if you didn't question your sanity in this process at least once, we would be worried about you.

Of course, it's easy for us to sit here in our Ivory Tower and tell you that you need to keep your "perspective" while you plan your wedding. In truth, perhaps many married couples take perverse joy in seeing engaged couples go through the anguish of planning a wedding. It's almost like a boot camp for marriage: if you can survive this, then you are fit to join the rest of us on the other side of the fence of marital bliss.

Even if weddings are some sinister plot to initiate the single into the married world, this doesn't excuse the fact that the entire U.S. wedding industry, your friends and relatives are trying to convince you that YOUR WEDDING DAY IS THE SINGLE MOST IMPORTANT DAY OF YOUR LIFE. And, of course, unless you get everything perfect, the wrath of the WEDDING GODS will be on your head.

Complicating this process is that green stuff with the presidents on it. As you are probably now well aware, weddings are darn expensive. Worse yet, as a consumer, planning a wedding puts you in a sometimes hostile environment. In a very short time, you must shop for products and services that you've never bought before and probably will never buy again.

We hope this book is useful as you plan your trip down the aisle. We sincerely appreciate your purchase of this book and we want to help you any way we can. If you have any questions about this book or just want to chat, see the "How to reach us" page at the end of this book.

In the face of all this, our message to you is quite simple: have a good time. Don't take this stuff too seriously. Remember that you are planning a party to celebrate you and your fiance's relationship. And, theoretically, people are suppose to have fun at parties. Even the guests of honor.

Appendix

Setting the Budget

The first step in setting the budget is prioritizing your needs. That's what the first section of this chapter is about. Next, you will set the overall budget you want to spend. Finally, we will show you how to budget money for each category according to your priorities.

Prioritizing Your Needs

We suggest that both you and your fiance or you and your parents (depending on who will be contributing to this event) sit down together with separate sheets of paper and make a list like this:

APPAREL	$ _____
FLOWERS	$ _____
CAKE	$ _____
RECEPTION/CATERING	$ _____
PHOTOGRAPHY	$ _____
VIDEOGRAPHY	$ _____
INVITATIONS	$ _____
MUSIC	$ _____
MISCELLANEOUS	$ _____

Once you've each made up priority worksheets, rank each category in order of importance from one (most important) to nine (least important). Be sure not to confer on your choices until everyone is finished.

In order to understand exactly what each category entails, the following is a brief explanation, including average costs.

1 APPAREL. This includes the bride's gown, veil, shoes, accessories, undergarments, and alterations. It may also include a separate going-away outfit. The groom's formal wear is also

part of this category. The average cost for apparel is $1175 ($1100 for the bride and $75 for the groom's formal wear rental). Yet, as you read earlier in this book, if you get carried away with accessories, the bride's tab alone could top $1300.

NOTE: For parents who are paying for the wedding, include the price of your gown and/or tux in this section. Also, some couples or their parents may pay for siblings' formal wear. Include such extra apparel expenditures in this category if necessary.

2 FLOWERS. This category includes "personal" flowers such as bouquets, boutonnieres, corsages or even hairpieces. Ceremony flowers may include candelabrum, altar arrangements and aisle decorations. For the reception, flowers may be used as table and buffet centerpieces, and even to decorate the wedding cake. If it's alive and blooming, include it in this category. Most weddings average about $800 but elaborate floral decorations can cost $1000 to $2000 or more.

3 WEDDING CAKE. The wedding (or bride's) cake is the obvious item we're talking about. However, in some parts of the country, a groom's cake or a dessert table may also be included. Using our example of 200 guests, the average cake costs about $500.

4 RECEPTION/CATERING. Basically, this category includes all food (except the cake), beverages, labor and rental items. Charges to rent the reception facility are included here, when applicable. For a basic sit-down dinner or hors d'oeuvre buffet, we've budgeted about $42 per person—that includes beverages and gratuities. This average can be deceiving—in Boston, for example, a sit-down dinner reception can cost $125 per guest. On the other hand, a simple "cake and punch" reception in a smaller city can cost just $5 per person.

5 PHOTOGRAPHY. The bride and groom usually only need to budget for their album and possibly a bridal portrait. The average couple spends about $1500 for professional wedding photography. Parents should include a separate album in their budget as well as any additional photos they will want.

6 VIDEOGRAPHY. If you want your wedding and reception videotaped by a professional cameraman, add in this category. Also budget for extra copies for parents if necessary. A rough estimate for a professionally-shot video is about $500 to $1000. However, prices can range from $200 up to $5000.

7 INVITATIONS. First, you buy the invitations and/or announcements. Add on any extras like reception or

response cards and other enclosures. Don't forget napkins, programs, and favors if you want them. You'll need informals (a.k.a. thank you notes) for all those gifts, and you may want to add in calligraphy. Don't forget to account for postage too. When you add in all these extras, the average expenditure here is about $200.

8 MUSIC. Ceremony music may consist of as little as a church organist or as much as a string quartet and a soloist. As for the reception entertainment, choices range from a pianist to a professional DJ or band. Music costs average a $1000 for entertainment at both the ceremony and reception.

9 MISCELLANEOUS. This isn't actually a fair category because it covers many things, but we mention it anyway. Some areas to think about are ceremony fees, blood tests and/or marriage license fees, accessories like guests books, beauty make-overs, transportation, or even lodging for members of the wedding party. A fair average for this category is about $1000—that figure can also cover cost overruns in one of the other categories if necessary.

Two other items not included in our calculations are the engagement and wedding rings. For the curious, the average engagement ring costs about $2500 and wedding rings now average $1000 for the pair.

Now compare worksheets. Are everyone's priorities the same? Probably not! In fact, by using the priority worksheet, you may be able to spot possible conflicts before you get started.

For example, Mom may think that flowers are extremely important to make a wedding festive; the bride may be more concerned about her dress, while the groom's priority is the reception music. Now is the time to discuss differing opinions before they cause major problems with your wedding planning.

The Overall Budget

As you read in the introduction, the average wedding in the U.S. today costs about $15,000! But, of course, you can spend half as much and still have a wonderful wedding.

The cost involved is dependent on several items: how far in advance you can plan, what time of day and day of week you want your wedding, where (in the U.S.) you get married, what time of year you choose, and what your priorities are.

❦ *How far in advance.* When you have little or no time to plan in advance, you may have to accept what is available regardless of quality or price. Bridal gowns are a good example. Many wedding gowns in traditional bridal shops require from three to six months to special order. If you don't have that much time, you may have to settle for a sample gown that is not in the best condition. The more time you allow yourself, the more choices you will have and the more flexibility for your budget.

❧ *Time of day, day of the week and time of year.* Typically throughout the U.S., the most popular day of the week to have a wedding is Saturday. If you choose a Saturday to get married, you will have to compete with many more brides than if you choose a Friday evening or a Sunday. Weekdays will be even more open. Some bridal businesses offer discounts for non-traditional days. For example, bands and DJ's will often accept work on Friday night or Sunday and give you a discount at the same time.

Time of day is also an important factor with your budget. If your budget is very tight, consider having your wedding in the morning or the afternoon instead of the evening. Food is the largest expense for most wedding receptions and dinner is the most expensive meal to serve. A late morning brunch or afternoon tea reception may save considerable money. These options and even a cake and punch reception are perfectly acceptable alternatives to the high expense of evening receptions.

❧ *Time of the year.* If you plan on having a holiday reception (such as Christmas or New Years), you should also plan on higher expenses. For example, flowers are more costly during December because of high demand and limited availability. Caterers are also busy with corporate parties at this time of year, as are bands and DJ's. As a result, prices are higher than at other times of the year. Other holidays such as Memorial Day, Valentine's Day, Labor Day, and Thanksgiving weekend may be similarly more expensive.

❧ *Number of people invited.* Since we noted above that food is your highest expense, it makes sense that cutting down on your guest list will save money. Enough said.

❧ *Your priorities.* When you look at your priority list, remember that you want to spend a larger part of your budget on the highest priorities. For example, if the reception catering is a high priority, this could be as much as one-third of your total budget. Even more if you are serious about food.

And that leads us to our next section: allotting money. First, before we do that, you need to come up with a total figure you want to spend on your wedding. We do not recommend that you go into debt to have the kind of wedding you want. In fact, there is no reason you should have to. There is also no magic formula for determining an overall amount. Look at what you can *afford* and determine the total from there.

Allotting Money

Again, take up your illustrious priority worksheet. At the top write in your total budget figure. Begin to allot your money to correspond with your priorities. Spend money where you think it is important. The following is a sample priority worksheet with a budget.

TOTAL BUDGET: $10,000

	Priority	Your Budget
APPAREL	1	$1,000
FLOWERS	5	600
CAKE	6	350
RECEPTION/CATERING	3	4,500
PHOTOGRAPHY	2	1,000
VIDEOGRAPHY	7	500
INVITATIONS	8	300
MUSIC	4	900
MISCELLANEOUS	9	850
	TOTAL	**$10,000**

With this sample, the reception, the photography and the dress are the highest priorities, therefore we are going to spend $6500 or 65% of our budget on these three items. You may decide you don't want to spend this much on the dress for example, and you will order a gown through a discounter. Instead you may want to spend more money on the flowers because you want a bright garden-like wedding. And so on. The choices are up to you! That's what makes planning a wedding both exciting and challenging.

Here's another good tip: open up a new checking account for wedding expenses. By separating out funds from your personal monies, you'll be able to get a better grip on the budget and expenditures.

Tradition vs. Reality

Traditionally, the bride's family paid for nearly the entire wedding and the groom's family paid for the rehearsal dinner. Of course, that was in 1955. Today, couples are writing their own rules. In some cases, families split the expenses 50/50. Other wedding budgets are split three ways among the families and the couple. Still other couples pay for the entire wedding themselves. Obviously, this is a personal decision.

ONE MORE THING WE'D LIKE TO ADD: We believe that it is too easy to get caught up in the planning and paying for a wedding. Even with our own wedding, we found ourselves having to step back from the event and remember why we were getting married in the first place. In fact, it's good to keep in mind that all you really need to get married is a license, a bride, a groom and an official. All the rest is fluff. If you keep this in mind and remember that the wedding is the beginning of your lives together, instead of a huge social event used to impress your friends and family, it will be easier to keep calm and cool throughout the planning period.

About the Authors

Let's be honest here—while it is the sincere hope of the publisher that this book will save you money on your wedding, we realize it most likely won't alter the way you look at the planet. It probably won't change your life. But this book sure has changed the authors'.

When Denise & Alan Fields wrote their first book on weddings, they weren't even married. Nope, what we had here were two fresh-faced kids with newly-minted college degrees who had zero job prospects. One year later, they were on Oprah, who told her viewers that "if you're getting married, you need this book." Shazam. Instant celebrities.

You be might be wondering, how did this happen?

Let's take a look at the background of these characters to see if there is any clue to their current status as "America's wedding watchdogs."

Denise Fields (a.k.a. Denise Coopwood) originally wanted to be a ballerina when she grew up in Loveland, Colorado. At age 13, Denise switched career paths and decided to become a doctor. She later abandoned this goal after learning that to become a doctor you had to dissect cats at some point along the way.

As a Colorado native, Denise developed an appreciation for the outdoors, the mountains and the absurd. She decided to attend college at the University of Colorado at Boulder—a place that has all three of the above qualities. Denise received a degree in European History, specializing in Elizabethan England. Only after graduation did Denise learn that the unemployment rate for Elizabethan scholars was approximately 132%. Sensing an impending financial crisis, Denise called a career audible: hey why not write books for a living? Denise had written some poetry in college and newspaper articles before that—so she did have writing experience.

Which is more than we can say about the second author of this book: Alan Fields. Alan had authored a newspaper column for the University of Colorado's student newspaper—but the seven people who regularly read the column would probably be hard pressed to call it "award-winning" writing. This is probably explained by the fact that Alan's career ambition was originally to become a television weatherman. This dream came to an abrupt end when someone pointed out to Alan that to be on TV, you couldn't look goofy.

Alan grew up in Dallas, Texas—which perhaps accounts for his particularly warped sense of humor. Fields was admitted to the University of Colorado in an administrative error, according to a university official who refused to be identified.

While in college, Alan met Denise in a chance encounter in the hallway of Kittridge West Dormitory. Two years later, Alan popped the question to Denise. While trying to plan their wedding, the couple came to the conclusion that this whole process is TRULY INSANE. After talking to other engaged couples, Denise and Alan realized that what the world really needed was a consumer guide to planning a wedding.

Denise and Alan moved to Austin, Texas and set about the process of researching this book. The first draft of this book was written in a basement apartment appropriately located on Bridle Path (mis-spelling intended) in West Austin. The first edition of *Bridal Bargains* sold in the high two figures.

Then, Oprah called.

Some 200,000 copies later, the Fields decided to move back to Boulder. They live there, happily ever after, with their son, Ben and dog, Zuzu.

Index

Keep up-to-date on Bridal Bargains!

I t's the Murphy's Law of guide books—as soon as we go to press, something in this book changes. To keep you on top of the latest bargains and news on nuptials, we've created two great ways for you to get updates:

1. FaxFacts. If you've got a fax machine, you can get the latest news on *Bridal Bargains!* **Call (303) 442-3744!** You'll hear a menu of choices, enter your fax number and poof! Our fax-on-demand system will send you the updates in a matter of seconds. All you pay for is the call. Get updates when it's convenient for you—FaxFacts is available 24 hours a day, 7 days a week!

2. On the Web. If you've got access to the World Wide Web, check out our home page at this address: http://www.usa.net/~adfields. (If this address isn't active, call our office at 1-800-888-0385 for the latest location).

What you'll find:

- New bargains suggested by our readers.
- Hints and tips from recently-married couples.
- Corrections and clarifications.
- The latest news on tying the knot!

Of course, if you have any questions that are not answered by these updates, feel free to contact the authors at (303) 442-8792.

Bridal Bargains
It's more than just a book.
It's a nuptial adventure.

Bridal Bargains 301

"Baby Bargains"

*Secrets to saving 20% to 50%
on baby furniture, equipment,
clothes, toys, maternity wear
and much, much, more!*
by Denise & Alan Fields!

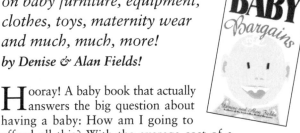

Hooray! A baby book that actually answers the big question about having a baby: How am I going to afford all this? With the average cost of a baby topping $5000 for just the first year alone, you need creative solutions and innovative ideas to navigate the consumer maze that confronts all parents-to-be. *Baby Bargains* is the answer! Inside, you'll discover:

- How to Save Up to 25% on brand-new, designer-brand baby bedding.

- Five Wastes of Money with baby clothes and which brands are the best.

- Seven tips to Saving Money on Cribs, plus in-depth reviews of the top crib makers.

- How to get a name-brand car seat for Free!

- The Truth About Strollers—and which brands work best in the real world.

- Dozens of Safety Tips to affordably baby proof your home.

- The Top 10 Best Baby Gifts and five gift don'ts.

- Name Brand Reviews of toys, monitors, high chairs, diapers and more!

- Seven Creative Sources for maternity clothes—and a national outlet that offers 40% savings!

Money-Back Guarantee: If *"Baby Bargains"* doesn't save you at least $250, we will give you a complete refund. No kidding!

As seen on Oprah!

Just
$11.95
(Plus $3 shipping)

Call toll-free to order!
1-800-888-0385

Mastercard, VISA, American Express and Discover Accepted!

How to Reach the Authors

Have a question about

Bridal Bargains?

*Want to make
a suggestion?*

*Discovered a great bargain
you'd like to share?*

*Contact the Authors,
Denise &Alan Fields
in one of five ways:*

**1. By phone:
(303) 442-8792.**

**2. By mail:
1223 Peakview Circle,
Suite 7000,
Boulder, CO 80302.**

**3. By fax:
(303) 442-3744.**

**4. By electronic mail:
adfields@aol.com**

**5. On our web page:
http://www.usa.net/~adfields**
*(If this address isn't active,
call our office at 1-800-888-0385
for the latest location).*

Join Our "Preferred Reader" List!

We've got lots of new books and special reports coming out over the next few years! Just jot down your name and address below, mail in the coupon and we'll keep you up-to-date!

Best of all, we have "early bird" DISCOUNTS especially for BRIDAL BARGAINS preferred readers!

Name _____

Address _____

City _____ State_____ Zip_____

Wedding Date_____

How did you hear about our book?_____

_____

What was your favorite section or tip? _____

_____

How can we improve this book? _____

_____

_____

_____

_____

Mail To:

BRIDAL BARGAINS
1223 Peakview Circle
Boulder, CO 80302
or fax to
(303) 442-3744

QUESTIONS TO ASK
Reprinted from
The *Bridal Bargains* book • Fields

APPAREL FOR THE BRIDE AND BRIDAL PARTY

❏ Who is the manufacturer of this dress?

❏ How long will it take to get the dress in?

❏ What are your payment policies?

❏ Can I have a written estimate for alterations?

❏ What free services are available?

CEREMONY SITES

❏ Do you have my wedding date available?

❏ What are the restrictions, set-up times and clean-up requirements?

❏ Who will be my contact at the site?

❏ What is the expected honorarium, donation or fee paid to the church/officiant? When is this normally paid?

❏ What kind of equipment must be rented for my wedding?

❏ Is any pre-wedding counseling required?

❏ For officiants, are there any travel charges, rehearsal fees, or other costs? Do you offer different ceremony options?

WEDDING FLOWERS

❏ Is my date available? Is there a deposit needed to hold the date?

❏ Do you have actual photographs or samples of your past work?

❏ Do you offer any silk or dried flower arrangements?

❏ Is there a delivery or set-up fee?

❏ How many weddings do you do in a day?

❏ Are you familiar with my ceremony site location?

❏ What rental items do you have? How are they priced?

❏ Can I attend one of your weddings during set-up for a look at your designs?

❏ What time will you be at my ceremony/reception sites to set up my wedding?

❏ Will you merely drop off my flowers or stay through the ceremony?

INVITATIONS

❏ How many different lines do you carry?
❏ Given my wedding and reception, what is your opinion of having response cards?
❏ Can I see some samples of actual invitations?
❏ Who is responsible for any errors that occur?
❏ Can I see a proof of the invitation?

RECEPTION SITES

❏ How many guests can the space accommodate?
❏ How many hours does the rental fee cover?
❏ Is there an in-house caterer or a list of approved caterers? Or can you bring in any caterer?
❏ Are there any cooking restrictions?
❏ Is there a piano available? What about other items like dance floors?
❏ What else is happening at the site the day of my wedding?
❏ Are there any union rules we must follow?

CATERING

❏ Can we have a taste test of the foods on our menu?
❏ Can we see one of your weddings during set-up?
❏ Do you provide a written estimate and contract?
❏ Are you licensed?
❏ Do you specialize in certain cuisines or types of menus?
❏ Where is the food prepared?
❏ When is the menu "set in stone?"
❏ How is your wait staff dressed?
❏ For cocktail or buffet receptions, how often will the food be replenished?
❏ Given the style of my reception, how many waiters do we need?
❏ How is the charge for labor figured? Is the clean-up extra?
❏ How much does a dessert table cost? Is the wedding cake price included in the package?
❏ What are your cancellation/ postponement policies?
❏ Do you have a liquor license?
❏ Are you familiar with my reception site?
❏ Do you receive any commissions from services you recommend?
❏ Will you guarantee these price estimates?